# A BRIEF HISTORY OF ARGENTINA

## JONATHAN C. BROWN

### University of Texas at Austin

Checkmark Books®
*An imprint of Facts On File, Inc.*

A Brief History of Argentina

Copyright © 2004 Lexington Associates

All rights reserved. No part of this book may be reproduced or utilized in any form or by any means, electronic or mechanical, including photocopying, recording, or by any information storage or retrieval systems, without permission in writing from the publisher. For information contact:

Checkmark Books
An imprint of Facts On File, Inc.
132 West 31st Street
New York NY 10001

**Library of Congress Cataloging-in-Publication Data**

Brown, Jonathan C., 1942 –
   A brief history of Argentina/Jonathan C. Brown.
      p. cm.
Includes bibliographical references and index.
   ISBN 0-8160-4959-9 (hardcover)
   ISBN 0-8160-5719-2 (pbk)
   1. Argentina—History. I. Title.
   F2831 .B88 2002
   982—dc21                2002006459

Checkmark Books are available at special discounts when purchased in bulk quantities for businesses, associations, institutions, or sales promotions. Please call our Special Sales Department in New York at (212) 967-8800 or (800) 322-8755.

You can find Facts On File on the World Wide Web at http://www.factsonfile.com

Cover design by Semadar Megged
Maps and figures by Dale Williams

Printed in the United States of America

MP Hermitage 10 9 8 7 6 5 4 3 2 1

This book is printed on acid-free paper.

# CONTENTS

# LIST OF ILLUSTRATIONS

# LIST OF MAPS

# LIST OF TABLES

v

# LIST OF FIGURES

# ACKNOWLEDGMENTS

I have benefited immensely from a wealth of literature on the history of Argentina in both Spanish and English. The Argentines have developed one of the most lively and professional historical traditions in Latin America, and they have a talent for seeing themselves with clarity and wisdom. They practice their studies at a number of fine institutions of higher learning and research institutes both in Argentina and abroad. Moreover, the Argentine historical community has welcomed foreign scholars to its archives and libraries so that the English-language literature ranks among the richest for any country of Latin America.

In addition, my students and former students assist me—indeed, they challenge me—in staying on top of the latest research. They themselves have contributed five doctoral dissertations and 15 master's research projects about Argentine history that have enriched my knowledge and understanding of that country. They will recognize in these pages where I am beholden to their research. I owe special thanks to Joan Supplee, Gil Ramírez, Ricardo Salvatore, Rukhsana Qamber, and Barbara Ganson for their doctoral work. Among those who have turned out fine master's projects are Kevin Kelly, Barbara Boczek, John Rochford, Andrea Spears, Lisa Cox, Barbara Pierce, Alfredo Poenitz, Yao-Sung Hsiao, Matthew Faddis, Wayne Magnusson, Jesús Gómez, Greg Hammond, and Byron Crites. I am indebted to María Celina Tuozzo for her keen insights on Argentine labor history. Michael Snodgrass graciously permitted me to draw from his superb analysis, especially on the relationship between Juan Perón and his working-class followers, which appears in Chapter 8. Both Celina and Michael contributed essays about Argentine workers in *Workers' Control in Latin America, 1930–1979* (Chapel Hill: University of North Carolina Press, 1997).

In Buenos Aires, I profited from the expert assistance of Daniel V. Santilli of the Instituto de Historia Argentina y Americana "Dr. E. Ravignani." He searched among several different sources in Buenos Aires to find many of the illustrations that grace this book. During the December 2001 crisis, I corresponded frequently with Torcuato Di

Tella, Ricardo Salvatore, and Cuatro Tolson, who kept me abreast of events. I benefited also from the Reuters news dispatches from Argentina that were written by a former student, Brian Winter. In addition, Gil Ramírez has shared jokes and insights over the years, Byron Crites donated a critical labor document, and Marcos Tonatiuh Aguila M. provided e-mail news on the December 2001 political crisis.

I have been fortunate over the years to have the advice and counsel of my own in-house editor and muse, Lynore Brown. I must also acknowledge my debt to the editor of this book, Ed Purcell. He first convinced me to write this brief history, then guided me through the process, correcting my occasional poor choice of words as he read through the manuscript. Unless otherwise noted, translations that appear in this book are my own. All the above contributed to making this a better book, though they cannot be faulted for its shortcomings.

# INTRODUCTION: THE ARGENTINE RIDDLE

Their fellow Latin Americans like to tell a joke about the Argentines. "Would you like to know how to become rich overnight?" they ask. "It's quite simple. Just buy an Argentine for what he's worth and sell him for what he *thinks* he's worth."

The joke, often repeated among Argentines themselves, seems to sum up one aspect of the "Argentine Riddle." The country once had one of the most vibrant economies in the world. In the 1920s, Argentines compared themselves favorably to France in terms of economic wealth and individual well-being. Children of the Argentine landowning class were known in London and Paris as the original jet-setters of the early 20th century. Now, Argentines count themselves among the underdeveloped nations of the world. Great-grandchildren of European immigrants now seek to repatriate themselves to the homelands of their great-grandparents. Argentines themselves are deeply disappointed about the supposed gap between the country's possibilities and its intractable problems, such as economic stagnation, chronic unemployment, political violence, and sharp class antagonisms. This is the Argentine Riddle.

What is wrong with Argentina? Argentina has a population that ranks among the most educated and skilled in Latin America, and its citizens have made major contributions to the world. Illiteracy scarcely exists among even the poor and working-class citizens, and Argentina's middle class historically has been large and politically engaged. Moreover, the humid and temperate Pampas are among the largest and most fertile plains areas in the world. With a topsoil running 50 feet deep in some places, the Pampas easily support rich grazing for cattle and sheep and produce bountiful harvests of wheat, corn, and sorghum. The interior provinces foster hundreds of world-class vineyards, fruit farms, sugar plantations, a timber industry, and cultivation of the famous *yerba* leaves from which Argentines love to brew the tea known as *mate*. The country's second-largest city, Córdoba, has spawned industrial development with its metallurgical and automobile industries; its third-largest city, Santa Fe, dominates a vibrant river shipping industry that connects Atlantic commerce to seven Argentine provinces, Paraguay, and parts of southern Brazil. Argentina has cooperated with neighboring countries to develop the hydroelectric potential of the many rivers of the Paraná River basin, most notably near the Iguazú (Iguaçu in Brazil) Falls. In the south, the Patagonian region attracts tourists fascinated by the natural beauty of Andean lakes, the whales and walruses of the Chubut coastline, the glaciers of Ushuaia, and the ski slopes of Bariloche. Walt Disney gained inspiration for his movie *Bambi* in Patagonia's mountain forests, and U.S. president Dwight Eisenhower delighted in playing on the world-famous golf course at the Hotel Nahuel Huapi.

The national capital, Buenos Aires, remains one of the great cultural centers of the Americas. Gracious boulevards intersect the elegant downtown shopping districts and are lined with imposing public buildings such as the Casa Rosada ("Pink House," the national palace), the neo-Hellenistic congressional building, and the great opera hall of the Teatro Colón. Barrio Norte, the most prestigious neighborhood of Buenos Aires, features many residential palaces that rival those found in Paris's Faubourg St.-Germain and London's Knightsbridge.

Argentina has always been politically influential beyond its borders, as evident in the following pages. The streak of independence and individualism that runs through the nation may be traced to the struggle between the indigenous peoples and the Spanish settlers to dominate the Pampas. Argentina's reputation for wealth and power began in the late colonial period, when nearly the entire colony partook in the export of silver and hides. The nation became one of the first in Latin America to shake off the colonial yoke of imperial Spain, spreading the liberation movement to neighboring countries as well. In the 19th century, it prospered in the promotion of agricultural exports, technological modernization, and European immigration (some historians claim that first-generation Italian immigrants fared better in Argentina at the turn of the 20th century than in the United States). Latin Americans have consistently looked to Argentines such as the liberator José de San Martín and presidents Hipólito Irigoyen and Juan Domingo Perón for ideological inspiration and political models. Although controversial, Evita Perón and Ernesto "Che" Guevara continue to inspire. Argentina can also boast having had the first female head of state in the Americas.

In addition to the natural resources and the rich urban and political culture of Argentina, one must also recognize the accomplishments of individual Argentine citizens. During the past two centuries, thousands of Argentine singers and dancers helped develop the distinctive musical genre of tango; singer and actor Carlos Gardel spread the Argentine tango to Europe and elsewhere in the 1930s. Argentine citizens have been awarded five Nobel Prizes, more than any other Latin American nation. In medicine, Bernardo Houssay received a Nobel in 1917, and César Milstein, in 1984. Luis Federico Leloir earned the Nobel Prize in chemistry in 1970. The foreign minister Carlos Saavedra Lamas won Argentina's first Nobel Peace Prize in 1936 after successfully negotiating a peace accord between Bolivia and Paraguay that ended the bloody Chaco War. Adolfo Pérez Esquivel won this same prize in 1980 for his work on behalf of human rights. In literature, Argentina has given the world its most enigmatic literary figure, Jorge Luis Borges. There are few epic poems equal to *El gaucho Martín Fierro* by José Hernández, and few romantic novels compare to *Don Segundo Sombra* by Ricardo Güiraldes. Argentine universities still turn out renowned scientists, physicians, economists, engineers, architects, and social scientists. Many teach and practice in Spain, France, England, the United States, and Mexico.

Nor do the Argentines lag behind in sports. Guillermo Vilas and Gabriela Sabatini have scored big in the world of professional tennis, each winning the U.S. Open championship. The world also knows Argentines for their prowess in soccer. Since 1978, the Argentine national team has won the World Cup twice, ranking just behind the Brazilian and Italian teams. Fans called Diego Maradona "the Magician" for his inspired play and knack of scoring, as in the miraculous "Hand of God" goal on the way to winning the 1986 World Cup in Mexico City. Though less well known, Argentina's polo players dominate the world's professional circuit. No doubt this tradition of horsemanship derives directly from the famous gauchos (cowboys) of the Pampas. Ten of the world's top 12 polo players are Argentine born and bred, and the country's horse ranches also turn out the finest Thoroughbred polo ponies. When the top two domestic teams face off each November in the final of the Argentine Cup at Palermo Park, most of each

Argentinean Adolfo Cambiaso, in the foreground, taking a nearside stroke, is the world's premier polo player. He is shown here during the 2001 Argentine Open tournament. (Alex Photo)

team's four players hold the coveted and rare 10-goal handicap. All eight are also native born. Many consider the daring Adolfo Cambiaso to be "the Magician" of polo.

All these achievements, and Argentines still feel disappointed. They know their country can do better than the 20 percent unemployment, shrinking middle class, and leaders seemingly more intent on looting the treasury than governing the nation. The following pages will explore both the accomplishments and failures in the historical forma-tion of the Argentine nation. The text will quote directly from the assessments of the country's greatest statesmen and writers as well as of people on the street. This *Brief History of Argentina* will also suggest an answer to the Argentine Riddle—though not a remedy, which is left to the Argentines themselves.

The answer to "What is wrong with Argentina?" lies in the coincidence of political power and economic privilege. It is a society suffused with prejudice and rigid class structures. In many ways, this South American nation has never overcome its colonial heritage of racism, social discrim-ination, and political arrogance. Those who assumed governance of the newly independent nation in the 19th century continued to use violence to maintain social order and to divide up wealth. True enough, economic growth and European immigration transformed the country at the turn of the 20th century, yet the political culture and social conventions remained remarkably unaffected. Immigrants adopted traditional Argentine values in far greater measure than they nurtured new ones.

These conditions persisted into the 20th century. The democratic reforms of Irigoyen and Perón introduced elements of social justice to a discriminatory society, but they never succeeded in establishing a firm institutional underpinning for reform against a violent opposition, often aided by the military. Therefore, the old problems of discrimination and privilege re-emerged in every succeeding period of economic growth. What resulted was a violent challenge by leftist guerrillas in the 1970s, followed by a far more violent Dirty War waged by a military govern-ment. The return of democratic elections in 1983 brought little relief to Argentines. Each of the last three elected presidents began his term in a mood of national euphoria and ended with great disillusionment. Two of these presidents did not remain in office to the end of their terms.

In this regard, the observation of the 19th-century constitutional architect about his countrymen seems timeless. "Liberty was in their hearts," said Juan Bautista Alberdi, "but the old bondage was neverthe-less perpetuated in their habits and, moreover, they were not united among themselves" (Alberdi 1877, 46–47).

# 1

# ANCIENT ARGENTINA AND THE EUROPEAN ENCOUNTER

If the Argentines today take pride in their individuality and independence, they would do well to credit the indigenous inhabitants of the land, as well as the first Spanish settlers. Only a minority of the native peoples of the region ever submitted to the outside authority of the far-reaching Inca Empire based in present-day Peru, and for those few the submission was certainly mild in terms of loss of autonomy and transfer of wealth. Indeed, the pre-Columbian peoples of the region now called the Southern Cone—the lands that form a cone shape descending to the tip of South America, consisting of the modern-day countries of Argentina, Chile, Paraguay, and Uruguay—had little wealth compared to the well-known civilizations of the Inca of Peru and the Aztec of Mexico. This relative poverty guaranteed their independence for many millennia.

The area that became modern-day Argentina covers a large and diverse section of the Southern Cone, stretching nearly half the length of the South American continent, from the tropic of Capricorn all the way to the southern tip. To the north and northeast are the modern nations of Paraguay, Brazil, and Uruguay; to the west and northwest, Chile and Bolivia. A line of high Andean mountains runs down the western side of Argentina and has historically presented a formidable barrier to travel and commerce. The land descends east from the mountains through a region of foothills and eventually to a large flat area of fertile plains known as the Pampas. To the north of the plains is a semi-arid region called the Gran Chaco, bordered on the east and northeast by a great river basin comprising several large rivers and the estuary of the Río de la Plata. A long Atlantic coastline leads down the eastern edge of Argentina to the Patagonian region.

# Modern Argentina

SOUTH AMERICA

ARGENTINA

BOLIVIA

JUJUY
Jujuy

SALTA
Salta

GRAN CHACO

PARAGUAY

Río Bermejo

FORMOSA
Formosa
Asunción

CHILE

Tucumán

TUCUMÁN

CATAMARCA

SANTIAGO DEL ESTERO

Río Salado del Norte

CHACO
Resistencia

Corrientes

Iguazú Falls

MISIONES
Posadas

Catamarca
Santiago del Estero

LA RIOJA

SANTA FE

Río Paraná

CORRIENTES

BRAZIL

La Rioja

SAN JUAN
San Juan

SIERRAS DE CÓRDOBA

CÓRDOBA
Córdoba

San Luis

Santa Fe
Paraná

ENTRE RÍOS

Río Uruguay

URUGUAY

Pacific Ocean

Santiago

Mendoza

SAN LUIS

MENDOZA

Buenos Aires

Colonia
Montevideo

La Plata

Río de la Plata

Punta del Este

Río Salado

ANDES

Santa Rosa

LA PAMPA

PAMPAS

BUENOS AIRES

Tandil

Mar del Plata

Río Colorado

Bahía Blanca

Neuquén

NEUQUÉN

Río Negro

L. Nahuel Huapi

RÍO NEGRO

San Carlos de Bariloche

Viedma

PATAGONIA

CHUBUT

Rawson

Atlantic Ocean

Comodoro Rivadavia

SANTA CRUZ

Río Chico

Río Gallegos

Straits of Magellan

TIERRA DEL FUEGO

Ushuaia

Cape Horn

Port Stanley

Falkland Is. (U.K.)

0       200 Miles
0       200 Kilometers

N

- - - - - - -  Modern national boundaries
............  Modern provincial boundary

2

| Estimated Population of Indigenous Peoples of the Southern Cone, 1492 | |
|---|---|
| Location | Estimated Population |
| Argentina | 900,000 |
| Paraguay–Uruguay–southern Brazil | 1,055,000 |
| Chile | 1,000,000 |
| Total | 2,955,000 |
| Source: William D. Denevan (1992, xxvii) | |

The original inhabitants of the region that became modern Argentina were either agriculturists who had to supplement their diets with hunting and gathering or nomadic peoples who subsisted entirely on hunting and gathering. They may have numbered almost 1 million people in 1492, when Columbus arrived in the Caribbean.

They lived dispersed over an area that now supports 37 million Argentines. Today one might wonder why these indigenous peoples were so impoverished when they inhabited a land of such rich and now-proven agricultural potential. The answer lies in their lack of technological sophistication. Before the arrival of the Europeans, the native inhabitants used only Stone Age technology. Their chiseled rock tools and their chief agricultural implement, the wooden digging stick, could not cut the deep roots of the Pampas grasses or clear the land to cultivate crops. Instead, they carried on agriculture only in the softer valley soils of the Andean highlands. The prairies remained rich only in animals and birds for the hunt. The ancients did not have tempered metals, draft animals, or the wheel. For that matter, they did not suffer from the diseases that ravaged Europe, Asia, and Africa and so had no immunity to them.

These early inhabitants did not form a cultural or ethnic whole. There existed many separate language groupings and dozens of ethnic and cultural differences, giving rise to intensive political decentralization. In each region of the Southern Cone, one cultural and ethnic group might have predominated, but it always had to share—unwillingly for the most part—the fringes of its territory with smaller groups of different cultures and ethnic identities. They observed basic political and religious loyalties at the village or clan level. These peoples recognized only their local leaders and disputed with arms over territory and resources even with other groups of the same culture and language. Every male hunter or cultivator was also a warrior. Every female subordinated herself to the rigid requirements of group survival and maintenance of the warrior male. Some groups enlarged their territories while others retreated to the poorer lands to form a complex and fluid map of ethnic and linguistic diversity across southern South America.

What the indigenous inhabitants of the Southern Cone had accomplished in terms of establishing their lives of group autonomy on the land would determine how the first Spaniards established their hold of the region. Unlike Mexico and Peru, each of which fell within a few years of Spanish arrival, it took the better part of the 300-year colonial period for Europeans to become established in Argentina; after all, there was no empire to conquer in Argentina and certainly no wealth had existed to sustain a large population of Europeans. Therefore, the Spaniards had to settle the region through a long series of small conquests over the indigenous inhabitants, all the while developing a European-style commercial and agricultural base. They had to painstakingly defeat nearly each and every decentralized group in piecemeal fashion. The defeat of no one clan group resulted in the submission of their indigenous neighbors. Even then, several important native groups continued their successful resistance for 400 years following the arrival of the first Spaniard. A summary survey of the pre-Columbian peoples of the Southern Cone will suggest the reasons that individualism and independence have become so entrenched in Argentine society.

## The Agriculturists of Northern Argentina

Scholars believe that the Americas remained uninhabited by humans until a drop in the level of the Pacific Ocean uncovered a land bridge from Asia where the Aleutian Islands of Alaska are presently located. Commencing approximately 50,000 years ago, several Asian peoples of different origins and ethnic backgrounds migrated in successive waves across the Bering land bridge. Subsequently, the sea levels rose and covered the land, leading the migrants to develop culture and technologies on a wholly separate path from those of the so-called Old World of Asia, Europe, and Africa. By 13,000 B.C. these migratory hunter-gatherers had moved through the Darién jungles of Panama and established encampments on the Peruvian coast and in Chile. Separate peoples crossed the Andes, slowly occupying the Amazon Basin, from which they moved north and settled the Caribbean Islands. Farther south, the migrants fanned out thinly over the Pampas and Patagonia of present-day Argentina. In the time of the pharaohs of ancient Egypt, approximately 1,000 B.C., the Mesoamericans of lowland Mexico were developing agriculture around the cultivation of maize or corn. The fisher peoples of coastal Peru adopted the cultivation of maize, while the highland Andeans of Peru subsequently perfected the cultivation of several varieties of potato. These hearty peoples also nurtured the only domestic livestock known in the Americas, the llamas and alpacas. Some of these Andean developments reached the peoples of Chile and northwest Argentina. Indigenous influences from the area of modern-day Brazil, in the meantime, had spread into the area of modern-day Paraguay. There the Guaraní cultivated cassava (also known as yuca or manioc) as their basic food product. The rest of the indigenous peoples of the lower Paraná River basin, the Pampas, and Patagonia remained hunters of game and gatherers of fruits and berries. (See map on page 11.)

## The Diaguita

The peoples of northwest Argentina, particularly in the Salta and Jujuy regions, reflected the Andean culture they shared with the Inca peoples of highland Peru. Our knowledge of them comes from the evidence of early archaeological sites and the information gathered by the earliest Spanish priests and settlers.

The Diaguita were agriculturists who used the digging stick as their principal tool and cultivated corn, beans, and peppers. Potatoes did not grow well in the lower altitudes. Similarly, they herded llamas and alpacas as sources of protein and of wool for making clothing. The Diaguita lived in houses of stone masonry like other highland peoples. They arranged their modest family-sized dwellings along the streams and fields with pathways between them. They did not build great cities, as were found elsewhere among the various pre-Columbian peoples of the Andes.

The early inhabitants of northwest Argentina shared a semiarid landscape dominated by high plateaus suitable for grazing, valleys suitable for tilling, and mountain peaks that rose above the snowline. Snowmelt represented the zone's water resource that these peoples harnessed for irrigation. The Europeans would later convert the land to cattle grazing, stock breeding, the growing of sugarcane and grapes, and the mining of copper. The original peoples made coiled basketry, wove ponchos and skirts from llama wool, and shaped pottery in geometric designs similar to their Andean neighbors in Bolivia and Peru.

5

Some of the cultural groups shared language patterns, but most Diaguita spoke a language different from the Aymara and Quechua dominant in the Andean highlands. The Diaguita built granaries of small stone houses. They built dams on rivers and streams to divert floodwater into marshlike depressions around which they planted crops, especially corn. Their principal crop originated in present-day Mexico and migrated through Peru to northwest Argentina well before the birth of Christ. The ancient Argentines of the northwest also hunted turkey and other small game, fished in the streams and rivers, and collected *algarroba* pods and prickly pears to supplement their diets.

Characteristically, while the Diaguita remained the dominant group of the region just before the European incursion, northwest Argentina supported an abundance of cultural diversity. Peoples of many cultures, such as the Atacameño, Humahuaca, Chicha, and Lule, shared the landscape, all of them living in a kind of harmony with the Diaguita, enforced by the imperial Inca hegemony.

They chewed the coca leaf as a mild stimulant and as an important cultural mark. A mildly intoxicating beer was made from wild *algarroba* beans that formed a variation of the corn *chicha* still prevalent today in the Andes. (*Chicha* is an alcoholic beverage popular among Andean peasants. Traditionally, women prepare *chicha* by masticating the *algarroba* pods or corn in their mouths and fermenting the resulting spittle mix.)

The tunic, a shirt of woven llama wool, was the principal garment of men and women, though the women's tunics were ankle length. In the winter, a woolen cape provided warmth. Everyone wore Andean-style sandals on their feet. Though agriculturists, the men still reveled in their status as warriors. They wore their hair long and adorned their heads with feathers and headbands as a mark of their warlike status. The main weapons were spears, bows and arrows, stone-headed clubs, and the distinctive weapons of the plains hunters, the bolas.

Among the Diaguita, there apparently existed none of the caste structure and social differentiation common among the imperial Inca, and they possessed little in the way of sumptuous goods such as gold and silver ornaments. Diaguita families formed into clans descended from a common ancestor. Important clan leaders may have had two wives (a principal indication of wealth among them), but most men were monogamous in marriage. In the absence of a well-organized priesthood, the shamans took charge of religious ceremonies and passed along the folk medicines from one generation to the next. They remained a relatively decentralized agricultural people, in which the chiefs of small units generally wielded modest political powers, although several chiefs did unite into informal political and military alliances. A Spaniard testified, "It is notorious that no village which has a cacique is the subject of another cacique or pueblo" (Steward 1946, II: 683)

Most chiefs inherited their leadership status from their fathers and uncles and confirmed that leadership with valor in battle, thereby putting his political authority in absolute terms. Otherwise, a council of elders shared decision-making power within the group; however, a chief who showed cowardice in battle soon lost his authority completely. The Diaguita's political decentralization meant that any large valley might be inhabited by several different groups, each in tense and hostile contact with the others. They fashioned fortresses of stone at important mountain passes, as warfare over limited resources became a feature of development down through the millennia. The imperial alliance may have mitigated the competition among the various clans of the Diaguita, although the stone walls that still dominate the narrow passages between the valleys of northwest Argentina give vivid testimony to the tenuous political relations among these agricultural peoples.

The Argentine northwest came very late into the Inca Empire. The emperor Topa Inca (1471–93) gained the submission of the indigenous groups of the region, but Inca influence never penetrated across the Córdoba mountains to the Pampas or through the Gran Chaco into modern-day Paraguay. Some chieftains of the Diaguita came to understand the Quechua language of the Inca, but the imperial powers rested lightly among these comparatively poor agriculturists. On the opposite side of the Andes, the Argentine Diaguita's counterparts inhabited most of present-day Chile down to what is now the city of Santiago. They too submitted to the Inca. But farther south, another agricultural group of different ethnic and linguist stock, the Araucanians, resisted the ancient Peruvians. These peoples—the Huilliche, Picunche, and especially the Mapuche—would also become important later in Argentina, rallying all remaining indigenous groups on the Pampas in resisting the Spaniards.

## The Mapuche

In the long transition from hunting, the Mapuche of what is today southern Chile benefited from the agricultural breakthroughs among the Diaguita. The Mapuche gradually adopted the cultivation of maize, potatoes, and peppers—each plant acclimated to conditions found in the temperate forests and valleys along the southern coasts of Chile. Game and fish supplemented their diet, enabling the Mapuche to settle into relatively permanent villages. Their deities represented the forces of nature and the harvest, and the shamans sought to appease them with offerings of food and sacrifices of domestic llamas. Masked dancers warded off evil spirits. With stone tools only, the Mapuche harvested the wood with which they constructed homes, corrals for llamas and alpacas, and the defensive palisades. These people occasionally carried out raids on neighboring villages, even though those attacked may have been of the same cultural and linguistic family.

Their forts and warlike independence served the Mapuche well when, in the 15th century, Topa Inca extended his conquests into the central valley of Chile. The outside threat sufficed to unite the competitive southern Chileans for an effective defense of their territory. Usually, the leaders had little control over their subjects and warriors, much like the decentralized political system among the Diaguita. To stop the Inca armies, however, the Mapuche elected war leaders, formed larger allied war groups, and mobilized great numbers of warriors. These same Mapuche later were to effectively and aggressively maintain their autonomy from European conquest, not submitting to outside authority, the independent nation of Chile, until the 1880s. During this long period of resistance, the Mapuche adopted the battle techniques of their European enemies and even engaged in defensive expansion across the Andes into the Patagonia and Pampas, which will be studied in subsequent chapters.

### The Guaraní

To the east of the lands of the Diaguita, beyond the Gran Chaco, lay the homeland of yet another agricultural warrior people, the Guaraní. Known for facilitating European encroachment rather than resisting it, the Guaraní's origins and survival do much to explain their reaction to the Europeans.

Bands of Guaraní occupied the semitropical forests of present-day Paraguay, southern Brazil, and northeastern Argentina. They had probably emigrated from the Amazon Basin of Brazil around 200 B.C., displacing and marginalizing the previous indigenous groups. The Guaraní peoples of the forests and rivers developed a civilization based on hunting, fishing, and slash-and-burn horticulture. They cut the trees, burned off the underbrush, planted and harvested crops for several years, then moved on, leaving the forest regrowth to replenish the fertility of the soil. Cultivation fell to the women, who raised maize, beans, sweet potatoes, peanuts, squash, and cassava.

Living patterns in the forest differed from the Andean pattern of the Diaguita. Extended families of Guaraní lived together in large, long straw-thatched huts. As many as 50 family members might live in the house of an important leader. They slept in hammocks suspended from the poles that supported the roof. Wooden palisades surrounded a village of 20 to 30 long houses, reminders of the incessant competition for resources and territory among native groups. Clothes made of feathers and animal skins warded off the winter's cold. In the summer months, men and women customarily went about their chores entirely naked. Spanish men later mistook the casual style of dress as a sign of libidinous.

The Guaraní, much like other indigenous groups throughout the Americas, observed strict roles defined by gender. Besides working in the fields, women took charge of preparing the meals, rearing the children, making pottery, and weaving baskets. Guaraní women also made the beverage *chicha,* which they infused with their own saliva before cooking and fermentation. Men developed skills as warriors and contributed to the diet through hunting and fishing. Guaraní boys customarily carried bows and arrows from childhood and used hunting as a way to perfect their combat skills. Chieftains and the more accomplished warriors practiced polygamy, having extensive households of several wives. Most men, however, had only one wife. Women faced death if caught in adultery, though they were allowed to separate from abusive or neglectful husbands.

Like their Brazilian cousins, the Guaraní were animistic in their religious beliefs. They identified natural forces such as the sun, sky, thunder, lightning, and rain as deities. Deities took on the forms of animals, especially birds, which held sacred meanings for the forest peoples. Shamans invoked these spirits in order to bring success in love, battle, and the harvest. Offerings, ritual dances, chants, and charms were used to ward off the darker forces of the universe.

Politically, the Guaraní maintained decentralized political units within their territories. Each group inhabited a defined area of territory throughout which its clans could fish, hunt, and engage in slash-and-burn cultivation. Fighting between groups was not uncommon. Raiding and stealing formed part of the struggle for survival, and individual warriors shared political authority with shamans and chieftains. They used bows and poison-tipped arrows, wooden clubs, and spears as the weapons of choice for hunting and raiding. Few material possessions seemed to separate the Guaraní leaders from the followers, for tropical agriculture yielded the same low level of surplus as among the Diaguita. The hereditary chiefs and shamans did enjoy some material advantage over commoners, a difference counted in the number of wives they had since each wife represented field labor and personal service.

The more-or-less permanent settlements of these agriculturists made the Guaraní prey to raids and depredations of boat peoples who thrived along the riverbanks and the nomadic peoples of the Gran Chaco. The precariousness of life among the Guaraní explains why they later accepted Spanish warriors, who seemed to have magical weapons, as allies against their traditional rivals.

## The Southern Hunters

In contrast to the Guaraní, the many groups of nomadic hunters and gatherers of the vast archipelago stretching from the Gran Chaco, through the Córdoba hills and Pampas into Patagonia, acquiesced to neither Inca nor European encroachment. The hunter-gatherers presented no fixed target to be conquered by one another, much less by the Inca armies or European adventurers.

Spaniards were later to consider the vast territory of the Gran Chaco to be "a desert" and settled it only in narrow strips meant to connect more important centers of European civilization. The Europeans became comfortable with the military and family alliances with the Guaraní and with exploiting the slender surplus production of the Diaguita, but they had little use whatsoever for what they viewed as the "impoverishment" of the southern hunters. Nor did the warlike nomads tolerate the Spanish settlers whom they resisted for well over three centuries.

Argentina's southern hunters contrasted with the agricultural peoples to the north and west because they accumulated no surplus whatsoever. They wandered in dispersed and migratory groups, developed only weak political leaders, battled constantly among groups for control of hunting areas, and survived within the narrow constraints of the harsh natural environment. Because they followed game and the seasons, the groups resided in small, temporary encampments made up of eight to 10 *toldos,* round tents covered with animal skins. The southern hunters also glorified warfare as the necessary attribute of survival and relished preying on their enemies in lightning raids. Their chieftains shared decision-making responsibilities with community councils, and

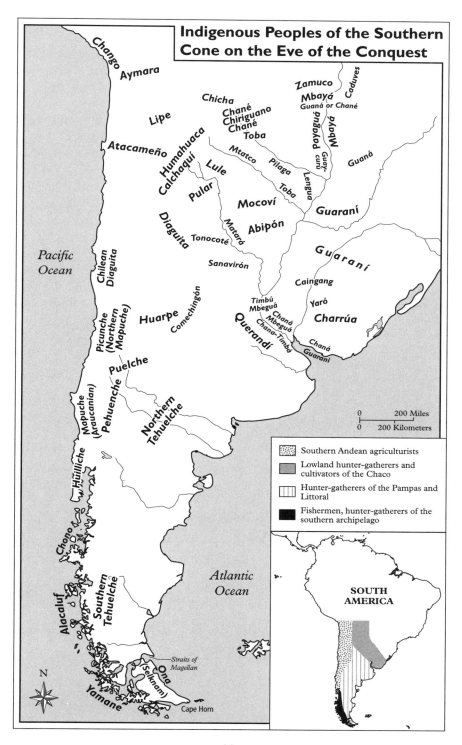

## Indigenous Peoples of the Southern Cone on the Eve of the Conquest

Chango
Aymara
Lipe
Atacameño
Chicha
Zamuco
Caduves
Mbayá
Guaná or Chané
Chané
Chiriguano
Chané
Toba
Mtatco
Pilaga
Guaná
Humahuaca
Calchaquí
Lule
Toba
Pular
Mocoví
Guaraní
Diaguita
Matará
Abipón
Tonocoté
Guaraní
Chilean
Diaguita
Sanavirón
Caingang

Pacific
Ocean

Timbú
Mbeguá
Yaró
Huarpe
Comechingón
Chaná
Mbeguá
Charrúa
Picunche
(Northern
Mapuche)
Querandí
Chaná-Timbó
Chaná
Guaraní
Puelche
Mapuche
(Araucanian)
Pehuenche
Northern
Tehuelche

Huilliche

Chono

Alacaluf
Southern
Tehuelche

Atlantic
Ocean

SOUTH
AMERICA

N

Straits of
Magellan
Ona
(Selknam)
Yamane
Cape Horn

0        200 Miles
0        200 Kilometers

Southern Andean agriculturists
Lowland hunter-gatherers and cultivators of the Chaco
Hunter-gatherers of the Pampas and Littoral
Fishermen, hunter-gatherers of the southern archipelago

11

their shamans specialized in paying homage to and influencing the numerous spirits. The shamans developed the knowledge of folk medicines and practiced the animistic rituals that made sense of the arbitrariness of nature.

Several but not all of the innumerable hunter bands were culturally and linguistically related to one another; however, the complete lack of large-scale territorial or political organization among them meant that no one group (or outside imperial force) could conquer the others and impose common beliefs and language. Each hunting group remained independent and mutually antagonistic to the other indigenous hunters. Despite the ethnic hostilities and language differences, the hunter-gatherers of southern South America did trade among themselves and exchanged practical knowledge. But in their adaptability to the harsh environment and in their political decentralization lay the secrets to their independence and autonomy. These hunting peoples pursued lives of splendid, if impoverished, individualism.

### Peoples of the Gran Chaco

The first major group of the southern hunters resided in the Gran Chaco, the great territorial depression between the Bolivian Andes, the Brazilian massif, the rocky hills along the upper Paraguay River, and the Córdoba mountains of Argentina. The Gran Chaco is not a region conductive to tilling. Its numerous marshes spill into and flood the surrounding grasslands during the rainy season, leaving a thin crust of salt on the land. During the rest of the year, the unrelenting sun dries up the vegetation, except for the thick tropical woodlands that bound the Gran Chaco on the east. Numerous cultural and linguistic groups contested for living space within this sparse landscape. At the time of European contact, the Chaco groups displayed much variation among themselves.

From study of the Inca it is known that people from the Gran Chaco came to the border villages of the Andean empire to barter animal skins and ostrich and egret feathers for ornaments of gold, silver, and copper. Through trade, these same Andean products found their way east and south to the hunting groups on the Pampas. Few peoples of the Chaco cultivated crops, the Guaná being one of the exceptions, for they cultivated root crops, especially the cassava plant, and tobacco. The Guaná dried and crushed tobacco into a coarse powder, which they smoked in pipes. (Apparently, few Chaco groups chewed coca leaves like their Andean neighbors.) Conquered by the Mbayá, the Guaná villages had

*A 19th-century depiction of a group of indigenous people of Argentina's Gran Chaco region* (Leon Pallière, 1858)

to pay tribute in tobacco to their conquerors. In return, they received the Mbayá's protection from the depredations of other groups.

Each of the seven major and numerous minor cultural and linguistic groups in the Gran Chaco maintained rituals representing beliefs about their relation to the cosmos. Certain rites of manhood and menstruation initiated youth into full participation in village affairs. Like all other indigenous groups, the people of the Chaco were polytheistic. Good and evil spirits existed everywhere, in nature, in animals, and in the heavens, so that the shamans had to chant and lead dances in order to placate the harmful spirits and bring good luck to the camp. The knowledge of herbs and the art of chanting confirmed the authority of the male, and in some cases female, shamans in curing the sick.

Each clan in the Chaco divided gender tasks: The men followed athletic and warrior pursuits, and the women, domestic and reproductive roles. Women constructed the temporary shelters, wove baskets, and made crude pottery. Monogamy prevailed among most men; only the headmen had more than one wife. The warriors honed their skills at warfare by hunting deer, peccaries, tapir, jaguars, and nutria. Boys customarily fished with bows and arrows. Besides using tobacco, all groups consumed *chicha*.

As was true among other nomadic peoples, the typical Chaco hunting band of 50 to 100 members made major decisions by consensus. The chieftain merely carried out the decisions of the band's adult males. Although individuals may have attempted to live in concert with nature in so far as possible, these hunting groups never existed in peace and harmony among themselves. Seasonal variations in the availability of game and even the slightest variation in rainfall left the hunters vulnerable to feast or famine. These factors placed the small bands under constant pressure to expand their living space and to raid and conduct warfare with neighboring groups. The Payaguá, for example, who lived at the headwaters of the Paraguay River, were particularly adept at handling canoes, which they used in fishing and hunting and in raiding the long houses of the Guaraní downriver.

The Jesuit missionaries, who were the first Europeans to study the hunters of the Chaco region, recorded oral histories that told of how armed rivalry between groups was a regular part of life. When a leader summoned his warriors to avenge the death of a kinsman, the warriors selected a young chieftain to lead the raid on a neighboring encampment, preferably in the early morning. Warriors killed their rivals, and in some cases took heads as trophies, later converting the skulls into drinking cups. The hostilities were frequent but did not approach extermination of one band by another. The raiders of the Chaco usually retreated after suffering a few casualties and brought captured women and children into their bands when possible, and the constant raids caused the groups to either take land from rivals or retreat to marginal territory. These nomadic hunters preferred to live in the vicinity of their ancestors' burial sites, but over time they were forced to move and adjust to one another. And the paucity of resources discouraged the Spaniards, who avoided the Gran Chaco for more than 300 years, especially after some early and disastrous encounters with these hunting peoples.

### The Charrúa

Another major group of southern hunters who had early hostile relations with the Europeans were the Charrúa. These peoples consisted of five distinct groupings, all of whom were related linguistically and who inhabited the region of present-day Uruguay, southern Brazil, and northeastern Argentina. The Charrúa, like other southern hunters, shared a disdain of agriculture and lived on game, fish, wild fruits, and roots. They made their houses of woven mats hung between pole frames. The Charrúa dressed in skins during the winter and wore a

*The Charrúa* (Delaunois, 1832)

15

leather apron in the summer; the males tattooed and painted their bodies, particularly before battle. The Charrúa also pierced their lips, ears, and noses, in which they placed feathers and shells. They built large canoes for fishing on the rivers and in the estuary of the Río de la Plata. The canoes of the Charrúa, according to an early European mariner, measured "10 to 12 fathoms [approximately 69 feet] in length and half a fathom [a little more than 3 feet] in width; the wood was cedar, very beautifully worked; they rowed them with very long paddles decorated by crests and tassels of feathers on the handles; and 40 standing men rowed each canoe" (Steward 1946, I:193). The men of the Charrúa hunted with bows and arrows, spears, and bolas (described below). They were also very skilled at slinging jagged stones at game.

Political and social decentralization was the rule among the Charrúa also. These hunting groups resided in small dispersed groups on the grasslands of Uruguay and on the riverbanks of the lower Paraná Basin. Eight to 10 people inhabited each family hut, and a band of nomads comprised eight to 12 families altogether. Two or more groups might band together for warfare but otherwise kept to themselves. According to the first European missionaries who attempted to convert them to Christianity, the chieftains did not have a great deal of authority in the hunting bands, where fistfights between individuals sufficed to settle disputes. In battle, the warriors were merciless to enemy warriors and incorporated captured women and children into their bands as slaves or family members.

### Peoples of the Pampas and Patagonia

In the expansive prairies that presently make up the eastern and southern provinces of Argentina, small bands of hunter-gatherers predominated. They hunted native animals such as deer, guanacos, armadillos, prairie dogs, and South American ostriches. In the woodlands of Patagonia, gathering seeds and hunting deer formed the basis of existence. The coastal peoples of Patagonia hunted seals and fished from canoes. For many centuries, life was much the same for these peoples. They too lived in small bands, celebrated their independence, and confounded the first Europeans.

Just before the Europeans arrived, the larger cultural and linguistic groups of the Querandí, Puelche, and Tehuelche inhabited large sections of the Argentine Pampas and Patagonia. These peoples moved mainly on foot and set up camps based on the seasons and hunting opportunities. They were little encumbered by material goods. Their tools were simple, usually bone and stone weapons and scrapers, products of their Stone Age existence. The peoples of the Argentine prairies, however, would become known for one unique weapon: the bolas. Made of three round stones covered by animal skin and connected by leather cords, the bolas, flung by a skilled hunter, could bring down guanacos, ostriches, and other large game. The hunter whirled the bolas around his head and flung them at the legs of his prey. He then moved in on the hobbled animal to make the kill with a spear or club.

The principal bands of the Pampas and Patagonia were quite small, made up only of a few families or clans. In this sense they were like other southern hunters. There existed no confederations of tribes or a

---

# ROLE OF WOMEN AMONG THE ˙PUELCHE, C. 1760

The women, who have once accepted their husbands, are in general very faithful and laborious; for, besides the nursing and bringing up their children, they are obliged to submit to every species of drudgery. In short they do every thing, except hunting and fighting; and sometimes they even engage in the latter. The care of all household affairs is left entirely to the women: they fetch wood and water, dress victuals, make, mend, and clean the tents, dress and sew together the hides, and also the lesser skins of which they make their mantles and carapas, and spin and make ponchas or macuns [two types of cloaks]. When they travel, the women pack up every thing, even the tent-poles; which they must erect and pull down themselves, as often as occasion requires: they load, unload, and settle the baggage, straiten the girths of the saddles, and carry the lance before their husbands. No excuse of sickness, or being big with child, will relieve them from the appointed labor: and so rigidly are they obliged to perform their duty, that their husbands cannot help them on any occasion, or in the greatest distress, without incurring the highest ignominy. The women of quality, or those related to the Caciques, are permitted to have slaves, who ease their mistresses of the most laborious part of their work; but if they should not have any slaves, they must undergo the same fatigue as the rest.

■

*(Falkner 1935, 125)*

---

rigid differentiation of their societies between warriors and hereditary leaders. Yet, these peoples did observe sharp gender differentiation, with women subordinated to men, who for the most part were monogamous. Women cleaned game, cooked, cared for and disciplined the children, put up the *toldos,* wove baskets, and made simple pottery. Men and women alike shared duties of gathering and preparing food and may have discussed basic decisions within families before the men met in council. As warriors and hunters, the men dominated the formal decision-making processes and carried out raids on neighboring groups.

## Overall Characteristics

The characteristics of the indigenous population influenced greatly the subsequent history of Argentina. Even the most elemental ethnography of the region could predict at least the general outlines of the coming encounter with the Spanish. The population dispersion, political decentralization, and lack of surplus wealth ruined the best-laid plans of the first Spanish adventurers. There could be no quick conquest of the Southern Cone, no fortuitous and intrepid capture of an emperor to cause discord and disillusionment among the indigenous defenders of the Pampas. No invaders could build towns and cities directly over the ruins of indigenous settlements they had just destroyed. The Europeans could not tap into existing agricultural and commercial networks. No one in Argentina could mimic the rapid conquest of the Aztec and Inca Empires.

Why? Because where the pre-Columbian populations lived in dispersed and decentralized patterns, the subsequent European settlement demanded a longer-term commitment and substantial rearrangement of social and economic relationships. The newcomers of necessity took their time, settling regions over the span of several centuries. They created towns and farms directly out of the wilderness. Europeans in the Southern Cone settled the homelands by bringing in new agricultural technologies, livestock husbandry, and techniques of combat.

Finally, pre-Columbian traditions endured the gradual European settlement. The languages, gender relationships, religious beliefs, preexisting rivalries, ethnic diversity, and varying cultural and material contributions—all of which were thousands of years old—survived. All indigenous peoples of the Southern Cone had already accumulated

# DESCRIPTION OF THE INDIVIDUALISM OF THE PEHUENCHE PEOPLE OF MENDOZA

This nation, which considers itself independent of the rest, does not have any strict alliance; nor do its members subordinate themselves to their own chiefs except through a kind of tolerance, so that no one is abused.

Only the oldest elders or the richest are those who are called caciques, or *guilmenes*. This title, which is earned by one's deeds, if those of one's ancestors were also recommendable, impresses the subjects more. According to this procedure, the son of a cacique who is not worthy, who does not make himself rich, [and] who has not accomplished great feats, is nothing. He is viewed as a contemptible *motetón* [commoner]; and then the staff of the cacique is inherited by the Indian of the village who is the most handsome and who speaks well and easily.

The caciques do not have any jurisdiction either to punish or to reward anyway. There each person is the judge of his case and, consequently, respects no one else's opinion. In this manner, if a *guilmén* wants to abuse a *motetón* and the latter feels more vigorous, he will attack his chief, stab him, do whatever he can. And far from meriting punishment, he will be considered a strong man for having proved his ferocity. If the cacique has more relatives than the *motetón*, they will go all out to right wrongs and assault the *motetón*, in order to pay him back and do the same to him. This action is the only restraint that they have; but in any case, the merit of having maimed the cacique will not be considered a loss, even if the *motetón* may lose his possessions.

■

*Luis de la Cruz, "Tratado importante para el perfecto conocimiento de los indios peguenches" (Angelis 1969, I:449–50)*

experience in the arts of resistance and independence. Certain tools, foods, habits, modes of transportation, religious beliefs, and social relationships of the ancient Argentines in fact influenced and transformed the European invaders, because these established indigenous traditions best suited the environment.

## The Encounter between Native Argentines and Europeans

The Río de la Plata (River of Silver) region was the focus of much of the Spanish encounter with the native population in what became modern-day Argentina. In truth, the Río de la Plata is not a river at all, but rather an estuary of the great Paraná River drainage system. Moreover, the name is used to refer to the greater region stretching westward from the estuary all the way to the Andes Mountains. The historic Río de la Plata includes the modern nations of Uruguay and Paraguay, as well as Argentina, and for the entire period of the encounter and colonial era, the histories of these three countries were closely intertwined. They were all part of overlapping entities, so it is inevitable to refer to and discuss events and conditions in Paraguay or Uruguay, as they are of signal importance to understanding the history of Argentina.

The Río de la Plata was ever at the fringe of an empire. Most of the region lay outside the great Andean empire of the Inca, and it was to be of secondary interest to Europeans, too. Fringe areas lacked wealth and humanpower, and Spaniards occupied them more slowly than they had in the territories of the great empires of the Aztec and the Inca, which had been seized in a matter of months. Rich in silver and indigenous labor, Mexico and Peru formed the core of Spanish interest in the Indies for the next several centuries. The Río de la Plata had neither of these riches so coveted by the colonists. Rather, the natives lived in decentralized agricultural or hunting groups, and they had no precious metals to offer the Spaniards. For complete settlement and domination settlers had to laboriously defeat the indigenous peoples one group at a time in a process that took centuries. Spaniards wishing to be supported as great lords could not easily capture the labor and services of the Charrúa and Querandí. The Spaniards therefore never conquered the Río de la Plata; they settled it.

### The Founding of Asunción

In 1492, Christopher Columbus, with his exploration of the Caribbean Islands, commenced an incomparable period of European expansion and empire building. He died believing that he had reached Japan and China. Other adventurers soon realized that they were not exploring Asia but two new continents. An Italian mariner who came to the coast of Brazil soon after Columbus's death returned to Europe and published a map that named the continents after himself, Amerigo Vespucci. Thus the so-called New World came to be known as North and South America.

European cartographers first began to fill in the contours of southern South America on their sailing charts following the 1516 discovery of the estuary of the Río de la Plata by the navigator Juan Díaz de Solís. Early explorers of the regions waded ashore in the estuary and explored the Paraná River, where they traded with the natives for objects made of silver. The Europeans referred to the peoples they encountered in the New World by the generic term *indios*, or *Indians*, which derived from Columbus's initial mistake in believing he had reached Asia, calling the place "las Indias," or "the Indies." This strange, erroneous nomenclature has been perpetuated by Europeans and their descendants ever since.

Explorers in the Río de la Plata region quickly learned that the source of these objects in precious metals came from the great Inca Empire to the west. Hence, the estuary and the entire region came to acquire the equally erroneous name of the River of Silver. In 1520, Ferdinand Magellan passed along the coast of Argentina and around the southernmost point of South America to Asia on the first circumnavigation

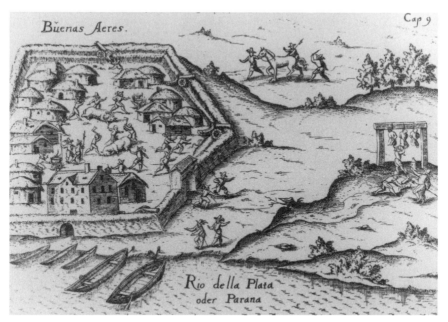

*A depiction of the fractious and chaotic first Spanish settlement at Buenos Aires, around 1536. While some of the colonists are shown in everyday endeavors, such as slaughtering and cooking livestock, others race about in obvious agitation. Note the macabre scene of execution and mutilation on the outskirts of the settlement. (Ulrich Schmidel, 1891, courtesy Emece Editores)*

21

of the earth. He bequeathed his name to the straits through which ships still pass between the Atlantic and Pacific Oceans at the tip of the Southern Cone.

To lay claim to its hoped-for wealth and also to keep the Portuguese in Brazil from settling the Río de la Plata, the Spanish Crown in 1534 commissioned a colonizing venture. It was one of the few expeditions sent directly from Spain. A Spanish nobleman with no prior experience in the Indies, Pedro de Mendoza, led this voyage of 1,600 men and 16 ships. They established a small settlement called Buenos Aires, for the "good airs," or fair winds, at the edge of the Argentine Pampas. Because the Querandí and Charrúa refused to provide food for them and had no

## THE FIRST BATTLE BETWEEN EUROPEANS AND THE INDIGENOUS PEOPLES OF RÍO DE LA PLATA, 1536

These [Querandí] brought us daily their provision of fish and meat to our camp [at Buenos Aires], and did so for a fortnight, and they did only fail once to come to us. So our captain, [Pedro de Mendoza], sent to them a judge, named [Juan Pavón], with two foot-soldiers, for they were at a distance of four miles from our camp. When they came near to them, they were all three beaten black and blue, and were then sent back again to our camp. [Pedro de Mendoza] . . . hearing of this from the judge's report . . . sent Diego, his own brother, against them with three hundred foot-soldiers and thirty well-armed mounted men, of whom I also was one, straightaway charging us to kill and take prisoners all these Indians and to take possession of their settlement. But when we came near them there were now some four thousand men, for they had assembled all their friends. And when we were about to attack them, they defended themselves in such a way that we had that very day our hands full. They also killed our commander, Diego [de Mendoza], and six noblemen. Of our foot-soldiers and mounted men over twenty were slain, and on their side about one thousand. Thus did they defend themselves valiantly against us, so that indeed we felt it.

■

*(Schmidl 1891, 7–8)*

22

gold for the taking, the ill-prepared settlers grew hungry and fractious. Several bands of warriors attacked this first Spanish settlement, and the colonists had to contemplate abandoning Buenos Aires. They had already sent an exploratory party upriver from Buenos Aires in search of the Inca Empire, which unbeknownst to them, had already fallen to a small group of Spaniards led by Francisco Pizarro. More than 170 men ascended the Paraná and Paraguay Rivers in an attempt to reach Peru by crossing the Gran Chaco. The Payaguá killed them all. Only one beleaguered indigenous group found it expeditious to help the Spaniards.

After losing a battle against another small Spanish party from Buenos Aires, the agricultural Guaraní of what is now Paraguay accepted the Spaniards as great warriors and allies in their own struggles with the surrounding bands. The Guaraní assisted the Spaniards of the Mendoza expedition in founding Asunción in 1537. It was to be the first permanent Spanish settlement in the Río de la Plata, as within four years, the remaining 350 inhabitants of Buenos Aires abandoned the settlement and moved to Asunción. Since there were only four Spanish women in Asunción, the Spanish men emulated the native leaders and took Guaraní women to serve them as concubines, servants, and food suppliers. Guaraní chieftains were made to offer their daughters to Spaniards in exchange for a military alliance against native enemies.

Having found no gold, the Spaniards sought to acquire the work of the indigenous women as a sign of wealth adopting the native custom. "[I]t is the women who sow and reap the crop," one Spaniard observed (Service 1954, 35). Their children were mestizo (of mixed Native American and European ancestry) and grew up speaking Guaraní rather than Spanish; however, these first-generation mestizos came to see themselves as European and remained loyal to the king of Spain. Eventually, the first- and second-generation mestizos became the gentry and leading citizens of Paraguay, and in the decades following the abandonment of Buenos Aires, they provided the leadership for the numerous military expeditions against neighboring Indian groups, gaining greater wealth and status with the number of Indian slaves captured in battle.

## Settler Politics and Society

Pedro de Mendoza died on his return voyage to Spain, and in his place the king dispatched Alvar Núñez Cabeza de Vaca to govern the small, landlocked colony of Paraguay. (*Paraguay* originally referred to the

Spanish-held area around Asunción. In the following centuries the term was extended to encompass territories to the north and at various times included regions beyond the boundaries of the modern-day nation of the same name.) Cabeza de Vaca was famous for his earlier adventures as one of only three survivors of Juan Ponce de León's expedition to Florida and the Mississippi River; after being stranded in a shipwreck in the Gulf of Mexico, Cabeza de Vaca had walked across Texas and Mexico all the way to Mexico City.

Cabeza de Vaca brought more European settlers, all male. Together the Spaniards and Guaraní warriors subdued rival tribes in the surrounding territory, but in an attempt to cross the Chaco region, Cabeza de Vaca nearly exhausted the resources of Asunción. Meanwhile, the settlers belatedly learned that Pizarro had already claimed the wealth of the Inca. Subsequently, because it was a land with no gold, Paraguay lost its attractiveness for Spanish immigration, and few additional Europeans arrived to challenge the influence of the original settlers. Dissension nonetheless broke out among members of the Spanish community, many of whom disliked Governor Cabeza de Vaca.

At issue was the division of the dwindling number of Guaraní. Soon after the Europeans arrived, diseases previously unknown to the American natives ravaged the indigenous population. Mestizos gained the immunities to European diseases from their fathers, and their population in Paraguay expanded as the number of Guaraní women and servants declined precipitously. In the semitropical environment of Paraguay, the native death rates from successive epidemics of smallpox, influenza, and other diseases rose to 40 percent within just one decade. For this very reason slaving expeditions were sent out to replenish the numbers of indigenous servants and concubines of the Spaniards and later of the mestizo gentry.

The economic crisis caused by the decline of the Guaraní population and the unpopularity of Governor Cabeza de Vaca spurred a faction of Spanish settlers to mount the first coup d'état in the Río de la Plata. The victorious faction returned Cabeza de Vaca to Spain in chains. A veteran of the original Mendoza expedition, Domingo de Irala became governor. The Guaraní too had grown desperate by their situation, ravaged by disease and the excessive Spanish demands for Indian servants, female labor, and foodstuffs. A number of Guaraní rebelled against the Spaniards in 1545, but the settler community put down the uprising with the aid of "loyal" Indians.

In the relative poverty of Paraguay, the settlers enjoyed political autonomy from Spain and freely established a social system to their own liking. Governor Irala divided the Guaraní into *encomiendas* (grants of Indian labor and tribute) among the individual Spanish settlers. These *encomiendas* became a kind of permanent serfdom for the indigenous peoples under Spanish rule. Spaniards in Asunción passed these grants on to their mestizo sons. Succeeding generations of mestizos moved from Asunción to establish other towns and other *encomiendas* on the frontiers of Paraguay. Decline of the Guaraní population, however, reduced the original size of the *encomiendas,* and by 1600, a mere 3,000 Indians remained in Asunción. The *encomiendas* tended therefore to involve personal labor more than tribute, giving the settlers in Paraguay a reputation for laziness. "Having plenty of all things good to eat and drink," one observer said with some exaggeration, "they give themselves up to ease and idleness, and don't much trouble themselves with trading at all" (du Biscay 1968, 11).

### Return to Buenos Aires

The Paraguayan settlers nonetheless desired the European goods symbolic of their rank and sought to reestablish the river link to the estuary of the Río de la Plata. The mestizo citizens of Asunción took it upon themselves to establish the river port of Santa Fe in 1573, and in 1580, they went downriver again to the estuary of the Río de la Plata. Mestizos of relatively high social status in Paraguay figured prominently among the 75 founders of the second permanent settlement of Buenos Aires. They were led by Juan de Garay, a Paraguayan descendant of one of the original members of Mendoza's expedition of 44 years before.

European settlements in the region established the Paraná River as a lifeline from Paraguay to Spain as well as to the rest of the Americas. Since the independent native inhabitants of the Gran Chaco barred a direct trade route between Paraguay and Peru, Buenos Aires soon supplanted Asunción. Its growth as the major Spanish port in the Río de la Plata would subordinate Paraguay to Buenos Aires's commercial orbit. In fact, during the next two centuries of the colonial period, Buenos Aires would become the Atlantic portal to nearly all of South America. As historian Juan Agustín García writes, "Buenos Aires was commercially oriented from its beginnings" (García 1955, 104).

The foundation in 1580 of this small port on the estuary of the Río de la Plata brought to an end a remarkable period of European expansion in the Americas. Nearly all the great cities of today's Latin America had been established between 1492 and the second founding of Buenos

Aires in 1580. Thus, the conquest phase in Spanish America ended at Buenos Aires, 88 years and 4,000 miles from the scene of Columbus's original contact. It was, however, only the beginning of a 300-year struggle for Argentina between the land's tenacious first inhabitants and the European interlopers.

# 2

# THE COLONIAL RÍO DE LA PLATA

**M**any Argentines have neglected their colonial past. The reasons are fairly evident: Subsequent economic modernization and immigration radically changed the outward appearances of the nation, and the colonial past is simply not as visible in Buenos Aires as in other Latin American capitals such as Lima or Mexico City. Yet the colonial period established many more fundamental elements of Argentine life and society than modern residents may care to admit.

Certainly, in the colonial legacy of the Río de la Plata (a region encompassing modern-day Paraguay and Uruguay as well as Argentina), one can find ample evidence of official corruption as well as hostility and warfare between the native peoples and the European settlers. This conflict persisted without solution for more than three centuries. There are also examples of political conflict within the Spanish colonial community. In terms of social inequality, the colonial period was formative. Spaniards marginalized the nonwhite laborers and exploited them in the interest of economic development. The import of African slaves contributed a mighty pillar to the edifice of a fundamentally inequitable social order.

Yet, a historian would be remiss not to mention the remarkable successes and vitality of colonial Argentina. The region had not been blessed with readily disposable resources, such as lodes of silver ore and large numbers of sedentary native agriculturists, the features that had made Mexico and Peru the centers of the Spanish Empire. Argentina was a fringe area. It depended on colonial activities elsewhere, especially in the silver mining region of today's Bolivia. Nonetheless, the settlers successfully developed Argentina into a prosperous and productive colony, despite the many obstacles. By the time the long colonial period came to a close, Argentina had become one of the jewels of the Spanish Empire.

## Potosí and the Silver Trail

In the 17th and 18th centuries, the Bolivian city of Potosí was the silver mining capital of the world. Its fabulous mountain of high-grade silver ore attracted a transient mining population, which, at times, numbered more than 100,000 people. Potosí easily was the most populous place in the hemisphere. The largest number of residents consisted of indigenous Peruvian laborers brought to the mines under the draft labor system called the *mita*. By 1700, however, mining operations were largely supported by a more or less permanent workforce made up of mestizos and African slaves, as well as Basque, Genoese, and Portuguese laborers. While most workers camped on the outskirts of the city, Spanish officials, merchants, and clergymen, numbering anywhere from a quarter to a third of the population, inhabited permanent buildings downtown. The Imperial City of Potosí boasted of some 4,000 buildings of stone, several with two stories. The Catholic religious orders housed themselves in well-made monasteries and convents decorated with the silver plate and tapestries befitting the wealthiest mining area in the world.

Without the silver mines, however, no one ever would have established such a metropolis in this Andean wasteland. The mining district lies between 12,000 to 17,000 feet above sea level. Few trees or grass,

*Mule trains, such as this one shown taking a break while crossing the Bolivian cordillera, provided transportation between the Argentine port of Buenos Aires and the silver mines of the Andes. The route was long and arduous and required hard trekking by tens of thousands of mules and thousands of muleteers.* (Leon Palliére, 1858)

let alone crops, can grow within a radius of 22 miles. Provisions for the population and supplies for the Spanish mines had to come from across the high sierras. Consequently, commerce in mercury, mules, food-stuffs, and consumer goods of every description required extensive trade contacts with Peru, Chile, and the Río de la Plata. One 17th-century traveler explained that everyone in Potosí, whether gentleman, officer, or clergyman, seemed to be engaged in commerce.

The city that minted a great part of the world's supply of silver coins for approximately 260 years supported a large volume of local trade. Each day the roads leading to Potosí were choked with mule trains, lla-mas, indigenous pack carriers, and herds of sheep and cattle. High transport costs raised the price of foodstuffs in Potosí to twice the price of victuals anywhere else in the region. As the terrain forbade wheeled vehicles, mules served to transport loads of silver, mercury to process the ore, and foodstuffs. Annually, more than 26,000 mules were driven to Potosí.

The Potosí market sustained the original settlement of the Río de la Plata, supporting groups of Spanish settlers who intended to establish commercial lifelines to the silver city of colonial Bolivia. Europeans from Peru first descended into the Río de la Plata to settle Santiago del Estero in 1553. Tucumán, some 140 miles back toward Potosí on the road, was founded 12 years later. Córdoba's foundation in 1573 extended the land route to the edge of the Pampas. The establishment in 1583 of Salta and Jujuy, closer to the highland markets, secured the road to Potosí.

Other trading routes were founded in the meantime to link the Río de la Plata to Spanish settlements in what are now modern-day Chile and Paraguay. From the Pacific coast, Spaniards crossed the Andes to found Mendoza and San Juan in 1561. Similarly, Spaniards from the Paraguayan settlement at Asunción went down the Paraná River to secure towns at Corrientes in 1558, at Santa Fe 15 years later, and finally at Buenos Aires in 1580. (See map on page 2).

## The Mule Fair of Salta

Befitting their positions as gateways to the Peruvian highlands, Salta and Jujuy became the foremost commercial cities of the colonial period. Salta's principal commercial attraction was its famous mule fair, held each February and March on the meadows at the edge of the Lerma Valley. The fair annually attracted hundreds of buyers from Peru and equal numbers of sellers of mules, corn, cattle, wines, beef jerky, tallow,

# TESTIMONY ON THE RISKS OF THE MULE BUSINESS, 1773

Those [mules] purchased on the . . . pampas, from one and one-half to two years old, cost 12 to 16 reales each [up to 2 pesos]. [In Potosí, mules sold for 9 pesos per head.] . . . The herds taken from the fields of Buenos Aires comprise only 600 to 700 mules. . . .

The purchaser who is going to winter the horses [in Córdoba] may also turn them over, at his expense to the ranchers, but I do not consider this wise because the attendants who round up and guard the mules maim the horses for their own purposes and those of the owner, an act in which they have few scruples. The aforementioned 12 men necessary for the drive of every herd of 600 to 700 mules, earn, or rather they are paid, from 12 to 16 silver pesos . . . and in addition they are provided with meat to their satisfaction and some Paraguay mate. . . .

Now we have a herd capable of making a second trip, to Salta, where the [mule fair] is held, leaving Córdoba in the end of April . . . so as to arrive in Salta in early June, making allowance for accidental and often necessary stops for the animals to rest in fertile fields with abundant water. In this second journey the herds are usually composed of from 1,300 to 1,400 mules. . . .

These herds rest in the pastures of Salta around eight months, and in selecting this locale one should observe what I said at the outset about . . . the illegal acts of the owners [of the pastures], who, although in general they are honorable men, can perpetrate many frauds, listing as dead, stolen, or runaways, many of the best mules of the herd, which they replace with local-born animals . . . not suited for the hard trip to Peru.

For every herd, two droves of horses are necessary; one to separate and round up the animals, and 4 reales a day per man must be paid to the owners, even if each one rides 20 horses, crippling them or killing them. . . . Each herd leaving Salta is comprised of 1,700 or 1,800 mules.

■

*(Concolorcorvo 1965, 112–15)*

and wheat. Tents and field beds of merchants spread out over the mud, and corrals nearby retained the thousands of animals for which they bargained. Obviously, the main commodity was the mule; yearly sales of the beast of burden varied from 11,000 to 46,000 animals.

Ranches for pasturing cattle and mules dotted the countryside of Salta and Jujuy in support of this annual commercial event. The largest estates could brag of wine presses, brandy distilleries, flour mills, soap-making equipment, and stores of wine and wheat. Inhabitants specialized in the livestock trades to such an extent that they seldom cultivated enough vegetables to supplement their beef diets. One traveler noted that Salta's commerce supported a town of 400 houses, six churches, 300 Spaniards, and three times that number of mulattoes and blacks.

Jujuy also depended on the mule trade. The town's position on the road between Salta and the highland valleys made it the terminus of the overland cart route from Buenos Aires and Córdoba. Teamsters had to transfer their freight to mules here for the trek up the rocky passes leading into the Bolivian highlands.

All this commercial development transformed the old homeland of the Diaguita agriculturists. While the Spaniards easily overcame their resistance, the Diaguita did not disappear. True, European disease reduced their numbers to about 15 percent of their precontact population, but the Diaguita remained part of the new Spanish society of the Argentine northwest. They retained enough land for a meager subsistence, were converted to Catholicism by the Spanish friars, and served influential Spaniards as laborers. Some of the women among them contributed—certainly unwillingly—to the formation of the mestizo working class of Argentina. The progeny of these indigenous women and Spanish men became the bearers, drivers, cowboys, and agricultural workers who underwrote the wealth of Salta and Jujuy. While the Diaguita survived, they were denied opportunities in the development of new Spanish commercial enterprises.

## The Cattlemen of Córdoba

Commerce at Salta depended on trade through and production in Córdoba. Three cordons of low mountain ranges run north to south through the present-day provinces of Córdoba and San Luis. They form both the easternmost fringe of the great Andean cordillera and the border between the semiarid uplands of western Argentina and the humid Pampas to the east. Consumer goods from these locales flowed to market through an integrated commercial pipeline of riverboats, oxcarts, and mule trains, which featured numerous customs collection points and not a little contraband. The extended overland routes economically united the faraway cities of Mendoza at the base of the Andean mountains and Buenos Aires, the port to the Atlantic Ocean.

For most of the colonial period, Córdoba served as the economic and administrative capital of the Río de la Plata. It was the most populous district in the region, and its residents eventually numbered more than 40,000 people. As the Spanish administrative and religious center, Córdoba boasted elegant government houses, churches, convents, and monasteries. Both the governor and bishop lived here, and the colonial university and headquarters of the College of Jesuits were also located in Córdoba. Cattle and mule production supported the city's prestige and importance. Spaniards (and Portuguese) settled on cattle- and mule-breeding estates on the Pampas east of the city. Córdoba's Jesuit college operated several *estancias* (ranches) that yearly dispatched approximately 1,000 mules.

Córdoba's merchant community was large. In 1600, merchants imported slaves for the Potosí market, paying in specie and flour for export. These tradesmen later dealt in as many as 30,000 mules and 600,000 pesos' worth of commerce annually. Merchant factors (agents) from Córdoba came to Buenos Aires to buy mules from local breeders at 3 pesos per head. After marking the mules with their distinctive brands, the factors had them driven overland to Tucumán and Salta to be wintered prior to the next year's fair. In Potosí, these same mules brought up to 9 pesos per head. Cattle too were rounded up and driven overland in much the same fashion.

Spanish commercial development at Córdoba marginalized the original inhabitants of the area, known as the "bearded" Comechingón. Early Spaniards never explained the mystery of the natives' facial hair, for indigenous peoples did not have beards, or the origin of their unique name "Skunk Eaters." The Comechingón did not easily yield their homeland to the Spaniards, nor were they pre-pared, like the agricultural Diaguita, to accommodate themselves at the bottom of Hispanic society. Instead their resistance was particu-larly fierce. They fought in squadrons of as many as 500 men but only at night and "they carried bows, arrows, and spears" (Steward 1946, II: 683–84).

Smaller cultural groups like the Sanaviron and Indama of the Sierras of Córdoba and San Luis were interspersed among the groups of the dominant Comechingón culture. The Spaniards could count on these independent and mutually hostile groups to remain disorganized and to offer little resistance; therefore, the Spaniards, with their technological advantages of steel weaponry, gunpowder, warhorses, and Indian alliances, powerfully outmatched the Comechingón. But neither did the Spaniards totally annihilate these so-called bearded Indians. Those

# A SPANIARD'S ACCOUNT OF WAR WITH THE INDIGENOUS PEOPLE OF CÓRDOBA

[We] went to the province of the Comechingones [Córdoba], who are bearded and very hostile Indians; and Captain [Pedro de] Mendoza went to the said river of Amazona [sic] with half of the men, and I remained in the camp in that province of the Comechingones, where during the period of 20 days these Indians attacked us four times, killing 20 of our horses. Seventy of us remained there in that camp, and each week half of us would go out to look for food, and once, seeing us divided, they came to the camp; but for bad luck they would have attacked us at night, because they would always fight at night and with fire. And at the time they came to do this, I [Pedro González de Prado] and Francisco Gallego were on watch, and these Comechingones came into the camp, and seeing this, I and the said Francisco Gallego charged at them alone, and since we were no more than two and this squadron had more than 500 Indians, placed in good military order with the squadron closed up and carrying bows, arrows, and half lances, when I charged into this squadron, they gave my horse a blow on the head so that he was stupefied and fell with me in the middle of this squadron, and the Indians would have killed me with their arrows if it had not been for the good armor I was wearing, and they took me alive and suspended me in the air, and killed my horse, who was very good, with five arrow wounds. And they should be asked if they know that if I and the said Francisoco Gallego had not charged at them, they would have burned the town and might have killed many of us; and while they were occupied fighting with us, our other companions had time to come out so that the Indians were defeated and many of them killed.

. . . I remained with the Captain Nicolás de Heredia, where we had many battles with the Indians and they killed many horses. We managed to build a fort with logs and branches and kept watch at the gates of it, and one night these bearded Indians came to attack us and got in through some gates that were closed, seeing us divided because the other companions had gone for food; and I was one of the first who came out to these gates to fight with the Indians, and the 30 of us Spaniards who were there defeated them and killed many of them.

■

*"Capítulos de una información de servicios prestados por Pedro González de Prado, que entró en las provincias del Tucumán y Río de la Plata"*
*(Parry and Keith 1984, V:426–27)*

who survived the warfare and disease of the 16th century found refuge on the Pampean frontier.

## Towns and Trade

Potosí's market stimulus provided the commercial basis for the formation of trade routes extending thousands of miles across mountains and plains. Santiago del Estero, Tucumán, Santa Fe, and Mendoza owed their economic well-being to the passage of goods and livestock to the highlands and of the return cargos of silver. Along the extended freight routes lay small villages, farms, and post houses that served teamsters and muleteers and their draft animals and the cattle drovers and their herds.

Indian warfare by no means disappeared following the Spanish occupation of the northwest. Typically, the Spanish governors ratified and even enhanced the traditional power of some Indian chiefs, whom the Spaniards called caciques (a term picked up by the Europeans from the Taino of the Caribbean). But occasionally, renegade Spaniards mobilized Indian rebellions for their own benefit. Pedro de Bohórquez, for example, called himself "Inca" and he united 117 native caciques, whose followers then rose up in arms against the Spaniards in the area of Tucumán in 1657.

The combatants on both sides attempted to destroy the economic assets of the other. The native warriors burned the wheat fields of the Spaniards just before harvest; the latter set fire to the cornfields of the indigenous peoples. Captives on both sides suffered prolonged and severe torture during which indigenous warriors played native musical instruments, such as reed panpipes and wooden trumpets, until the death of prisoners.

To settle once and for all the indigenous resistance, the Spanish at Tucumán resorted to an Inca system of social control: They exiled recalcitrant groups to distant colonies. One group from La Rioja walked back from their exile in Potosí to continue their struggle, but the Spaniards successfully resettled another group, the Quilmes, to a location just south of Buenos Aires. Quilmes is now the name of a suburb of the capital and one of the leading local beers.

Tucumán and Santiago del Estero, both lying midway between the economic and administrative center of Córdoba and the Salta mule fairs, were important trading intermediaries in the colonial era. Santiago found early prominence as a center of exchange, boasting of some 40 plazas for trade. According to a commercial summary of 1677,

34

*Women working at traditional tasks in Santiago del Estero, which became an important center of commerce in the late 17th century. The town was strategically located between Córdoba and Salta and came to serve as an exchange for goods, mules, and laborers.*
(Leon Pallère, 1858)

the commodities that passed through Santiago on the way to Potosí included 40,000 head of cattle, 30,000 mules, and 227 tons of *yerba* (leaves used to make the popular tea *yerba mate*).

Tucumán eventually supplanted Santiago as a more important commercial community. Early on, Spanish traders organized the indigenous agriculturists to produce "Indian cloths" to be sold in Potosí, but the population of sedentary native peoples dwindled due to epidemics of European disease in the mid-17th century. The city's merchants then turned to the mule trade, buying mules in Córdoba and selling them at the Salta fairs. Soon the dominant economic concern became oxcarting. *Estancias* in the area specialized in breeding and breaking oxen for the great cart trains passing between Jujuy and the port of Buenos Aires. Working with local timbers and leather, Tucumanos constructed Spanish-style carts with wheels nearly 20 feet in diameter (the better to pass over muddy roads) and with a carrying capacity of more than 1 ton.

The commercial route that formed a great arch from Potosí south to Córdoba turned east to connect with the Paraná River at the port of Santa Fe. This river town served as the link to Paraguay's production of *yerba* and tobacco. Paraguayans sent their goods downriver in canoes, rafts, boats, and sailing barks because the hunting peoples of the Gran Chaco wilderness prevented contact with Bolivia. Major river travel occurred between February and August, when the spring rains swelled the river's channels. Other Paraguayan products descended as far as Buenos Aires in the same fashion. From Santa Fe, cart trains carried Paraguayan tea and other products to Córdoba for further distribution west to Mendoza and Chile or north to Potosí.

## Farmers of Mendoza

Mendoza served as the commercial link between the Río de la Plata and the secondary market at Santiago de Chile. Abundant sunshine and steady water supply from the Andean snowmelt proved ideal for growing crops through irrigation. Mendocinos engaged in viticulture and wheat growing as auxiliary economic activities, but commerce remained foremost. Paraguayan *yerba* and imports from Buenos Aires passed through Mendoza bound for Chile. In Mendoza, goods were transferred from oxcarts to mule packs to be guided across the Andean passes during the summer transport season. The weeklong trip covered

*The main plaza at Mendoza, a city favored by location and climate, which made it a thriving place in the late 17th and early 18th centuries. Mendoza's surrounding fertile countryside provided crops such as grapes and wheat, and it was also the point where goods bound to and from the Andes were transferred from oxcarts onto pack mules, or vice versa. (Edmond B. de La Touanne, 1826, courtesy of Emece Editores)*

160 miles from Mendoza to Santiago de Chile. Chileans sent their products to Bolivia via Mendoza. The local farmers here added their own wheat and wine to the cargos. Although produce of the vine such as the grape brandy aptly called "fire-water," or aguardiente, found a low-end market even in Buenos Aires, the wines of the Andes foothills merely supplemented what the market lacked in their overseas trade with Europe.

Along the extensive trade routes between the great market and production areas, travelers found auxiliary economic services—roadhouses, remounts, forage, and country stores. Farmers along the roads provided teamsters with lambs, eggs, squash, and watermelons. People even made a living from ferrying goods across large streams. They furnished ox-hide tubs and swimming horses for baggage and passengers alike. These services completed the regional trading complex of the colonial era, but they did not earn their workers large fortunes, which is why the Spanish merchants and landowners left them mainly in the hands of mestizos and mulattoes.

## Gatherers of *Yerba* in Paraguay

Another great production center in this far-reaching commercial network was located up the Paraná River. Though they lived only 620 miles by land from Potosí, Paraguayans could not communicate with Bolivia because of the hostility of the natives of the Gran Chaco, so Paraguay existed on the very administrative and economic fringe of the Spanish Americas. The silver of Potosí, however, attracted the commercial interests of every settler group in the Río de la Plata. The gentry of Asunción found their commercial salvation in the leaf of the *yerba* tree of Paraguay's rain forests. *Yerba* was found to make a distinctive tea called *mate*, which soon gained favor among the residents of Peru, Chile, and Argentina. (Many people in the Southern Cone still drink *mate* daily.) One sipped the liquid either through a silver straw from a sterling cup or through a wooden straw from a gourd, depending on social status. Most of the earliest *yerba* traffic flowed through Asunción downriver to Santa Fe, then overland to markets either in Chile or Peru. *Yerba* remained Paraguay's principal export throughout the colonial period. It brought in six times the revenue of the second most important export—tobacco.

The demand for *yerba mate* throughout the Southern Cone brought about the transformation of its production in Paraguay. The first exporters in the early 17th century merely organized their Guaraní workers to go into the forest to pick and then toast the leaves from wild *yerba* trees. Later, Jesuit missionaries began to cultivate the tree as a plantation crop. Eventually, the Jesuits and their mission Indians nearly supplanted the inefficient forest gathering of *yerba* by merchants. The commercial advantage of the missionaries aroused the envy of the gentry in Asunción, causing a long-festering breach between the Spaniards in Paraguay.

## The Jesuits

By the 1620s, the Jesuits had established missions among the Guaraní Indians in the region east of Asunción in present-day Brazil. The missions, of course, had always been an issue of contention between the missionaries and the settlers over control of the Indians. The Portuguese settlers at São Paulo had taken to enslaving the Guaraní because of their reputation as good agricultural workers. The first Jesuit missions had gathered groups of Indians together into large settlements; therefore, the Brazilian slave hunters liked to attack the mission Guaraní, carrying off hundreds of slaves. In response, the Jesuits successfully obtained permission from the Spanish Crown to arm the Guaraní Indians. This was a momentous decision reestablishing the pre-Columbian heritage of military prowess among the Guaraní. In 1641, 300 colonists from São Paulo and 600 native allies attacked the missions. The Brazilian expedition suffered a decisive defeat. But the Jesuit arming of the Guaraní also annoyed the settlers at Asunción, for it closed off to them this source of indigenous workers.

By the 17th century, many missionary priests had received their training and ordination in the Americas. These native-born priests and nuns were exclusively Creoles, Americans born of European parentage. People of mixed blood, Negroes, and Indians were excluded from the priesthood. The schools at which novices studied eventually became the first universities of the Americas. Among these was the University of Córdoba, founded in 1613, which eventually opened up to Creole young men who did not intend to prepare for the priesthood but aimed for careers in law and bureaucracy.

Financial support for these schools and for proselytizing came from a number of sources. The regular orders obtained from the Spanish Crown land and the rights to Indian labor in order to support their work. The Jesuits in particular became known as the most savvy of the religious businessmen. Jesuit headquarters in Córdoba oversaw a nearly self-sufficient economic system that included haciendas for wheat, farms for food crops, ranches for cattle and sheep, plantations for sugar and cacao, warehouses for the export of silver and the import of wine and slaves, wool-weaving shops, teams of mules for transport, and rental properties in both rural and urban zones. As important economic entities, these religious estates also owned African slaves: The Jesuits were the largest slaveholders in Argentina.

The missionary orders in Latin America, therefore, were well supported and wielded considerable temporal as well as spiritual power, attracting no small degree of envy. Their economic assets bothered many merchants and landowners who had to compete either with the missionaries for labor and markets or with each other for scarce church finances. Merchants at the city of Asunción resented paying taxes on the transport of their *yerba mate,* while Jesuit missionaries sent bundles of *yerba* leaves tax-free down the Paraná River to Santa Fe and Buenos Aires.

In theory, public officials intended for Christianity to bind together a fractured and heterogeneous colonial society, providing a common element to the governors and the governed, the privileged and the dispossessed, the rich and the poor. Certainly, the Jesuits understood something about power over subject peoples. They built churches in villages, directed the Indians' work, and tried to keep other Spaniards away. They learned native languages in order to preach among indigenous groups. But the friars never accepted natives into their mendicant orders as priests, because they did not consider the Indians to be their equals. They preached instead the doctrine that their long-suffering Indian subjects would receive rewards later, in heaven. Thus, Catholic orthodoxy was a mechanism of social control, and religious instruction prepared Indians and the poor to accept their permanently subordinate role in colonial society.

## Slavery

Slavery in colonial Argentina differed from slavery in other parts of Latin America, such as Brazil and the Caribbean islands, which demanded huge numbers of African slave workers. Colonial Brazil, for example, imported as many as 2.5 million Africans to work as cane cutters on sugar plantations under brutal conditions, as well as thousands more to provide the mine labor required by a gold rush in the 18th century. The late-18th-century sugar boom in the Caribbean led to the rapid growth of African slavery there: Cuba's slave population, for example, quadrupled in the decades between 1790 and 1820.

Consequently, black Africans and native-born blacks of African ancestry came to outnumber whites in several Latin American colonies, especially those with sugar and gold mining economies. By contrast, colonial slave owners in the Río de la Plata used slaves merely to supplement scarce supplies of indigenous and mestizo labor. Slavery operated alongside the imperfect free labor regime in colonial Argentina.

In the 17th and 18th centuries, an estimated 100,000 African slaves arrived at the port of Buenos Aires, a number probably equal to the total numbers of white Spanish immigrants. From Buenos Aires, the internal trade carried slaves upriver to Paraguay and overland to Chile, Bolivia, and the interior provinces of Argentina. Landowners in Tucumán produced cane sugar and used African slaves in the milling process more than in the arduous work cutting cane in the fields, where itinerant Indian and mestizo laborers toiled. Mendoza hacendados used slaves in their households, truck gardens, vineyards, and wheat fields. In the cattle and mule-breeding haciendas of Córdoba and Buenos Aires, African slaves served as year-round laborers tending to the livestock, wheat harvests, and general maintenance.

Compared to Brazilian and Cuban plantations, Argentine rural estates made less harsh demands on their slave field workers. Argentine stockbreeding operators, for example, permitted relative mobility and freedom for slaves. Landowners commonly locked up newly arrived African-born slaves, called *negros bozales,* at night and strictly supervised them by day at first, but once acclimated, the slaves gained increasing privileges and responsibility. Africans who mastered Spanish might serve their owners by supervising itinerant peons in the planting and harvesting of wheat or in the branding and slaughtering of cattle. Many rural landowners came to trust their long-serving slaves and granted requests for extra rations, tobacco, clothing, and horse tack; owners even sought suitable wives for favored male slaves from among both slave and free women. African slaves did sometimes run away from their owners but found it difficult to mix with the mestizo and indigenous peoples since their distinctive physical appearance and African accents betrayed them as runaways. Africans in Argentina established no runaway slave communities as they did in Brazil and Cuba.

Urban slavery in Argentina was perhaps more important and certainly more concentrated and visible than rural slavery. Colonial policy forbade the enslavement of indigenous persons except in unusual circumstances, so wealthy Spanish families often purchased African slaves for household work, seeking women, in particular, as cooks, nurse-maids, house cleaners, and laundresses. Spaniards purchased males to serve in livery or the families' urban businesses. Merchants and artisans bought male slaves in small numbers for carrying merchandise, baking bread, and learning the rudiments of a craft. Urban slaves in Buenos Aires and Córdoba had relatively greater freedom to mingle on the streets and formed associations among themselves based on their many different African languages and origins. On Sundays, urban slaves attended their own Catholic services, which they enlivened with the songs and dances of Africa.

As elsewhere in the Americas, the slaves of Argentina did not reproduce in large numbers, so maintaining a slave workforce depended on continued imports of Africans. Men normally outnumbered women in the African slave trade by a ratio of three to one. The genders were separated when the newly imported slaves arrived at the slave markets: Male slaves were purchased predominantly for rural labor and the females for urban household duties. Spanish householders regarded outside male slaves with suspicion and kept their young female slaves secluded and off the public streets, although older, trusted female slaves walked the streets selling sweetmeats and hawking wares for their owners. The female household slaves were much more likely to fall prey to the sexual attentions of Spanish men than to enjoy freedom of choice from among African males outside the house. On the other hand, black male slave workers on rural estates had relatively free association with indigenous women and women of mixed race.

These conditions in Argentina fostered racial mixing, which resulted eventually in a free working class of mixed Spanish, African, and Indian heritage. A child fathered by a male slave but born to an Indian or to a mestizo mother was considered free. Mulatto children born to slave mothers served in slavery, but their familiarity with Hispanic customs and idiomatic Spanish usually gave them greater opportunity for manumission or for running away and hiding within the free, racially mixed urban populations. "This month a mulatto slave named Francisco Antonio has escaped," reported one majordomo in 1799. "Despite my writing to the *alcaldes* of [several communities in the Banda Oriental], there has been no news about him" (Salvatore and Brown 1989, 744). Therefore, generation upon generation of newly arrived African slaves contributed to the process of racial mixture among the Argentine working classes.

## Corruption and Tax Evasion

Freight rates inhibited much interprovincial trade in the Río de la Plata, to be sure. Cart trains traversed the 1,450-mile route between Buenos Aires and Jujuy in about three months' time. Riverboats on the Paraná were small, had to sail laboriously upriver, and could move in both directions only during the rainy season. Freight rates therefore were high and could not be avoided, and the merchants passed on the cost of transport to all consumers. Even commoners saved a few reales (a common coin equal to one-eighth of a silver peso) by avoiding what few taxes they could, but corruption and large-scale tax evasion was a privilege of the rich and powerful.

The tradition of tax evasion became well established during the colonial period for two reasons. First, the king of Spain had outlawed direct international trade between Europe and the Río de la Plata. Second, the king's officials in the Río de la Plata, not to mention his subjects there, could only make a living by ignoring the restrictions on trade.

The royal court in the 16th century had concluded that silver was not only its most precious import from the Americas but also the basis of Spanish power in Europe. Moreover, the silver trade earned large tax revenues for the Crown in terms of mining concessions, minting charges, sales taxes, and port duties. Spain therefore attempted to protect silver shipments from foreigners and decided that the port of Buenos Aires was too vulnerable to the Portuguese from nearby Brazil and to Dutch and British maritime power. The Crown ruled that the silver of Bolivia was to be exported not from Buenos Aires but from Lima. The resulting official South American trade route was inefficient, indirect, illogical, expensive, and laden with corruption—and it lasted for 200 years.

In the mid-16th century, the Crown decreed that all South American trade was to be carried on the *flota*, or fleet, system. Mule trains transferred silver bullion from Potosí over the Andean cordillera to Lima. The silver then moved by ship to Panama City and overland through the Isthmian jungles to merchant vessels in the Caribbean. The illogic did not end there. All Spanish merchant ships were to meet once per year at the port of Havana and be escorted by warships in a fleet formation across the Atlantic Ocean to Spain. European merchandise, much prized among settlers in the Americas, was to return along the same route in fleet formation, also once a year.

Furthermore, the king's loyal subjects in the Río de la Plata could carry on import and export commerce with Spain only through Lima!

Direct Atlantic trade from Buenos Aires was not permitted. So, if the governor of Córdoba wished to purchase the best Spanish wine for a dinner party, he had to pay the transport cost and taxes of its travel overland from Lima. If a mule merchant wished to dress his wife in the latest European fashions in order to attend the governor's party, he had to ship the cloth across the Andes from the import houses of Lima. Spanish officials and merchants at the Atlantic port of Buenos Aires were expected to do the same.

## Illegal Trade at Buenos Aires

The humble village of Buenos Aires would never have developed into Spain's greatest port in South America if it had depended on Spanish policy. The fleet system did not work as effectively as royal officials had hoped; scarcity and high prices led to smuggling in many areas. There began early in the 17th century a common complaint that was to endure the entire colonial period: Río de la Plata merchants and cattlemen should be allowed free and direct trade to Spain and Europe.

Royal authorities responded grudgingly by permitting only a small number of ships into the harbor at Buenos Aires. Eventually they gave licenses to trade between Argentina and Brazil—but not in silver bullion. Foreign vessels could only put into the estuary of the Río de la Plata for repair, not for trade. Later, the Crown permitted the import of African slaves to Buenos Aires, again under costly official licenses. Each small concession led to abuses of fantastic proportions. In the end, Spanish officials were powerless to stop contraband, and containment of smuggling proved impossible. Underpaid local Spanish officials, therefore, chose the sensible alternative: They, too, engaged in illegal commerce. *Porteño* governors (*porteño*, from "port," was the term residents of Buenos Aires used for themselves) freely granted permission to foreign and unlicensed ships to put in at Buenos Aires and also bought and sold merchandise, using their political positions to avoid the usual customs charges. Participation in contraband commerce reached all levels among the well-to-do. Local merchants short-manifested their cargoes and paid customs agents to look the other way. The Jesuit college at Buenos Aires was said to have been one of the largest clearinghouses for the illegal export of silver specie.

From almost the beginning, foreigners have played an important role in the commercial development of Buenos Aires. The Portuguese were the first, and their favored commerce was in African slaves. That the Spanish royal court extended the slave trade monopoly to a Portuguese

43

# KING CARLOS II DENOUNCES THE CORRUPTION OF PUBLIC OFFICIALS IN BUENOS AIRES, 1672

In 1660, my predecessor the King sent four orders concerning notices that were being received from England and Holland about how much the vassals of those states were engaged in commerce with the Ports of the Indies and particularly with that of Buenos Ayres, about the great returns of silver that they gained from the exchanges that they carried out, and about the growing profits that they were having due to the tolerance of the Governors; each day the excess was becoming greater. And His Majesty ordered that his counselors investigate the situation and arrive at a remedy, and that the above orders be issued (conforming to the consultation by the Junta of State) that would be useful in applying vigilance in Buenos Ayres, with precise instructions to seize the ships of all nations that still carry on that commerce.

On that occasion it was recognized that where the most excess had occurred had been Buenos Ayres, during the time that Pedro de Baygorri governed that city; there had been many English, French, and Dutch ships which had been admitted, introducing goods to Spaniards and carrying away great sums of silver from that which was extracted at the mines of Potosí . . . weakening the power and strength of Spain and raising those of the enemies. . . . There was imported more than twelve million pesos in merchandize on which were paid very little taxes for the Royal Treasury but great sums to the Governors on the pretext of permitting ship repairs, all very malicious . . . and creating discord between the Bishop and the Governor, the latter of whom was giving preference to the business dealings of the Jesuits.

■

*(Carlos II c. 1672, 1–2)*

merchant house only encouraged illegal trade. The slave license authorized the Portuguese to exchange slaves for local Spanish American products—such as hides, (poor-quality) wine, and wheat—but not for silver bullion. Yet, silver smuggling consumed much of the Portuguese efforts. In the early 17th century, the Portuguese traded so much at Buenos Aires that several of them took up residence and married into local families of the white gentry.

Spanish officials at Buenos Aires willingly collaborated with illegal trade organized by the Portuguese. Authorities regularly confiscated unlicensed imports of merchandise and slaves, only to sell the goods back to the original owners at a mock auction. This deception provided importers with the proper documentation to transport illegal cargoes to the interior regions. Between 1606 and 1625, approximately 450 slaves annually passed through Buenos Aires, even though 90 percent of them lacked the proper royal licensing. In exchange, Portuguese ships carried away Bolivian silver bullion.

By 1640, Portuguese traders began to lose their hegemony at Buenos Aires to the Dutch. As many as 22 Dutch ships might be anchored off Buenos Aires at any one time, receiving full cooperation from local Spanish officials. Even the Jesuits had few qualms about dealing with the Protestant shippers of Amsterdam. The Castilian monarch certainly knew of the illegal trade at Buenos Aires and chastised the *porteños* for their corruption and consumers for their taste in European imports. Despite the Crown's displeasure, smuggling at Buenos Aires continued unabated into the 18th century, when the British arrived.

In 1713, the British South Sea Company gained the exclusive monopoly from the Spanish Crown to import slaves into the Spanish dominions. The company established a warehouse in Buenos Aires and imported more than 18,000 Africans over the next 27 years. Its monopoly contract stipulated that the British were to deal only in slaves in exchange for local products, but no merchandise or silver. The South Sea Company did not keep the bargain. By sharing its illicit profits with local officials, British merchants gained sanction for illegal imports of merchandise and exports of bullion.

It became a mark of social status in cities as disparate as Salta, Córdoba, and Buenos Aires to have African men and women as servants. Artisans also owned slaves, as did small farmers. Widows and spinsters of modest means even used slaves as a form of social security: They sent their slaves into the marketplace as peddlers, sellers of sweetmeats, and prostitutes. The slaves then brought home to their mistresses the revenues earned in such trades. African slaves and black servants lived with their employers, most of whom were white. Slave imports to the Río de la Plata rose throughout the colonial period because demand always outstripped supply.

All this illegal trade satisfied so many powerful persons in the Río de la Plata that it could not be stifled. Spanish officials and merchants became wealthy dealing with those very foreigners they were pledged to keep out of the empire. Likewise, local cattlemen gained outlets for

# THE BRITISH ROLE IN THE SLAVE TRADE AND CONTRABAND, 1740

The commerce of Buenos Ayres is very extensive, and indeed such a commerce as no other port in the Spanish West Indies can boast. . . . The trade carried on betwixt Buenos Ayres and Europe should be only by the register-ships from Spain; but besides this, there is carried on a contraband trade to England and Spain; and there is another with the Portuguese who possess the opposite shore of the Rio-de-la-Plata, by means of little vessels, under cover of sending their own commodities, but really European goods.

Besides the different branches of trade carried on here, already mentioned, there was still another very considerable article, namely, the importation of negro slaves, which was done by other nations in the following manner.

The first assiento [sic], or farm, was a treaty, or contract made in 1702, between the King of Spain, and the French Guinea company, for furnishing the Spanish Dominions in South America with negro slaves: whereby the complement of negroes was to be 3800 yearly, during the continuance of the war about the Spanish succession, and 4800 in the time of peace; the duty being fixed at thirty-three pilasters and one third, or £ 5: 19: 5$\frac{1}{4}$ Sterling for every negro. But, by the Treaty of Utrecht, the French ceded the assiento treaty to the English, who

their dried cattle hides. The cartmen of Tucumán and muleteers of Mendoza gained profits in transporting slaves and silver, while public officials in Córdoba and Salta collected more taxes on the movement of goods over the major trade routes of the Río de la Plata. Paraguayans found larger markets for *yerba* and tobacco among those who made their living from trade. Yet no place thrived on the illegal trade quite so much as the city of Buenos Aires. Its population grew exponentially between 1615 and 1770 according to population estimates (see table).

By 1776, Buenos Aires had become the leading port in southern South America. International trade had developed in the estuary because of economic rather than political sanction. The Portuguese presence across the estuary in southern Brazil and Uruguay posed a threat to the established (though illegal) trade routes to the silver

entered into a treaty with the Spaniards, for the furnishing of negroes, which was to commence the 1st of May 1713, and terminate in May 1743. The English South-Sea company undertook to supply Spanish Americans yearly with 4800 negroes, for which the same duty was to be paid, as had been settled by the French. The forty-second article of this treaty, which was the last and most considerable of all, was not included in the treaty with the French; for this article permitted the English assientists to send into the ports of Spanish America, every year the treaty was to subsist, a ship of 500 tuns [sic], laden with the same commodities the Spaniards usually send there; with a licence [sic] to vend the same, conjointly with them, at the fairs of Porto-Bello and Vera Cruz; which was a concession diametrically opposite to the ancient policy, and usual jealousy of the Spaniards, with regard to their American commerce. . . .

A very considerable part of the gold and silver of Peru and Chili [sic] is exported from Buenos Ayres to Europe; as also great quantities of hides and tallow, with such other commodities as are furnished by this part of America: for the importance of this place principally consists in its convenient situation for commerce; whereby the most valuable commodities, in the most distant provinces of the Spanish empire, are brought here to be exchanged for European goods.

■

*(Campbell 1762, 330–33)*

mines. Spain was thus confronted with the necessity of reinforcing its presence in the neglected fringe of its American empire.

Throughout the early colonial period, cattle raising was not a common occupation of settlers on the prairies south of Buenos Aires.

| Population Estimates for Buenos Aires, 1615–1770 | |
| --- | --- |
| 1615 | 1,000 persons |
| 1674 | 4,607 |
| 1720 | 8,908 |
| 1770 | 22,551 |
| Source: Jonathan C. Brown (1979, 22) | |

---

# A *VAQUERÍA* ON THE PAMPAS, C. 1760

The Spaniards, finding that the trade in hides was by far the most profitable to them of any, were possessed with a blind rage for killing all the [wild cattle] they could lay hands on. . . . The horsemen employed have each separate tasks assigned them. Some furnished with swift horses attack a herd of oxen, and with a long spear, to which is added a sharp semicircular scythe, disable the older bulls by cutting the nerve of the hinder foot; others throw the [lasso] on them whilst they are staggering, and others follow behind to knock down and slay the captive bulls. The rest are employed in stripping the hides off the slaughtered animals, conveying them to an appointed place, fixing them to the ground with pegs, and taking out and carrying away the tongues, suet, and fat. The rest of the flesh, which would suffice to feed a numerous army in Europe, is left on the plain to be devoured by tigers, wild dogs and ravens; and indeed one might almost fear lest the air should be corrupted by such a quantity of dead bodies.

■

*(Dobritzhoffer 1822, I:221)*

---

Cattle hides found their way into the holds of foreign vessels, but the erratic demand for this commodity could be satisfied by the cattle hunt, the *vaquería*. A leading citizen of Buenos Aires would organize an expedition of gaucho horsemen and oxcarts, which proceeded south onto the frontier where great herds of wild cattle and horses had multiplied. What the hunters desired most were hides for trade, tongues to supply to the local meat market, and tallow for candles and cooking. A large *vaquería* might last two or three weeks and produce several thousand hides. This wasteful method of production could not satisfy a rise in demand and by the late 18th century was largely replaced by more rational cattle raising techniques on the famous *estancias* of the Pampas.

## Reorganization of the Southern Hunters

The Spanish silver trail through the Río de la Plata did not become established nor did it function without challenge from the original inhabitants of the land. Tucumán and Córdoba represented a European wedge between two areas of indigenous hostility, and to the north extended the Gran Chaco, home of proud peoples whom the Spaniards neither conquered nor assimilated. Bands of seminomadic groups resisted displacement from their ancient hunting lands in Mendoza and Córdoba and periodically raided Spanish cart and mule trains and outlying cattle haciendas. Though disease was ravaging their numbers, these indigenous peoples nonetheless regrouped themselves to remain independent of Spanish rule throughout the colonial period.

The Indians of the Pampas were particularly adept at maintaining their independence and autonomy from the Spaniards. The Querandí Indians who lived on the southern shore of the Río de la Plata estuary had besieged the remnants of Pedro de Mendoza's expedition at Buenos Aires in 1536. Furthermore, the Querandí and other Pampas hunters were not frightened by Spanish warhorses. As hunters, the Pampas Indians were accustomed to bringing down big game, including horses and cattle that had escaped to the prairies from the first Spanish settlement and multiplied there, with spears, arrows, and bolas. The native peoples also changed their diet; in addition to their traditional fish and game, they added the meat of the growing herds of horses and cattle. So, by the time Juan de Garay returned to reestablish Buenos Aires in 1580, the Pampas hunters had adopted the horse into their own culture. (A Querandí war party ambushed and slew Garay in 1583.)

The horse permitted the native groups to expand their nomadic life, hunting far and wide across the virgin prairies. The men gave up their bows and arrows for the spear and the bola, which were more easily used from horseback. They mounted large hunting expeditions and raiding parties on other Indian groups and on European settlements. Their diets became richer in animal protein, and they converted the hides and leather into housing and implements. The men raised or raided for cattle to sell in Tucumán and Paraguay or to Araucanian groups in Chile. Indian traders established an extensive system of cattle trails over the Andes, including corrals and mountain pastures for fattening the cattle for Chilean markets. The women were relegated even more narrowly to hand labor, freeing the men for hunting. They manufactured handicrafts such as feather goods, skins, and saddlery from the wildlife of the Pampas. These specialty "Indian crafts" provided items of commerce between the natives and the settlers. Indians traded among themselves and with Europeans for *yerba mate*, tobacco, brandy, arms, metal tools, sugar, and European clothing.

*An indigenous tolderiá, or encampment. The prominence of horses and the adoption of cattle hides to make their toldos show the impact on these indigenous people of contact with the Spanish.* (Carlos Enrique Pellegrini, 1830, courtesy of Emece Editores)

The Indians periodically raided the settlements along the extended trading route from Potosí down to Buenos Aires. For the entire colonial period, the Spaniards could not establish haciendas on the fertile Pampas beyond a line running 60 miles south of Buenos Aires. Beyond this frontier, the southern hunters lived off the wild cattle that roamed the plains.

As time moved on, Indian society on the southern plains became more differentiated and complex. Fights against the Spaniards enhanced the status of the warriors, and the families of the best war leaders evolved into a line of tribal leaders. Group and tribal councils did not give way to authoritarian kings, but great battle leaders and those with oratorical skills consolidated rule over larger and larger conglomerations of indigenous peoples. Successful warriors and families also began to amass wealth in the form of horses, herds of cattle, and numerous personal followers and captives. Among the southern hunters of the Pampas and Patagonia, an important leader could acquire up to seven wives, each of whom linked him in political alliance to other warrior families. Hunting bands stressed capturing women and children, especially from settler communities, who could be used as slave laborers and concubines and for trade.

Likewise, the indigenous groups of the Gran Chaco soon were influenced by the European presence at Asunción. Through trade, they obtained desirable new commodities such as textiles, iron weapons and kitchenware, and alcoholic beverages. They adopted pork and beef into their diets and learned to weave cloth from wool, giving up their skin garments. These important changes in their material culture included the increased use of *yerba mate* and the horse. The arrival of the Jesuit missionaries in the 17th century certainly upset the shamans and annoyed the chiefs who had more than one wife (an annoyance for which many missionary priests met their martyrdom). But the Chaco hunters also learned to sow crops and domesticate livestock, thereby providing a more secure diet.

The horse, however, was the single most important European contribution that, once adopted, changed the lives of the Chaco Indians. The horse made the hunts easier and enabled indigenous groups to go beyond old territorial limitations. Previously migratory peoples became veritable vagabonds, and the horse enabled the more aggressive hunting groups to incorporate (even enslave) the marginal groups. Despite Jesuit exhortations to the contrary, the Abipón of the southern bank of the Paraguay River took to raiding over long distances. In the mid-17th century, they allied with another native people to attack the settlers at Santiago del Estero.

Intertribal rivalries also intensified, and weakened by the ravages of disease, some smaller hunter cultures disappeared or amalgamated with the aggressor groups. For example, the Abipón turned on some of their erstwhile Indian allies, after which these expert horseman looted the town of Santa Fe in 1751. "The Abipones imitate skillful chess-players," noted one missionary. "After committing slaughter in the southern colonies of the Spaniards, they retire far northwards, afflict the city of Asunción with murders and rapine, and then hurry back to the south" (Dobritzhoffer 1822, II:4). To a certain degree, the Abipón used the horse to stave off tribal extinction, for the diseases that began to ravage them in the 17th century had reduced their numbers from 5,000 to 2,000 members.

Warfare between settlers and Indians encouraged the continued militarization of both cultures in the Río de la Plata. Warfare was cruel and merciless. Nonetheless, coexistence emerged. The settlers remained in their towns and their lands nearby, and along the great cart trails. The north and south of this arc of settlements remained the world of the southern hunters. Where the two cultures meshed, along the frontier line, one found alternating cycles of trade and warfare. The colonial period proved to be the Indian summer of the southern hunters. Their violent resistance was destined to cost these hunting peoples their very cultural and linguistic existence.

# 3

# IMPERIAL REFORM AND CONFLICT IN THE RÍO DE LA PLATA

During the 18th century, the Río de la Plata, which had been on the fringe of possessions in Spanish South America, became one of the empire's most vibrant commercial areas. Trade flourished at the port of Buenos Aires, and most of Potosí's silver now passed over the extended mule and cart trails from Bolivia to the estuary on the Atlantic coast. Stimulated by exports, the area became an important market for foreign shippers. Mercury arrived here for the long trek overland to Bolivia's silver mines, and slaves also arrived in increasing numbers. The expanding commerce induced cattle producers on the Pampas to adopt more efficient methods. Population soared throughout the region, but particularly in the expanding province of Buenos Aires.

The economic expansion of the 18th century, however, caused a number of problems that the Spanish Crown felt compelled to address. Growth of the Hispanic population encroached on the frontier regions inhabited by the indigenous peoples, who themselves experienced a regeneration of political organization and population, and violence intensified on the frontiers. The commercial development also brought rising conflict between the Spanish-speaking colonists of the Río de la Plata and the Portuguese in Brazil. This international conflict involved the Jesuit missions of Paraguay, as well as their Guaraní acolytes, who were vying for the occupation of the riverine provinces and Uruguay. Finally, the Crown also had to confront the problem of contraband, since it received little in the way of tax benefits from commercial expansion in the Río de la Plata and Spanish kings had always considered the American empire their proprietary source of state revenues.

*A late 18th-century view of the skyline of Buenos Aires and the estuary of the River Plate, where cargo ships anchored to be emptied and loaded by small craft. The city was designated as the major Atlantic port of the Spanish colonial empire in the Southern Cone.* (Fernando Brambila, 1794, courtesy Emece Editores)

As for social inequities, commercial growth failed to lead to equality of economic opportunity and the democratization of the social order. The antagonism between the Hispanic and the indigenous cultures continued unabated. Under the circumstances, the white gentry accorded neither respect nor opportunity to poor nonwhites. The increasing size of a slave underclass within the Hispanic society also hardened social discrimination, and mestizos and mulattoes, who descended from native or African ancestors, suffered sharply. Even among the privileged white class, there was discrimination, since the newly arrived merchants and bureaucrats used their European birth and contacts to discriminate against the interests of the Creole gentry born in the Americas.

Eventually, the royal government began a series of administrative changes called the Bourbon Reforms that were intended to solve the problems of colonial defense and tax evasion; social inequalities remained untouched. The reforms legalized and expanded Spanish commerce at Buenos Aires; in fact, the Crown established a new viceroyalty within the Río de la Plata and made the port the administrative capital of this emerging region. Bolstered by fear of clerical power in the colonies, the government also expelled the influential Jesuit order and confiscated its extensive properties. As we shall see,

54

these reforms served to exacerbate existing political and economic problems every bit as much as they ignored social inequalities.

## Araucanization of the Pampas

Although they had not yet been "conquered" by European settlers, the autonomous Indian groups that inhabited the prairies and hills of the southern Pampas and Patagonia nonetheless underwent momentous changes, transforming their lifestyles so as to resist the pressures of the expanding European population. The indigenous peoples adopted some of the settlers' ways; for example, by the beginning of the 18th century, the Indians already had developed a brisk trade among themselves in European cattle and horses. They also began to congregate in larger and more complex groups, dividing themselves among wealthy chieftains and poor followers. Male hunter-warriors gained higher status, while women and older people correspondingly lost status.

Spaniards and gauchos alike had noticed the political and social changes occurring among the Pampas Indian groups, a process they called "the Araucanization of the Pampas." The Araucanians in this case were the Mapuche peoples of southern Chile, whose resistance continued to prevent the Spanish population there from spreading southward. The indigenous groups in Chile and the Patagonia had by the 18th century been trading with one another across the southern Andean passes for at least a century. Then the Mapuche began to mingle and intermarry with indigenous groups of the Patagonia and the Andean foothills. Araucanian social practices and rituals were adopted by native Argentines, as were the warrior societies and tighter political alliances. The process first occurred among the Pehuenche of the Upper Patagonia region.

Upon arriving in Argentina, the Chilean Mapuche gave up their horticulture completely and became herders of livestock, horses, and cattle. They even adopted the cultural practices of their Argentine hosts. They wore boots made from horsehide, roasted meat by placing hot stones on the inside of the carcass, preferred *chicha* made from the *algarroba* bean, lived in the conical hide-covered tent called the *toldo*, and used horse blood as a cleanser for the face and hair. They even took up smoking tobacco and inhaling the smoke to induce a kind of intoxication, and developed a taste for horseflesh. Still, these peoples moved in small groups, their camps typically numbering 10 large *toldos* and holding up to 30 warriors.

The original Argentine natives greatly admired Araucanian skills at war. From early on, the Chileans had adopted European tactics and equipment and had mastered warfare from horseback. These expert cavalrymen adopted the use of the long spear armored with tips fashioned from metal captured from the settlers. The spear even became something of a religious relic to the Mapuche.

The Mapuche first became interested in Argentina as a source of horses, and the first Mapuche arrived on the Pampas in 1708 at a meeting of war chiefs on the Quinto River. Their reputation for fighting the Spaniards impressed all the chiefs in attendance. Groups of Chilean traders and warriors stayed on, incorporating themselves into existing clans on the plains as warriors, husbands, and fathers. They first infiltrated the original Pehuenche and enabled this group to expand northward into central Mendoza. By 1725, Spanish officials in Buenos Aires began to notice them because Araucanian warriors were raiding outlying Spanish haciendas and stealing cattle. Within the next several decades, the Puelche of Mendoza became Mapuche speakers. By 1750, no Puelche remembered the old language. By the 1770s, the Mapuche

*During the 18th century, speakers of the Mapuche language from southern Chile, known as Araucanians, moved onto the Argentine pampas, where their culture changed the behavior and habits of the native tribes—a process called the Araucanization of the pampas. The most obvious change was the widespread adoption of aggressive cavalry warfare, as exemplified by these mounted warriors. (Leon Pallière, 1858)*

56

language had become the lingua franca among all the Indians of the Pampas region.

After Araucanization, powerful hereditary chieftains emerged, for the first time, to lead confederated bands of mounted warriors in raids on Spanish settlements for booty and captives. One such raid had been sparked by the usual sort of outrage committed in the two-century-old frontier war—a Spanish attack on a peaceful village of mainly native women and children. Two leaders, Cacapol and his son, Cangapol, rose to lead the Tehuelche. This group roamed along the Negro and Colorado Rivers in northern Patagonia, ranging up to the Tandil Hills on the southern Pampas. These two chieftains united many others tribes in the great uprising of 1740. More than 1,000 mounted warriors swept north to raid for cattle, horses, and human captives. According to the report of a Jesuit missionary, the Tehuelche seized more than 20,000 head of cattle and took many women and children. The raid came in response to the expansion of the Hispanic population onto the frontier south of Córdoba and Buenos Aires. Indigenous groups that had seemed pacified and missionized also rebelled, setting off a campaign against Jesuit missions in the Pampas in 1753.

# A MISSIONARY'S ACCOUNT OF THE 1753 UPRISING ON THE PAMPAS

There remained no other thing for the infidels to do but to get ready for the surprise assault on the Mission village. They set the plan of attack for the following morning, which was the 13th of January 1753. The enemies approached the village at two in the morning; on the road they encountered two sentinels, whom they beheaded. In order to terrorize those Indians who were within the Mission village, they placed the heads on lances, entering the village with loud shouts. They ran through the streets and took the lives of eight Guaraní Indian soldiers whom the field officer had left with 12 Spanish soldiers. The Pampas Indians, with the exception of a few who hid, discontented with what was happening, joined the infidels. The attackers were captained by Felipe Yahati, brother of the dead cacique José Yahati.

*(continues)*

It was about seven in the morning and tired of fighting, the barbarians and their many accomplices lost hope of their ability to carry out their designs. They resolved to abandon the field of battle and retire from the Mission. They headed to the hacienda or *estancia,* where there were not more than three Guaraní Indian shepherds, who defended themselves with arrows and fled to the woods on the bank of the Salado River, which borders the *estancia.* The infidels rounded up the horses, mares, mules and 6,000 head of cattle. Rich with booty, they retired to their lands, in which they were unable to enjoy the fruits of their plunder.

It was the case that the famous [Indian] cacique Bravo encountered the troop of thieves. He was the sworn enemy of Felipe Yahati, and envious of the booty that he was carrying, Bravo and his men sprang on them, took the lives of many of them, and despoiled them of all their stolen goods. In this way he repaid with death the cruel Felipe Yahati for his iniquities and hatred of Christianity. The men of the cacique Bravo captured an injured Yahati and the barbarian [Bravo], relishing in the blood of his rival, ordered that his warriors strike him with their lances little by little, giving him a slow and very cruel death.

■

*"Testimony of Padre Sánchez Labrador on the abandonment of three Jesuit missions south of the Salado River" (Furlong 1938, 204–5)*

A tense standoff developed between the indigenous peoples and the Spaniards when the government finally built in the 1770s a line of forts along the frontier. These forts performed several functions. As a line of defense, they prevented Indian warriors from raiding in the territory being settled by Hispanic landowners and cattlemen. The forts also became centers of trade between the two cultures. Government officials even instituted an effective policy of supplying the indigenous groups with cattle and horses, paying them "tribute" as a guarantee to peace. Nevertheless, this conflict would only intensify at the beginning of the 19th century, again in response to important events in the Hispanic world of Chile and Argentina. Then, even more warlike and powerful chieftains were to follow in the footsteps of Cacapol.

*Chiefs, known as caciques to the Spanish, assumed hereditary power and more prominent roles among the indigenous tribes of the Pampas after the assimilation of Araucanian culture. This early 19th-century view shows a chief at the head of well-armed mounted followers.* (Augustus Earle, 1820, courtesy of Emece Editores)

## The Jesuit Problem

Isolation preserved Asunción in a state of near economic lethargy throughout the 17th century. Few Spanish immigrants entered the region, and the mestizos, who called themselves *"españoles,"* established a familiar social hierarchy with the wealthier landowners and merchants at the apex and the indigenous laborers at the bottom. That these mestizo elites spoke the Guaraní language did not prevent them from exploiting the Indian population for labor and concubines. In the absence of Spanish women, sexual license became quite ingrained in this isolated setting. Here the mestizo elite jealously preserved its domination over the Indians with little interference from the colonial state, reason enough that the Jesuits came to be resented in Paraguay.

Having arrived at the end of the 16th century, the missionaries of the Society of Jesus accepted the "heroic" mission of bringing "civilization" to the Indians. The citizens of Asunción, however, did not wish them to take charge of the Guaraní villages close to that city. The Jesuits went instead into the wilderness regions up the Paraguay and Uruguay Rivers in territories that today form parts of Argentina and Brazil. In the course of the 17th and 18th centuries, they brought the Guaraní into mission villages and taught them the rudiments of Western civilization and religion. More than a few missionaries were martyred for their efforts.

For the most part, however, the indigenous forest peoples adapted to the new regime. They built villages and churches, cultivated cassava and maize, and learned to breed cattle, horses, and pigs. They also took to learning the catechism in their own language, which they embraced fervently. The Guaraní headmen were less eager to practice marital monogamy, but from the mission Indians' standpoint, the bargain was not entirely negative. The Jesuits did not reduce them to slavery nor did they convert the women into concubines. Moreover, the missionaries introduced the Indians to crops and farm animals, such as chickens and cattle, that enriched their diets. Tax rates on the mission Guaraní remained low, and the Jesuits offered them protection from their indigenous enemies, the Paraguayans and the Brazilian slave hunters.

The main Jesuit settlements lay south of Asunción between the Paraná and Uruguay Rivers, but the Jesuits also established seven missions in the present-day Brazilian states of Santa Catarina and Rio Grande do Sul, raising numerous cattle herds on the prairies. Mainly in an effort to protect Spanish interests in the Río de la Plata from the Portuguese in Brazil, the missionaries had turned the mission Indians into a formidable military force. However, arming the mission Indians did not sit well with secular residents at Asunción. Nor did the demographic resurgence of the Guaraní. The Indian population at the missions reached a nadir at the beginning of the 18th century, by which point the native population had developed immunities to European diseases. In 1710, approximately 100,000 Indians inhabited 30 Jesuit missions, rising to 130,000 by mid-century. In Asunción at about the same time, the number of Indians serving the Paraguayans reached only 12,000. (Although Paraguay had a semiautonomous governor, throughout most of the 18th century it was tied closely to the Río de la Plata, economically, socially, and defensively.)

The Jesuits helped integrate Paraguay and Argentina into the economies of the rest of colonial Latin America. Besides gathering together the frontier Guaraní and other native groups into mission

## DIRECTIVE TO THE JESUIT MISSIONS CONCERNING BUSINESS ACTIVITIES, 1738

In order to eliminate the disorders and the great discredit that the Society of Jesus has begun to experience (and greater ones are feared for the future), I order the Father procurators or whoever is in their place in the Office of the Missions in virtue of Holy Obedience under pain of mortal sin that they do not perform any act of buying for the purpose of selling nor any other act of business even though the goods involved belong to Indians, laymen, or clerics. Only those acts are licit and allowed that involve goods owned by the Society as long as they conform to the common precepts of the province and those specifically given to the Office of the Missions.

I order these same procurators and their replacement as well as all members of the Society in the college and Hospital of Our Lady of Belén under Holy Obedience that gold or silver (minted or not) not belonging to the Society or its missions, even though it arrive labeled or with letters for any of ours, be not admitted as belonging to us but it be manifested that it has another owner. The effect of this will be to dispel the notion that we or the Indians are rich and that a great deal of treasure passes through our hands.

These two precepts are to be included among those of the other provincials and read to the community once a year. Buenos Aires, August 24, 1738. Jaime Aguilar.

■

*Archivo General de la Nación, Buenos Aires, Compañia IX, 6-9-7*
*(Cushner 1983, 177–78)*

| Slaves and Livestock on the Jesuit Ranches of Córdoba, c. 1748 | | |
|---|---|---|
| | No. of Slaves | No. of Livestock |
| Santa Catalina | 317 | 7,400 |
| Altagracia* | 175 | 9,200 |
| Candelaria | 98 | 26,000 |
| Total | 590 | 42,600 |

* Figures for Altagracia are estimated based on statistics for preceding and succeeding years.
Source: Nicholas P. Cushner (1983, 54–56)

settlements, the Jesuits oversaw the planting of *yerba* trees. But, by the end of the 17th century, the friars' business practices annoyed many secular merchants living in Asunción so much so that the priests were ordered to observe the highest standards in their business practices.

The Jesuits enjoyed the typical religious exemptions from most colonial taxes and controlled much of the available Indian labor. In addition, the Jesuit missionaries enjoyed commercial links with other Jesuit institutions throughout South America—haciendas, chapels, schools, and urban headquarters called colleges. Finance capital arrived from the colleges, along with European and American textiles, ironware, and wine. Jesuits ranches in Córdoba provided mules and cattle (see table). The missions exported *yerba* and some handicrafts directly to other Jesuit institutions as far away as Ecuador. At the beginning of the 18th century, the Jesuits already had great advantages over their secular competitors at Asunción.

Therefore, as the domestic South American markets advanced on the strength of export and population growth, so did the commerce of Paraguay. The Spanish Jesuits extended their missions in a wide arc from what is now Minas Gerais, Brazil, through Paraguay down the Paraná River into the Banda Oriental of Uruguay. The order's large haciendas on the southern side of the Uruguay River produced cattle and mules, which were driven via Salta to the mining camps of Upper Peru (modern-day Bolivia). Jesuit haciendas along the opposite bank of the Paraná River specialized in producing hides for international trade at Buenos Aires and in wheat and other foodstuffs for the growing local market. The Jesuit estates brought in Guaraní workers from Paraguay and bought African slaves at Buenos Aires to staff these estates. By virtue of entrepreneurial talent and generous tax breaks, the Society of

Jesus became one of the most successful colonial economic institutions in the 18th century.

But as the economy of the Río de la Plata region became more complex, the Jesuit empire made more enemies. Penurious colonial officials at Asunción envied the order's exemptions from taxes, small merchants disliked its commercial advantages, and modest ranchers resented its control of Indian workers. The Jesuits were on guard to avoid antagonizing competitors with "unfair" trade practices; nonetheless, local political opposition grew, and in 1721, the so-called Revolt of the Comuneros, or "townspeople," broke out in Asunción against the Spanish governor who was perceived as being in the pocket of the Jesuits. The revolt was led by modest mestizo ranchers, farmers, and merchants, who rose up against the governor. The governor was killed and his place taken by locally born citizens. Indeed, on this occasion, the poorest elements among the mestizo farmers seemed to participate in local politics with such relish that even the local elite had second thoughts. Not until 15 years later, in 1735, did crown officials reestablish authority in Asunción.

The *comuneros* were not Guaraní. The Indians' loyalties remained with the Jesuits, their paternalistic benefactors; in fact, armed Guaraní from the missions helped reestablish Spanish authority at Asunción, no doubt adding to the humiliation of the Paraguayan mestizos. Subsequently, mission Indians helped build fortifications at Montevideo (in Uruguay) and Buenos Aires, and the Guaraní militias fought in 1742 to drive the Portuguese out of Colonia do Sacramento, a port the latter had established on the estuary of the Río de la Plata.

Despite Guaraní loyalty to the Crown, the 30,000 Indians who inhabited the seven mission towns east of the Uruguay River became angry when their own Jesuit superiors ordered them to retreat to Paraguay. Spain and Portugal had signed the Treaty of Madrid in 1750. It recognized Portugal's claim to Rio Grande do Sul and Santa Catarina in exchange for its renunciation of all designs on Uruguay. The Guaraní affirmed their loyalty to the Catholic Church and to the Spanish king but rebelled against their own priests. The Guaraní rebellion lasted from 1754 to 1756. Indian caciques ordered the wagons burned and shot arrows at Spaniards who attempted to move them from the towns. They turned their religious fervor against the very Spanish authorities who had forced Catholicism on them in the first place. The Guaraní claimed that God had given them the land and refused to believe that their beloved Christian king would make them abandon their churches to the godless Brazilians. "If the Portuguese want our towns and our lands," they told their priests, "then they will pay for them with their blood" (Ganson 1994, 235).

This second major disturbance in the region was not quelled until the Spanish and Portuguese mounted a joint military expedition against the Guaraní rebels. Even so, Spain later repudiated the treaty because the Portuguese did not completely abandon Colonia. Some Guaraní returned to their old missions in the 1760s, although the days of glory were over. The royal courts of both Spain and Portugal by then resented the Jesuits who had been granted great temporal powers in order to control the Indians. The earlier Paraguayan Revolt of the Comuneros as well as the subsequent Guaraní revolt seemed to indicate that the Jesuits were not the solution but the cause of social disruption in South America.

## Conflict with Portuguese Brazil

The Spanish Crown had been wary of the Portuguese in Brazil since the beginning of the Bolivian mining boom in the mid-16th century. But there existed such a large frontier buffer between the Portuguese coastal settlements at Salvador da Bahia and Río de Janeiro that a few Portuguese ships in the estuary of the Río de la Plata did not seem too threatening. However, that expansive buffer zone began to shrink as the settlement of both the Spaniards and the Portuguese gradually reduced the frontier. As previously noted, the Spanish Jesuits moved their missions north and east into territory claimed by the Portuguese. Likewise, the São Paulo slave-hunters of the 17th century gave way to miners seeking gold in the early 18th century. Suddenly, the Portuguese became protective of their frontier territories. The two colonial powers would clash over Paraguay and Uruguay.

The Portuguese had an alliance with Great Britain, while the Spanish monarchs maintained a "family compact" with Bourbon France. The first wars of the 18th century increasingly involved the Americas in Europe's disagreements, and Great Britain ultimately seemed to benefit most from the conflicts. The War of Spanish Succession, from 1700 to 1713, by which France's Louis XIV was able to place a Bourbon on the throne of Spain, resulted in a compromise in which British merchants gained the coveted monopoly to legally import slaves to the Spanish American colonies. Colonia do Sacramento, the Uruguay port for contraband across the Río de la Plata estuary from Buenos Aires, went to England's ally, Portugal.

Then came the so-called War of Jenkins's Ear (1739–48), so-named because of the loss of a British mariner's ear to a Spaniard's knife. The

British gave up the slave monopoly, and the Portuguese gave back Colonia do Sacramento. It was at the end of this conflict that the Jesuits had to pull back their Guaraní missions from southern Brazil. In this and the subsequent Seven Years' War (1756–63), the European powers continued to involve the indigenous peoples of the Americas in their disagreements. The Spaniards mobilized the Guaraní militias from the Jesuit missions to defend Buenos Aires. The Spanish raid on Colonia in 1762 surprised 27 English merchant vessels, which were trading in illegal Spanish silver. But the peace treaty ending this war returned Colonia do Sacramento to Portugal anyway.

The Spanish and French gained some revenge, however, in the war of independence in British North America (1775–83). French and Spanish troops both helped the American colonists in their struggle for freedom from Great Britain, despite the irony that Spain and France still retained their own colonial empires in the Americas. Spain also recaptured Colonia. These rising international contests increasingly involved South America in European conflicts. For these reasons, the Spanish monarch felt compelled to tighten imperial control in the increasingly valuable Southern Cone, but a problem arose. The colonial subjects in the Río de la Plata had become accustomed to their independence and autonomy. Each imperial reform thus seemed to them to be an assault on their loyalty and their privileges.

## The Bourbon Reforms

The Spanish kings decided to strengthen their empire through a series of administrative and economic reforms. In Spanish America, these became known as the Bourbon reforms, after the name of Spain's royal family. The reforms came gradually, one at a time in piecemeal fashion, and sometimes contradicting and countermanding previous reforms.

The basic long-term objectives of these reforms fell under several categories. First, the Bourbons sought to strengthen the administration of their colonial possessions, then they sought to capture control over trade and commerce. Part of these economic and administrative reforms involved rationalizing the collection of taxes and closing tax loopholes. Moreover, the Crown wanted their American subjects to participate more in the defense of the empire, through territorial expansion into the frontiers and also by serving in colonial militias. Finally, the reforms struck at the autonomy of colonial society. Plans were devised to curb the power of the local elites and to manage more effectively the volatile social resentments that might ruin the entire colonial enterprise. Because so many Iberian soldiers and officials were dispatched to reinforce royal authority, the Bourbon reforms have been termed the "Reconquest of the Americas."

Studying these reforms as a whole, one cannot escape the conclusion that they succeeded so well in the Río de la Plata that they ultimately undermined, rather than strengthened, Spanish colonialism. The Bourbon reforms gave focus to resentments at all levels of society. They provided the spark for several rebellions, but most of all, they fastened the colonies so securely to Spain that the colonial subjects in the Southern Cone became unwittingly involved in several European wars that eventually provoked what the reforms were intended to avoid— social unrest, rebellion, and political independence.

### The Viceroyalty of the Río de la Plata

In terms of colonial administration, the changes were far-reaching. The reforms scrapped the old setup that had divided Spanish America between the viceroyalties of New Spain (Mexico) and Peru. Many new administrative entities were carved out, particularly in South America. The Viceroyalty of New Granada, with its capital at Bogotá, was established in 1739, with authority over Ecuador and Venezuela, as well as Colombia. The Crown then detached extensive territories of the Río de la Plata to establish a third viceroyalty in South America with its capital at Buenos Aires. The citizens of Buenos Aires, the *porteños*, basked in their new status.

This administrative change seemed to confirm the logic of contraband, for Buenos Aires gained control of all the hinterland with which it had been trading—illegally for the most part—for more than a century. Uruguay, Paraguay, and Bolivia all became part of the Viceroyalty of the Río de la Plata, a momentous administrative change that removed Lima's control over the silver mines of Potosí. The Crown did extract a price for this new prestige. It staffed the top positions in the new viceregal government with Spaniards. Creoles, American born whites, could only share power in the town councils (*cabildos*) and even then only in positions subordinate to the wealthy Spanish-born merchants.

### "Free Trade"

Commercial relations had to change because Spain's mindless trade sanctions could not accommodate the economic expansion of the 18th century. The fleet system was in shambles, so the trade ministry loosened its grip in the 1740s and allowed individual ships to trade at

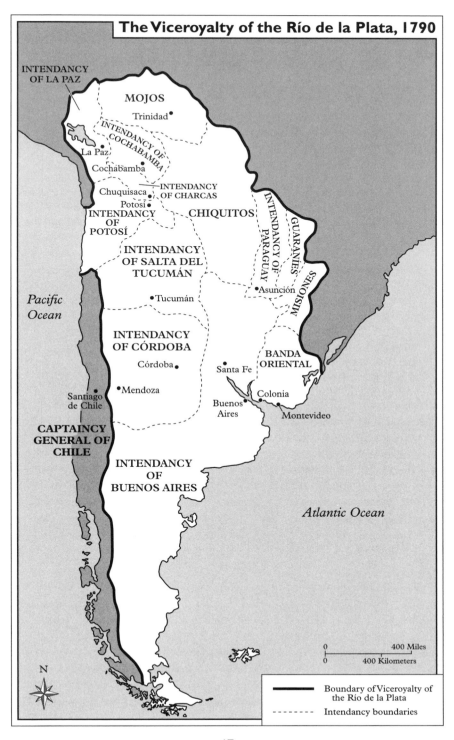

## The Viceroyalty of the Río de la Plata, 1790

INTENDANCY OF LA PAZ

MOJOS

Trinidad

INTENDANCY OF COCHABAMBA

La Paz

Cochabamba

INTENDANCY OF CHARCAS

Chuquisaca

Potosí

INTENDANCY OF POTOSÍ

CHIQUITOS

INTENDANCY OF PARAGUAY

GUARANIES

MISIONES

INTENDANCY OF SALTA DEL TUCUMÁN

Tucumán

Asunción

*Pacific Ocean*

INTENDANCY OF CÓRDOBA

Córdoba

Mendoza

BANDA ORIENTAL

Santa Fe

Colonia

Santiago de Chile

Buenos Aires

Montevideo

CAPTAINCY GENERAL OF CHILE

INTENDANCY OF BUENOS AIRES

*Atlantic Ocean*

N

| 0 | | 400 Miles |
| 0 | | 400 Kilometers |

—————— Boundary of Viceroyalty of the Río de la Plata

- - - - - - - Intendancy boundaries

# A DESCRIPTION OF THE PEOPLE OF BUENOS AIRES, 1783

According to reports that I [Juan Francisco de Aguirre] have been able to acquire, the population of Buenos Aires varies between 30,000 and 40,000 souls of all kinds of people. Among them the white or Spanish are the more considerable, at less than half the population; the other half consist of blacks, mulattos, and a few Indians from outside. The Spanish type is divided into two classes, Europeans and Americans, who dedicate themselves to commerce, to the mechanical arts and to agriculture. The people of color are almost only for service.

In commerce the most important merchants of the community come from the families of patricians and foreigners; the majority, 31, are of this sort. By way of their correspondents in Spain and mainly in the Port of Cádiz they supply the financing with which the stores and shops send goods throughout the viceroyalty and provision this city.

. . . In Buenos Aires . . . one sees the clothing styles of Spain and especially of [the Spanish province of] Andalucía, whose sons seem to be into many things in this port. Buenos Aires is a city which proves the refrain that says: "the father a merchant, the son a gentleman, and the grandson a beggar." Nevertheless, neither is the opulence excessive, nor is the poverty ragged and miserable. The dress jewelry of the great and common women of Buenos Aires consists of topaz; and because diamonds are scarce here, it is said in jest that the main adornments of women are caramels [the color of topaz]. Men is one species that Spain gives to America, to which they transmigrate for commerce and to improve their fortune; among them come some high-born men and many, many more who are not, and according to the profits with which arise in business, the houses and families also rise of this country, where the richest [and not the well born] are considered the highest order.

■

*"Diario de don Juan Francisco de Aguirre" (Luna 1995, III:264, 308)*

Buenos Aires. The more flexible shipping, an end to many trade restrictions, and lower tariffs in Latin America permitted Spain to respond to British commercial pressure. Many of these trade reforms, as well as many other changes, were instituted during the long reign of Charles III (1759–88).

"Free trade," as the Spanish reformers called it, was finally implemented in 1778. Henceforward, merchants and shippers could use 10 ports in Spain (instead of just Cádiz) and trade directly with Buenos Aires and all other major ports in Spanish America. At long last the official requirement that all trade in the Río de la Plata pass through Lima—a requirement that had never been observed—came to an end. Taxes on silver production were also reduced from 20 percent to 10 percent, and other tax rates went down, even though tax loopholes were closed.

The economic results of the so-called free trade reforms were dramatic. Spanish commerce with its American colonies rose 300 percent. The increase of trade was primarily the result of expanding external demand and only secondarily of the economic reforms. In the 18th century, the booming economies and rising populations of Europe increased the market for Latin America's primary products. For the Río de la Plata, this meant silver, hides, and beef jerky; therefore, the economy expanded on primary exports, with only secondary development of the manufacturing sector. The trade reforms represented Spain's belated attempt to regain control of its colonial commerce, but this it could not do. Most of the ships carrying this expanded colonial trade were non-Spanish. Merchants and shipowners ignored even the remaining restrictions and continued illegal trading.

The Bourbon crown also eliminated its longtime slave-trading monopoly and permitted open trade in African slaves throughout the empire. This trade "reform" and the economic boom of the late 18th century resulted in the peak of the slave trade through Buenos Aires. African

| The Racial Composition of the Population of Mendoza, 1812 | | | | |
|---|---|---|---|---|
| Racial Category | City | Country | Total | % of Total |
| White | | | | 44 |
|    Spaniards | 190 | 46 | 136 | |
|    Foreigners | 11 | 8 | 19 | |
|    Creoles | 2,629 | 3,054 | 5,683 | |
| Native Americans | 548 | 2,327 | 2,875 | 22 |
| Slaves and Free Blacks | 2,100 | 2,356 | 4,456 | 33 |
| Clergy | 109 | 40 | 149 | 1 |

Source: José Luis Masini (1965, 11)

contributions to the racial makeup of the region's population also rose. Some observers reported that half of the residents of Buenos Aires were African or mulatto. Even in the interior, the number of nonwhite residents increased. Whites were a minority population in Río de la Plata by 1810.

## The Colonial Militias

Defense of the empire remained a prime concern of Spain, and the Crown intended both to bolster colonial military forces and to shift the expense for defense onto the colonies. After 1760, new militias made up of part-time citizen soldiers were created throughout Spanish America, manned and paid for by the colonists themselves. Buenos Aires had 4,600 militiamen organized in the city within 10 years. To recruit militiamen, the authorities had to give new legal rights to mulattoes and mestizos, for the white colonials were attracted only to posts as officers. Ordinary citizens who brought suit against members of the militias now could do so only in military courts. For the first time, mulattoes and mestizos could bear arms and wear uniforms. The white elites were not pleased, for they resented those whom they considered their racial inferiors having received identical privileges to theirs. Moreover, Argentine-born white militia officers could not rise to the top military ranks; Spaniards reserved the ranks of colonel and general only for themselves. Therefore, the military reforms of the Bourbons appeared to be another in a long succession of attacks on the privilege and rank of white colonists. Later on, when the empire came into crisis, these white Argentine officers would take matters into their own hands.

## Taxation

Defense and many other reforms depended on enlarging the tax base and increasing imperial revenue. Royal monopolies, an old device seemingly at odds with the trade reforms, were imposed on a greater number of popular commodities. Tobacco, *aguardiente* and other spirits, gunpowder, salt, and other items were converted to monopolies, their manufacture and distribution run by Spanish administrators. Free workers and small producers of these products either became incorporated into the royal reorganization of the industry or faced elimination. The profits from the sale of tobacco and spirits, sold only in monopoly stores, now went into royal coffers. With monopoly control of these popular articles of consumption, the state had to raise prices in order to make more revenues from sales. It was small wonder, therefore, that a new form of smuggling arose in the Río de la Plata: the illegal trade in Paraguayan and Brazilian tobaccos.

Not only did tax rates go up, but the collection of taxes also was rationalized. Previously, so-called tax farmers (middlemen who had private contracts with the government) had assumed the responsibility of collecting taxes, and these individuals were often local merchants who received tax payments from shopkeepers and producers in exchange for a percentage of total collections. Such a decentralized system contributed to a great deal of evasion and preferential treatment, so an important element of the Bourbon reforms came in centralizing the collection of taxes.

Now a new group of professional bureaucrats connected to the administrative intendancy system assumed the burden of collecting taxes from the tax farmers. Again, Spaniards gained: The bureaucrats of the Intendancy were Spaniards, whereas many of the old tax farmers had been local merchants. Moreover, each new tax official had his own detachment of guards. Eight intendants were assigned to the principal cities of the Viceroyalty of the Río de la Plata in 1782. Thereafter, the Intendancy spread to the other Spanish American colonies.

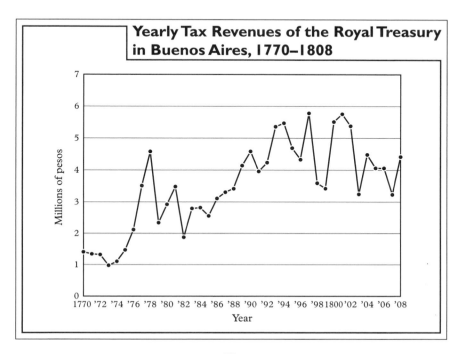

Tax revenues rose for the entire Río de la Plata region (see figure). This resulted more from the efficiency of collection than from economic growth, and no doubt, the tax burden rose for everyone in the region. For these reasons, smuggling and contraband never disappeared.

## Church-State Relations

As the civil authority expanded, the Crown also sought to exercise its patronage over the Catholic Church by reducing the clergy's temporal power in the colonies. The Jesuits became the first victims of this policy. Not only had the Jesuits caused resentment among some colonists with their success at controlling Indian labor and at tax-exempt commerce of products from their profitable mission estates, but also they had become implicated in Iberian politics. The Jesuits were perceived as more loyal to the pope in Rome than to the king under whose patronage the religious order had grown wealthy. The order was eventually expelled from the Spanish Empire in 1767.

In the Río de la Plata, the Jesuits were to leave their colleges in the major cities, give up their *estancias,* and quit the University of Córdoba. Likewise, the missionaries were to abandon their work among the Chaco and Pampas indigenous peoples. Carrying out the order in Paraguay was an especially delicate matter. The Jesuit missions there contained nearly 100,000 Guaraní Indians, who maintained their own armed militias. Special emissaries of the king, accompanied by cavalry units, conveyed the secret edict to Asunción. They arrested the Jesuit priests—some in the dead of night—and quickly packed them on riverboats to Buenos Aires for their exile to Italy. Few people learned about the royal orders until the Jesuits were already gone.

The reorganization of the militias paid off handsomely for royal officials when the Crown made the decision to banish the Jesuits from the Spanish Empire. Public officials charged with the expulsion order believed that the removal of the Jesuits might provoke rebellion by the Indians and slaves under their control, but the exile of the Jesuits came off without great violence. The authorities confiscated the missions and haciendas and distributed them to other missionary orders or to the merchant brotherhoods.

The great mission system of Paraguay deteriorated greatly after the Jesuits departed, whereas Paraguay survived the Jesuits quite easily. The economy and its principal export, *yerba mate,* continued expanding. Private entrepreneurs took up the cultivation and harvesting of the *yerba* leaves and established commercial links with merchants at the

72

expanding port of Buenos Aires. Now versed in Hispanic customs, the Guaraní made the transition from being wards of the church to being peons for Paraguayan agriculturists. Many also settled as squatters on the abundant land south and east of Paraguay.

The Jesuit agricultural estates, schools, and other properties, many of them large and containing hundreds of African slaves and Indian workers, now became resources for local officials to rent out to members of the gentry. Some estates were well maintained, others not. One of the largest Jesuit estates in Uruguay, the Estancias de las Vacas, was taken over by a lay brotherhood made up of wealthy Spanish merchants at Buenos Aires. The religious brotherhood sent out professional administrators and extra workers to the estate. The cattle herds proliferated. Cattle hides were sold for export, and wheat and dried meat were brought in to Buenos Aires to be sold in support of the orphanage and girls' school that the brotherhood also managed. Meanwhile, the king's officials collected the rent.

Local merchant groups applauded the humbling of the powerful Jesuit "state within a state," but certainly not all colonial whites liked the decision. By the 18th century, most of the Jesuits had in fact been born in the Americas and were from influential families; moreover, the sons of many wealthy local families owed their education to Jesuit schools located in nearly every city.

## Growth of Buenos Aires

Another result of the Bourbon reforms was the rise of a powerful group of Spanish merchants in Buenos Aires. Trade in contraband did not end as the Spanish Crown had wanted, but legal, Spanish-controlled commercial exchange burgeoned at the port. Agents of the great trading companies of Cádiz, Seville, and other Spanish ports arrived at Buenos Aires to establish local trading houses. Using their powerful connections to Spanish metropolitan commercial and political interests, the merchants moved into the collection of silver from Bolivia for export. They also imported mercury and African slaves. Hardware and textiles continued to come from northern Europe, but now through the warehouses of Spain and in greater volume. Likewise, these wholesale merchants collected and warehoused the major exports of the port: silver, hides, dried meat, and exotic commodities like nutria pelts and ostrich feathers for Europe's fashionable salons.

The growth of the great merchant families in Buenos Aires paralleled that of their peers in Mexico City and Lima. Young Spanish men, emigrating especially from the Basque provinces of northern Spain, began work as apprentices. Once successful, they then married the American-born daughters of older Spanish merchants. They invested in retail shops and transport facilities, established their relatives and kinsmen in the cities of the interior, joined the correct lay brotherhoods, gave to the church, and competed for political honors and offices. Their Creole sons were destined for the church, the shop, the low bureaucracy, and the military. Their daughters who had dowries were reared to marry other Spanish merchants, and those without dowries expected to marry families of upstanding Creoles, to go to the nunneries, or enter spinsterhood. In all respects, the merchants of Buenos Aires comported themselves with the same haughtiness and commercial behavior as those in Mexico City and Lima, save one peculiarity: They did not invest in haciendas. Land was too easily available and too cheap to offer big returns on investment—at least for the time being—and profits from the long-distance trade in silver, mercury, slaves, and merchandise were just too plentiful.

Below this group of Spanish commercial moguls existed a vast network of warehousemen and retailers. Approximately 600 retailers of cloths and imported goods operated in Buenos Aires, as did 700 taverns and general stores selling wines, spirits, candles, salt, bread, kindling, and other consumer items. These retailers—and the street peddlers who competed with them—often were beholden to rich merchants from whom they received goods on credit. Spanish immigrants swelled the ranks of artisans who especially served the luxury market with silver items, fashionable clothes, and European-style furniture. Mulatto freemen and African slaves owned by Spanish-born master artisans worked in trades such as baking, masonry, carpentry, tailoring, and shoemaking. A large body of free laborers, including tanners, lime burners, and sellers of kindling wood also hawked their trades in this port city. Porters were particularly visible, running around the streets, unloading merchandise from horse-drawn carts.

Increased legal commerce and relaxed trade restrictions did not resolve all the market conditions that gave rise to smuggling. Clandestine commerce continued on a smaller scale because the Bourbon reforms failed to eliminate high customs duties and the certain monopolies and did not permit unrestricted foreign shipping in the Río de la Plata. Smuggling was still a welcome vice among otherwise respectable colonial merchants. By trading in contraband now and again, they realized greater profits on their investments. *Porteños* (Buenos Aires residents) often dealt directly with foreign ships in the estuary and brought goods ashore

# RISE OF A SPANISH MERCHANT IN VICEREGAL BUENOS AIRES

Ventura Miguel Marcó del Pont was one of the Spanish merchants who connected Spain to the distant cities of the empire. Born in 1762 at the port of Vigo, in Galicia in northwestern Spain, Marcó moved to Buenos Aires and acted as the commercial representative of his father's Spanish merchant house. Using influence based on family ties and his Galician origin, Marcó actively directed a commercial network that included Lima, Santiago de Chile, Mendoza, and Córdoba in the west; Potosí in the northwest; Montevideo, Colonia, and the smaller river ports in the Paraná River basin; and Vigo and Málaga in Spain. In this kind of business, Marcó differed little from other successful Buenos Aires merchants of Spanish birth who maintained commercial ties based on kinship and credit.

Family ties and Spanish origin ensured both the political and the economic unity of the Spanish American empire. Marcó received shipments of European goods from his father's merchant house in Vigo. He shipped cargo and correspondence to Europe via Spanish ship captains with whom his family had ties. Marcó del Pont also fostered his connections with relatives who lived in Córdoba, Mendoza, Santiago, Lima, and Potosí. All these Spanish-born correspondents assisted one another in the exchange of goods throughout South America.

Despite its sophistication, the commercial system, even in the best of times, was vulnerable to distance and competition. Marcó owed his success to Spain's control of its own colonial trade. European war threatened to erode that control and permit Creole merchants and British shippers to encroach on the trade monopolies of Spaniards such as Marcó del Pont. As European warfare intensified in the first decade of the 19th century, the Spaniards began to lose their advantages in South American commerce. One Lima correspondent reported to Marcó del Pont in 1807, "Sales are fatal here on account of the numerous effects that the treacherous British enemies are introducing to us now with contraband and then with permissible trade, so that I do not lose sight of the many ways their treachery seeks to ruin us" (*Papeles Ventura Miguel Marcó del Pont* 1807, file 6).

to their warehouses under the cover of darkness. Contraband was never surreptitious enough to escape the notice of viceregal authorities. Indeed, without their compliance, smuggling could not have reached such heights. Those very functionaries charged with suppressing smuggling— customs officials, coast guard officers, and the viceroys themselves— profited from payoffs they received for ignoring it.

Owing to its population growth, administrative importance, and commercial wealth, Buenos Aires soon became the largest and most important domestic market in the entire region. Ponchos and cheap native textiles from Tucumán and Santiago del Estero found their biggest markets in the port city, where they were sent via oxcart in bundles of 50 ponchos each. Córdoba's leather industries supplied Buenos Aires and other provinces with chamois and suede. Paraguay also found greater markets in Buenos Aires for its hemp, fruits, vegetables, raw cotton, and native textiles.

The transport trades, benefiting directly from the commercial development of the port, flourished throughout the Río de la Plata. Legal trade between Buenos Aires and Potosí expanded significantly. In 1800, Potosí received goods worth 600,000 pesos from Buenos Aires and approximately only half that amount from Peru. This commerce redounded to the prosperity of trade centers between the two poles of the La Plata economy. Already, in the early 1770s, caravans of 20 carts or more regularly arrived in Buenos Aires with dried fruits, wines, brandies, flour, dried peaches, and passengers from provinces such as Mendoza and San Juan. Trade with Chile, formerly conducted through Lima, now flowed from Buenos Aires overland to Mendoza and through the Andes to Santiago de Chile. Tucumán and other trading towns participated in the export market of Buenos Aires as teamsters transported silver and vicuña wool from Jujuy to Buenos Aires for export overseas. Increased river trade in hides and domestic products gave rise to considerable boatbuilding not only in Buenos Aires but also in river towns closer to the forests, such as Corrientes and Asunción. The volume of such commerce in the interior of Argentina probably grew 20 times over during the latter half of the 18th century.

The Banda Oriental ("east bank," today the nation of Uruguay) also emerged as an exceptionally productive supplier to Buenos Aires. In the latter quarter of the 18th century, small and large landowners alike sent hides, dried meat, and wheat to Buenos Aires. The area's first cattle-slaughtering plants were located on the Banda Oriental. These plants, called *saladeros,* produced salted meat and hides in factorylike production for export. This was the first step in eliminating the time-consuming

| Population Growth in Colonial Argentina, 1777–1809 | | |
|---|---|---|
| Intendancy | 1777–78 | 1809 |
| Buenos Aires | 37,130 | 92,000 |
| Córdoba | | |
|   Córdoba | 40,203 | 60,000 |
|   Mendoza | 8,765 | 21,492 |
|   San Luis | 6,956 | 16,242 |
|   San Juan | 7,690 | 22,220 |
|   La Rioja | 9,723 | 12,619 |
|   Total | 73,337 | 132,573 |
| Salta del Tucumán | | |
|   Jujuy | 13,619 | 12,278 |
|   Salta | 11,565 | 26,270 |
|   Tucumán | 20,104 | 35,900 |
|   Santiago del Estero | 15,456 | 40,500 |
|   Catamarca | 13,315 | 24,300 |
|   Total | 74,059 | 139,248 |

Note: Three other intendancies of the viceroyalty—Paraguay, the Banda Oriental, and Chuquisaca (Bolivia)—are excluded from this table.
Source: Jorge Comandrán Ruiz (1969, 80–115)

and labor-intensive process of slaughtering cattle on the hacienda itself. But the age of intensive specialization in the cattle industry still lay in the future. As trade rose in the estuary of the Río de la Plata, Montevideo (founded in 1726) became a complementary port of call for foreign ships, especially for local produce and trade with Brazil. Many merchant houses in Buenos Aires also maintained branch offices and warehouses in Montevideo. The port of Colonia, recaptured from the Portuguese in 1776, served local shipping that carried ranch products from the Banda Oriental and along the Uruguay River to Buenos Aires.

Population growth rates indicate that all areas of the viceroyalty benefited from the late 18th-century growth (see table). But Buenos Aires province grew faster than all others. What is more remarkable is that the population in the countryside grew at a faster pace than in the port city.

## Settlement of the Pampas

South of Buenos Aires, colonial ranching remained a modest endeavor fit for Creoles who had some commercial connections and for many small farmers of immigrant or racially mixed backgrounds. Animal husbandry was replacing the *vaquería* cattle hunt as the chief method of rural livestock production, and these ranchers domesticated cattle herds, which, when slaughtered right on the ranch, provided the hides for export. Some cattle were sold on the hoof to supply the city with meat. These landowners also produced wheat, which they delivered to Buenos Aires in hide bags via oxcarts. The bigger ranch families tended to intermarry and act as bourgeois imitators of their wealthier Spanish cousins, but they were a rustic lot. The rancher and his sons worked at the branding and butchering alongside the hired gauchos, while the women pounded wheat into flour and churned butter or tended the orchards and gardens. Close to the city, small farmers harvested vegetables from truck gardens and produced milk and cheese from small herds of dairy animals.

In domesticating their herds, ranchers of the Pampas depended on two traditional Hispanic practices: the *rodeo* and the brand. Town councils granted both land and brands to prospective ranchers among its citizens. In the colonial period cattle ranches fell under the generic name of hacienda, but in the 19th century became known as *estancias*. On the hacienda, the rancher's men gathered the cattle into designated pastures, called *rodeos*, in order to accustom them to domestication. A hacienda might consist of several *rodeos* within its perimeters, each tended by one or two cowhands whose principal task was to ride the limits of their areas to keep the herds together. As yet, there were no fences on the Pampas. If several head of the hacendado's cattle strayed, he could reclaim them when all cattlemen in the vicinity rounded up their herds at branding time. Most agricultural and cattle production was located north of the Salado River; south of the river reigned the indigenous people.

Labor now became an important consideration, for the cattle owners needed cowhands to watch their herds yearlong. Itinerant gauchos—Guaraní Indians, free blacks and mulattoes, and mestizos—came to Buenos Aires from the interior provinces. Their jobs consisted of rounding up strays, branding and slaughtering, breaking and training the horses, and maintaining the corrals. They were adept at lassoing, horsemanship, and use of the knife and the bolas. Together, the hacendados and the itinerant cowboys produced the sun-cured cattle hides that increasingly entered foreign trade. Although their labor was needed, however, the rural workers did not gain respect among the Spaniards and Creoles of Buenos Aires.

# ONE SPANIARD'S VIEW OF THE HUMBLE COUNTRYPEOPLE, C. 1790

These herdsmen, servants in a desert, almost without communication, scarcely know friendship, and are consequently inclined toward distrust and deceit. When they play at cards, for which they have a great passion, they ordinarily sit over their heels, having hold of the reins of their horse in their toes, so that it does not wander off, and frequently they have at their side a blade or knife stuck in the ground, disposed to kill whoever gambles with them if they discover a minor trick, because in this point they are very knowledgeable and are not models of loyalty and honesty in the game. When they have lost all their money they gamble their shirt, if it is worth it, and he who wins generally gives his [shirt] to the loser if it is worthless, because among them no one has two. When they go off to marry, the future husbands ask to borrow white clothes, take them off on leaving the church, and return the clothes to those who lent them, going to sleep on the skin of a cow, because they do not generally have a house or furniture. . . .

These men are almost all thieves, and they even steal women. They carry them into the depths of the deserted woods, where they construct a small hut similar to that of the Charrúa, and they eat the meat of wild cattle that are found in the vicinity. When the couple is completely devoid of clothes, or when any other urgent necessity obliges them, the man departs alone and goes to steal horses from the Spanish farms; he sells them later in Brazil and returns bringing the necessities. I [Félix de Azara] have discovered and captured various of these thieves, and I have found the women they had stolen. One of the women, Spanish, young, and pretty, was 10 years old when she lived with this class of people. She didn't want to go back with her family and saw with emotion that I wanted to return her to the house of her parents. She told me that she had been taken by one called Cuenca, who was killed by another who was then killed by a third, this by a fourth, and that her last husband had run into the same bad luck. She never mentioned Cuenca's name without crying and without telling me that he was the first man in the world and that his birth had cost the life of his mother because he was so unique.

■

*Viajes por la América meridional entre 1781 hasta 1801*
*(Luna 1995, III:46–47)*

In the final analysis, the Bourbon reforms exacerbated existing problems. The reforms always carried additional restrictions, such as a prohibition of direct trade with non-Spanish shippers, which merely encouraged a continuation of extralegal commerce. Improved tax collections annoyed privileged white colonists unaccustomed to paying their proper share of taxes. So much of the economy's profits seemed to be shipped out for the benefit of Spain rather than remaining in the region. In addition, the arrival of Spanish-born merchants and bureaucrats challenged the autonomy previously enjoyed by the colonial white gentry. One might even conclude that the Bourbon reforms were undermining the very objective they meant to impose, Spanish control of the Río de la Plata region.

While the Bourbon reforms certainly increased the social tensions in the Río de la Plata, they were not sufficient to begin the independence movements. The social class most affected by the Bourbon reforms, the Creoles, was in fact the most conservative. Even though they suffered the indignities of taxes and loss of jobs to Spaniards and may have lost control over the nonwhite workers, the Creoles still remained privileged—and frightened. They feared a massive social upheaval and knew full well that imperial Spain protected their not insubstantial social privileges and wealth. The Bourbon reforms served only as the dry timber of insurrection. The actual spark that would set off the conflagration came from elsewhere.

# 4

# CRISIS OF THE COLONIAL ORDER AND REVOLUTION

The spark for revolution in Argentina came from Europe. It came from war. Being colonial possessions of major European powers meant that the Río de la Plata and other American colonies became venues of European military activity and, in particular, victims of the costs of warfare in the Atlantic. The rise of Great Britain and France as Europe's premier military powers in the 18th century involved the declining nations of Spain and Portugal in the competition. The Bourbon monarchs of Spain joined their French cousins in what was called the "Family Compact"; Portugal allied itself with Great Britain. All four European nations had colonies in the Americas. Naturally, North and South America became just another battleground in their on-again, off-again struggle.

This was particularly true for Spain's principal port in South America, Buenos Aires. In the last decade of the 18th century and first decade of the 19th century, European warfare disrupted commerce at Buenos Aires, exposed Spanish corruption in the Viceroyalty of the Río de la Plata, revealed imperial weaknesses unresolved by the Bourbon reforms, and permitted a resurgence of Creole power. Colonial military forces fought over real estate and strategic positioning in the Río de la Plata, where the Portuguese controlled Brazil and the Spaniards controlled Paraguay and Argentina. Then, the French Revolution intensified all military competition in the Atlantic and called into question the very foundations of "empire." The French Revolution attacked monarchy, the basis of empire; its advocacy of the Rights of Man undermined slavery; and revolutionary ideas questioned the right of one citizen to be placed over another. Two military actions connected to the French Revolution launched South America on a new trajectory: the British invasion of Buenos Aires and Napoléon's invasion of the Iberian

Peninsula. These two events set the Viceroyalty of the Río de la Plata on the course of civil war and independence.

And what was to result from independence? Not the republican paradise that the Creole leaders had envisioned, but rather political chaos and disunity in which several colonial social maladies would survive. Schooled by the colonial order in racial discrimination, social violence, and political corruption, the Creole leaders preserved many practices that had plagued Argentina since its settlement by the Spaniards.

## Revolution in France

The French Revolution of 1789 altered the balance of power that had characterized previous European warfare. After being defeated by republican France in 1795, Spain retained a tenuous partnership with the more powerful country while Great Britain's navy remained the guarantor of Portugal's independence. Therefore, whenever France and Great Britain engaged in hostilities, which they did frequently after the French Revolution, Portugal and particularly Spain were drawn in. These conflicts were too costly to Spain, whose empire lay across oceans commanded by hostile British fleets. In the wars lasting from 1797 to 1802 and from 1805 to 1808, British ships blockaded Spanish ports, cutting off its commerce with Buenos Aires just as colonial commerce was reaching its highest levels in 200 years.

In these times of war against Britain, the Spanish merchants in Buenos Aires and throughout the Río de la Plata were particularly on the defensive. Their advantage had always consisted of their monopoly ties to the powerful merchant houses in the Spanish ports. Imports of Spanish mercury dropped off, so consequently, silver production declined and tax collections slumped. Spain was forced to permit more foreign shipping into its colonial ports. Yankee and German vessels began to appear frequently and had few reservations about trading with Creole merchants eager to deal in contraband goods. Spanish merchants now had to compete with Creoles without the assistance of imperial advantages. The native-born merchants of Buenos Aires developed a taste for authentic free trade and requested that commerce be extended to non-Spanish vessels even during peacetime. They were turned down.

Because the wars following the French Revolution exposed the Spanish Empire's weaknesses, the most glaring of which was Spain's utter dependence on the financial resources of its colonies, Spanish officials made additional demands on taxpaying colonists. Looking far and wide for money, Spanish ministers chose to loot the wealthiest single institution in the Americas: the Catholic Church. For three centuries, the various church investments had been amassing capital in the colonies from bequests of money and real estate. Church authorities rented out haciendas and town houses and lent their accumulated liquid capital to landowners, taking mortgages at the rate of 5 percent per annum. These massive mortgage holdings became the target of a desperate Spanish wartime treasury. In 1804, the Crown ordered the church to call in its loans and send the proceeds to Spain. Before this order was finally suspended, in 1808, nearly all the colonies had suffered this form of imperial decapitalization. Colonial blood ran hot over this affair.

In the Río de la Plata, the collection of church assets illustrated well the sort of bureaucratic-commercial advantages that many influential Spaniards enjoyed. They assumed that public service and private profit were not mutually exclusive. Through his connections in the royal court, the Spanish-born merchant Ventura Miguel Marcó del Pont, for example, received the imperial commission to collect the special wartime taxes on church-held mortgages from Chile, Bolivia, and Mendoza. He was to remit the proceeds to Spain. This tax commission enabled Marcó del Pont to profit personally from the collection and transfer of public monies, as he had the right to deduct his fees from the total proceeds. Spain was raising unpopular taxes at the very moment that the colonial economy was declining, giving rise to much resentment from the colonists.

The collection proved successful, and Marcó del Pont soon came into the possession of some 101,000 pesos in cash and an additional 20,000 pesos that had been paid in hides. However, wartime events soon were to compound his profits when British warships and troops in the Río de la Plata prevented Marcó from remitting the tax revenues to Spain.

## The British Invasion

Another weakness of the empire was soon exposed in the Río de la Plata. When British troops invaded Buenos Aires in 1806, Spain's colonial defenses were shown to be vulnerable and her military officers incompetent.

Great Britain had suffered from the same trade disruptions that afflicted the Spanish Empire, and unsold goods piled up in the warehouses of Liverpool as Napoléon Bonaparte's armies closed off one European market after another to British commerce. The interruptions to Spain's trade with its overseas colonies affected Great Britain, too, because British ships carried so much of the merchandise from Cádiz and other Spanish ports to South America. After a decade of commercial frustration, the British invasion of Argentina in 1806 held promises for an economic recovery for the merchants of Liverpool and London.

Nevertheless, the military expedition of Commodore Sir Home Riggs Popham took the British government by surprise, since the invasion was Popham's own idea and executed on his own recognizance. Without prior authority, Popham sailed his force from South Africa across the Atlantic to the estuary of the Río de la Plata. He easily captured Buenos Aires in 1806, wrenching control from an unprepared and unsuspecting Spanish viceroy. No sooner had British troops disembarked at Buenos Aires than the viceroy, along with his highest-ranking Spanish commanders and the wealthiest Spanish merchants, fled unceremoniously from the capital.

Popham thought an attack on the viceregal capital would encourage the colonists to rise up against the "unpopular" Spanish rulers and wrote home to British businessmen that, "The conquest of this place opens an extensive channel for the manufactures of Great Britain" (Crump 1931, 183–84). Jubilant businessmen immediately fitted out 100 ships and dispatched them for Buenos Aires. But lower-ranking Creole officers had rallied the Buenos Aires colonial militia, 1,200 strong, which had expelled the British from Buenos Aires and captured the army commander, General Beresford. The British forces, meanwhile, had succeeded in capturing Montevideo and Colonia, which they held for nine months. Popham was recalled to stand court-martial.

Creole militia officers—commanding mestizo and mulatto soldiers and led by a French-born officer, Santiago Liniers—had stood and fought while the Spanish viceroy ran away. After they expelled the British troops, the militia officers pressured the *audiencia* (royal council) of Buenos Aires to depose the king's viceroy and elect Liniers to replace him. Meanwhile, some of the Spanish merchants were trading surreptitiously with British ships at Montevideo, rousing the resentment of the Creole militias who were laying siege to the British troops in the city.

In 1807, the British in Montevideo received reinforcements from England and launched a second attack on Buenos Aires. Apparently, the British political and military leaders still mistakenly believed that the Creole colonists wanted to exchange their corrupt and weak Spanish imperial masters for the more economically powerful British imperialists. Once again, the colonial militias at Buenos Aires repulsed the

# THE FIRST BRITISH INVASION, AS WITNESSED BY A CREOLE MILITIA OFFICER, 1806

It was more than 10 years that I [Manuel Belgrano] was a captain of the urban militias, more out of whim than affection for the military life: My first essays about it were from this era. The marqués de Sobremonte [viceroy of the Río de la Plata], days before the disgraceful incursion [by English troops], called me in order to form a company of cavalry, recruited from the young men of commerce, and to that end he gave me veteran officers to provide instruction. I looked for recruits, but did not find any, because there was much hatred toward the militia in Buenos Aires.

They sounded the general alarm, and imbued with honor I rushed to the fortress, the point of assembly; there one found no kind of order or organization, as it usually happens in groups of men ignorant of all discipline and without any kind of subordination. There they formed up some companies, and I mustered into one of them, feeling ashamed that the most trivial rudiments of the militia were being ignored.

The first company marched out to occupy the House of the Filipinas (the old slave-trading warehouse), while those remaining were disputing with that same viceroy that they were for defending the city and not going to the countryside.

The result was that there being no veteran troops nor disciplined militiamen to oppose the enemy, [the English] conquered the city with relative ease. When we went into retreat, I myself heard it said, "They do well in resolving to withdraw, because we are NOT PREPARED FOR THIS CHALLENGE."

∎

*"Autobiografia de Manuel Belgrano" (Di Tella 1994, 167)*

British. After a useless venture of two years in the Río de la Plata, the British forces finally abandoned Montevideo, too.

The Spaniards came back to Buenos Aires after it was all over, but the Creoles never allowed them to return to their old autocratic powers. The militias backed the *cabildo* (town council), dominated now by Creole members. The Spaniards who had collected funds from the church in Bolivia attempted to send them on to Spain, but the Creole-backed political authorities sequestered these revenues for use in Buenos Aires instead. Spain's wartime incompetence and greed had tried the patience of the Creoles.

Moreover, the participation of the Creoles as militia leaders in imperial defense ultimately undermined the social hegemony—and thus the commercial and political positions—of men like Ventura Miguel Marcó del Pont. As a Spaniard, Marcó ultimately became a victim of the American repercussions of European war. British traders expecting to reap profits flooded the import markets of the Río de la Plata with so much woolens, linens, glassware, footwear, rum, and furniture that prices plummeted below cost. Several local merchants, Marcó del Pont among them, sought to purchase cheap British goods and hold them in their warehouses for subsequent sale at marked-up prices. While the foreign troops were in Montevideo, Marcó's commercial agents and boat captains were dealing on a barter basis with British merchants. They exchanged British manufactured goods for hides and dried beef. Such acts may have made commercial sense, but they also could be construed as treasonous.

Most damaging of all, the British invasion interrupted Marcó's communication with Europe. The Spanish merchants could no longer ship colonial products back to their home ports in Spain. Marcó blamed "those malicious Englishmen" for the loss of the customary one-half percent commission on such transactions.

Marcó del Pont personally paid a much higher price for the British invasion. He had made an extraordinary loan of 70,300 pesos from his collection of church mortgages to help pay for the defense of the viceroyalty. He was never to retrieve this money. Then several boat captains complained to the new viceroy, Santiago Liniers, the hero of the reconquest of Buenos Aires, about Marcó's involvement in "false contracts" with British invaders. Despite his financial contribution to the defense of the Río de la Plata, Marcó and his agents had been compromised by trading with the enemy. Creole patriots who had defended Buenos Aires were lining up against the Spaniards who either fled or collaborated with the British.

## Creole Consciousness

In the four decades of commercial growth that followed the 1776 establishment of Buenos Aires as capital of the new Viceroyalty of the Río de la Plata, Spanish-born merchants in that city had become its leading citizens. *Porteño* society differed from that of many other Spanish

American cities in that Buenos Aires' wealthiest and most-respected citizens were not primarily government officials, miners, landowners, or the titled nobility. They were overseas merchants who, of necessity, cultivated political connections rather than land. These merchants controlled the importation of slaves and mercury and the exportation of silver and hides. Their credit supported the merchandising of European finished goods throughout the Southern Cone. Invariably marrying native-born daughters of older Spanish merchants in Buenos Aires, these Iberian-born *comerciantes* established families that diversified into local marketing and public office.

The powerful merchant community also assisted in the political administration of the colonies, financing public officials and collecting taxes and fees on commission for the Crown. In fact, much of a Spaniard's access to commercial wealth depended on his political influence. As the leading social group, the merchants supported the social institutions of the Spanish presence in the Río de la Plata: the church, Catholic charities, and the religious brotherhoods. They maintained correspondence and trade with Spanish kinfolk in Chile, Bolivia, and Peru. Without doubt, the *porteño* commercial class provided the sinews that held together Spain's vast empire in South America.

As a consequence of European war, however, Spain's colonial trade suffered a volatile series of booms and busts between 1790 and 1810. The volume of trade during two periods, 1797–1801 and 1805–8, fell to levels just 10 percent of what they had been in 1790. Contraband commerce with British and, increasingly, Yankee merchants helped make up the difference. Creole merchants now competed on an equal footing with Spaniards, who became disgruntled at the loss of their old privileges. "Free trade with the English has put our commerce in such a deplorable state," lamented one Spaniard, "because all of the English manufactured goods are so cheap; we will be left without any money or silverware" (Socolow 1978, 166).

By 1810, the power of the Spanish-born merchants had been reduced, and the group was unable to prevent the passing of political and economic power to their hitherto less-privileged Creole cousins. The result of this disintegration was independence. In the process of its precipitous decline, the Spanish merchant class at Buenos Aires lost control of its trade, its social ties throughout the region, its political power and, ultimately, its own wealth.

The economic resurgence of the Creoles contributed to the self-assurance of South Americans. Indeed, they had already been preparing for this moment by participating in the general European intellectual ferment of the 18th century. The Enlightenment in France and Great Britain questioned authority and promoted rational thought and experimentation. In Spain and Portugal, however, the kings' ministers adopted only elements concerning rational thought and experimentation. The Iberian brand of the Enlightenment promoted their ideas of agricultural development and their conceptions about strengthening administration and mercantilism, which meant milking the American colonies for raw materials and reaping trade revenues from an enforced commerce. In economic liberalism, for example, they discovered methods not of promoting industrial revolution but of reinforcing mercantilism. The Iberian crowns also entertained Enlightenment notions that promoted secular over religious power, the better to control the powerful institution of the church. However, other concepts such as popular sovereignty, the social contract, and consent of the governed, as developed by the French philosopher Jean-Jacques Rousseau, did not resonate among the imperial ministers.

These revolutionary ideas did make their way to Latin America, however. The books of John Locke, Isaac Newton, René Descartes, Voltaire, and Rousseau were illegally imported through colonial ports. Members of the elite, bureaucrats, and clergymen became familiar with the complete philosophy. Elite education proliferated in the early 18th century with the establishment of numerous universities in the major cities of the Americas. The older school in Córdoba was joined by the University of Chuquisaca (Bolivia) in 1725 and the University of San Felipe in Santiago de Chile in 1758. Mainly, these universities taught law and religious philosophy to prepare elite youth for careers in the lower levels of the bureaucracy and the church. The white colonists responded to these educational opportunities with alacrity. Furthermore, these universities disseminated the ideas of the Enlightenment without the imperial filter. But truth be told, these ideas came late to Latin America—in the 1790s.

When they did arrive, the youth of the elite immediately familiarized themselves with the tenets of the Enlightenment. In the emerging region of the Río de la Plata, the merchant's Creole son Manuel Belgrano, later a militia officer, read the new books from his study in Buenos Aires. Mariano Moreno, graduate of the University of Chuquisaca and a young Creole bureaucrat, who was to become part of the first Creole government in Buenos Aires, edited an edition of Rousseau's *Social Contract* "for the instruction of young Americans" (Lynch 1987,28).

Perhaps intellectual sentiments of greater power than the ideas of the Enlightenment or the American Revolution were those concerning simple identity. More Creoles began to identify themselves as Americans than as transplanted Europeans. The Bourbon reforms had increased the tax burden on the colonists without ending the corruption of the Spanish-born officials, which only heightened American nationalism. After all, the demographic trend favored the Americans even among the elite. White Americans outnumbered Spaniards in the colonies 20 to one, if not by more. Even so, Spaniards were immigrating to the American colonies in the 18th century in record numbers, taking up lucrative posts in the import-export houses and moving into professional and artisan positions. They especially were filling the bureaucratic positions now being denied to the "Americans." Creoles increasingly felt the sharp barbs of Spanish arrogance.

But the Creoles still were not quite ready for revolution. Something spectacular was needed in order to overcome the natural conservatism of the colonial elites. It occurred in 1807 and 1808, when Napoléon's armies invaded the Iberian Peninsula.

## Napoléon in Iberia

In November 1807, Napoléon sought to protect Europe from his British enemies by striking at Britain's ally, Portugal. The ministers of the Portuguese royal court escaped and fled to Brazil under the protection of a British naval escort, and the Portuguese royal family converted Rio de Janeiro from a viceregal to an imperial capital. The trade of Portugal's British allies enjoyed preferential status in Brazil, and imports of English manufactured goods and the exports of Brazilian cotton, sugar, and coffee prospered.

Politics were not so tranquil in the Spanish Americas, however, especially after Napoléon turned on his incompetent ally. He invaded Spain and imprisoned the entire Spanish royal family. French troops overran much of the Iberian Peninsula and installed Napoléon's brother as King Joseph of Spain. The once-powerful Spain was reduced to occupation by foreign troops and its once-autocratic and omnipotent kings to captivity. Imperial Spain had become rotten and weak over the course of three centuries and had mismanaged the riches of its empire. The corruption and depravity of Spanish officials in the colonies undermined the imperial base beyond remedy. Resistance in Spain, however, came ferociously from commoners who carried out a bitter and bloody guerrilla war against the invading French forces. The one country that rose to support Spain in its rebellion against the occupation of its former ally, France, was its longtime enemy, Great Britain. British warships and troops helped Spanish guerrilla forces drive the French from Spain.

## Elite Unrest in Spanish America

In the Río de la Plata, news of the capture of the Spanish king by French troops made all the difference. The breach widened between Spanish-born and native-born whites. It was a fairly rapid deterioration that undid once and for all those ties of family, mutual economic benefit, fear of domination by nonwhites, and allegiance to the king that had bound together the Spaniards and the Creoles.

The issue was political. Now that Napoléon's brother Joseph Bonaparte claimed the crown of Spain, did the colonials owe the same loyalty to him as to the Bourbons? In the absence of the Bourbon king, many Creoles asked where political sovereignty resided. In King Joseph? Did sovereignty reside in those incompetent and grasping viceroys who, like the one in Buenos Aires in 1806, had fled at the first sign of danger? Did sovereignty now reside in the *cabildos* that always had more Creole representation?

One might even say that the Spanish American revolts began with this essential breakdown of elite consensus between Spaniards and Creoles. For example, an influential Spanish merchant, Félix Alzaga, led a reactionary conspiracy in 1809 against the French-born viceroy Liniers in Buenos Aires. Even though Liniers had the backing of the local Creole-led militias, he was replaced. By 1810, however, the *cabildo* of Buenos Aires emerged as the most powerful local political entity, precisely because militia backing gave the Creoles a majority in the town council.

In Buenos Aires, Marcó del Pont also was soon to experience wartime unpleasantness. This Spanish merchant lost control of the church mortgage revenues as a result of the emerging Creole control of political life in Buenos Aires. The viceregal government already had spent the money he had donated, as its outlays to colonial militias led by Creoles like Cornelio de Saavedra and Manuel Belgrano were increasing steadily. The fall of Liniers in 1809 and his replacement by the pro-Spanish viceroy did not alleviate Marcó's commercial tribulations. First, Great Britain's military defeat during the invasion did not prevent British merchants from continuing to trade in the Río de la Plata. In 1809, while Great Britain and the Spanish independence fighters were allied against France, the British had introduced more than £1.2 million worth of goods into the Río de la Plata. Spanish merchants suffered from the overseas competition and demanded the expulsion of the British; however, the new viceroy sorely needed new revenues and was unable to restrict British trade without reducing customs revenues that financed his government. Fifty British merchants had taken up residence in Buenos Aires and Montevideo, and the continuing political crisis prevented the viceroy from repaying Marcó del Pont's "emergency" loans. He would soon part from the rest of his church revenues in the ensuing civil strife.

## Revolution in the Río de la Plata

The independence movement took hold early in the Río de la Plata but dissolved into chaos. Creole insurrectionary leaders could not maintain unity among themselves, and unable to overcome their racism, they lost the initiative to the popular rebellion from below. In the process, the artificial geographical unity of the Viceroyalty of the Río de la Plata came unglued.

Buenos Aires made itself the leader of revolution in the Southern Cone by virtue of the political and social changes resulting from the 1806 British invasion. The cowardly actions of Spanish officials during the foreign invasion had given a political lift to the Creoles. The leaders of the militias, in particular, acted as the spearhead of Creole political assertiveness. They formed a tenuous alliance with their own troops, whose numbers had grown to more than 3,000 in the city. These *pardo* (mulatto) and black militiamen now had weapons in their hands; received pay and rations, which represented a considerable redistribution of income; and marched through the city with new pride and self-importance. Not all Spaniards and Creoles were pleased, but the once powerful and wealthy Spanish merchants had fallen on hard times. The British and Yankee merchant ships drawing up to the city benefited Creole merchants and rural producers, with whom the Spaniards now had to compete on equal footing. So when the news arrived that the French forces in 1810 had invaded southern Spain, the Creoles were ready to act against the reactionary viceroy.

The militia leaders forced the viceroy to call a *cabildo abierto*, an open town meeting, that permitted "the populace" to advise the viceroy on how to respond to the new political developments. Armed supporters of the Creole leaders surrounded the *cabildo* building, intimidating the Spanish delegates, who stayed away. On May 10, 1810, a date celebrated today as Argentina's Independence Day, the *cabildo abierto* succumbed to pressure, voted to depose the viceroy, and appointed a ruling triumvirate, of Creoles, including the revolutionary intellectual Mariano Moreno. The triumvirate, however, was not yet ready to drop its allegiance to the imprisoned Spanish monarch and promised to return sovereignty to King Ferdinand VII as soon as he regained his freedom from French captivity. To many Spaniards in Buenos Aires, the commitment of Creole politicians to royal authority lacked sincerity.

Final Creole political victory, marked by the seizure of power in the *cabildo abierto* by militia officer Cornelio de Saavedra, further eroded Marcó del Pont's claim for repayment of his "loan" to the government.

# VENTURA MIGUEL MARCÓ DEL PONT LOSES HIS MONEY TO THE REVOLUTION, 1810

The political struggle that followed the victory over the British invaders separated the Spanish-born and the native-born whites. Perhaps Ventura Miguel Marcó del Pont, a Spanish-born merchant, had brought on his own trouble, in a way, by requesting that Viceroy Santiago Liniers return the 70,300-peso "loan" that Marcó earlier had made to the interim governor. Viceroy Liniers instead demanded a strict accounting of all the merchant's wealth. Marcó complied, admitting that he still had 31,000 pesos in cash, whereupon Liniers cited the "great emergencies of the time" in ordering that Marcó deliver the remaining money to the treasury. Within two months, Marcó received an order authorized by the Council of Castile (Consejo de Castilla) for the immediate remission to Spain of all funds belonging to Real Caja de Consolidación. But the *porteño* government already had spent the funds, as its outlays to Creole-led militias were increasing steadily.

Following the *cabildo abierto* on May 10, 1810, Marcó fled Buenos Aires, abandoning his Creole family. Marcó's wife had been born in Buenos Aires, as had his children. A son, Agustín, followed a *porteño* army into Alto Perú and eventually settled down in Salta as a patriot military officer, not as a merchant. As a Creole, Agustín, did not inherit the international social contacts of his father.

In an irony of empire, the Spanish side of the family was still to play a role in American affairs. Ferdinand VII appointed Marcó del Pont's younger brother, General Francisco Casimiro Marcó del Pont, as captain general of Chile. The younger Marcó faced the revolutionary Argentine general José de San Martín on the battlefield in 1817.

Within two weeks, Saavedra himself rebuffed a final effort by Marcó to regain the monies he had lent for the defense of Buenos Aires.

Clearly, the Creole political forces were no longer willing to allow colonial taxes to be sent to Spain. An additional element entered into the junta's decision to penalize the wealthier Spanish-born merchants like Marcó del Pont. Creole politicians were appealing to members of the popular classes, several thousand of whom were under arms in the city of Buenos Aires alone. In effect, the Creole leaders were redistributing wealth from the most elevated social groups to the lowest.

Part of that process involved removing the control of public monies from Spanish merchants and from semiofficial tax farmers, and Marcó del Ponte had served in both capacities. Simultaneously, the rebellion of the Creoles and their plebeian followers began to destroy the Spaniards' commercial and political network within the hinterland of South America. Military uprisings interrupted trade through the interior to Potosí, and Spaniards fled from Córdoba and Mendoza and later from Santiago, Lima, Potosí, and ultimately Montevideo. Commenting on the social chaos that resulted from the political breakdown, one British resident contrasted the once-prosperous *estancias* of the Banda Oriental to a revolutionary-era economy, "so depopulated and desolated, so immersed in misery and discontent" (Szuchman and Brown 1994, 85).

## Political Breakdown of the Viceroyalty

Several factors prevented a rapid succession of *porteño* revolutionaries from realizing their plan of gaining political control of the former Viceroyalty of the Río de la Plata in its entirety. First of all, they bickered among themselves, intriguing and breaking up into feuding factions. Their plans, enunciated in endless proclamations, were quite impractical. Despite their decrees ending the slave trade in Buenos Aires and declaring "Freedom of the Womb" in 1813, in which children born to slave women after that date would be free when they reached their 21st birthday, the Creoles held their own black and mulatto followers in contempt.

These leaders also had a tendency to turn on one another savagely. Mariano Moreno, for example, lost favor in 1811, and to get rid of him, his rivals sent him on a diplomatic mission to Europe, en route to which he died at sea. Others who lost favor were flung into jail. Vengeance even caught up to Santiago Liniers, hero of the British invasion and former viceroy. From his retirement in Córdoba, he voiced opposition to the arrogant manner in which the Buenos Aires junta treated the cities of the interior, for which transgression Liniers was seized and executed. The future hero of independence, General José de San Martín, formed an altogether unsympathetic opinion of the Creole politicians in Buenos Aires and stated, "I fear [utter ruin] not from the Spaniards but from domestic discord and our lack of education and judgment" (Lynch 1987, 68).

There was another reason why Buenos Aires could not effectively exert its leadership far and wide across the region. Creoles in other areas of the Río de la Plata wished to be governed not by their incompetent peers of the faraway port but by home rule, however incompetent it too might prove to be. Across the estuary at Montevideo, on the other hand, the Creole gentry preferred to support the Spanish governor rather than follow the dictates of the divided politicos of Buenos Aires. The *porteños* squandered initial support by sending three successive "liberating" military expeditions to bring the Bolivians under political control. The Creole military leaders twice sacked the mint at Potosí and once attempted to blow it up. Their excesses encouraged the black and mulatto troops from Buenos Aires to riot and pillage. In addition, the social liberalism of the invaders annoyed the Bolivian Creoles. The *porteños,* who had no experience with a sedentary and subordinate Indian population, misunderstood the social conservatism of their peers in the Andes. Even though they hesitated to outlaw slavery in Buenos Aires, the *porteño* invaders had no second thoughts about decreeing the end to the Indian labor drafts, the termination of Indian tribute, and equality between Indians and whites. Bolivian elites were not unhappy to see loyalist forces from Lima drive out each one of the military expeditions sent by Buenos Aires in 1811, 1813, and 1815.

Paraguay also resisted the political leadership of Buenos Aires. In 1811, the native-born gentry backed the Spanish intendant in defeating an expedition from the port. Afterward, however, the same Creole landowners overthrew the Spaniards. The Paraguayans were the first to actually gain independence from Spain in 1811 while simultaneously gaining autonomy from Buenos Aires.

## The People's Revolution

An additional factor prevented the *porteños* from establishing the political leadership of Buenos Aires over the entire former viceroyalty: the popular revolution. Given the ruinous bickering among the Creole leaders, the popular classes took matters into their own hands. These popular rebellions, occurring simultaneously in many regions, radically decentralized political leadership and led to a brief but intense period of direct seizure and redistribution of property. The landholding and merchant classes viewed these last two actions as robbery and pillage, but the rebels simply considered them redistribution of what others had made from the labor of the nonwhites during the colonial period.

We should not assume that these exercises of direct sovereignty of the mounted soldiers, the *montoneros*, amounted to popular democracy and socialization. Among these groups, power flowed from the tip of the lance, and small landowners and their families suffered from the rebels' depredations in greater measure than the elite. After all, the colonial order had not prepared persons of the popular classes for democracy and human rights. But in the process of the revolution, these popular rebellions advanced the political cause of federalism and pushed a social agenda that the Creole leadership otherwise would not have shared.

The *artiguista* movement of Uruguay and the riverine provinces of Argentina is a perfect example of the popular rebellions at work. The *artiguistas* were followers of José Gervasio Artigas, a revolutionary caudillo (irregular military leader) from the Banda Oriental. In the colonial days, on this rough and tumble frontier between Spanish and Portuguese territories, Artigas worked alternately as a cattle rustler, a landowner and cattle breeder, and the leader of mounted police forces that attempted to bring order to the countryside. Instability had abounded in the Banda Oriental, stirred up by Spanish and Portuguese conflict over control of the contraband trading port of Colonia. After Spain eliminated the Portuguese from the Banda Oriental in 1776, the area became a prosperous zone of cattle breeding and illegal trade in Brazilian black tobacco. The port of Montevideo developed as a commercial auxiliary to Buenos Aires (although Montevideo had a better harbor and its warehouses overflowed with hides and other pastoral products, Buenos Aires retained the commerce in slaves, mercury, and Bolivian silver).

The rivalry between the two sides of the Río de la Plata estuary continued into the period of revolution. In 1810, the *orientales*, or "Easterners," as they were known then, preferred to support the Spanish governor at Montevideo rather than submit to the Creole junta at Buenos Aires. However, Spanish officials in 1811 raised their tax demands on the cattlemen—even questioning their property rights— then invited a Portuguese expeditionary force from Brazil to help fight Buenos Aires. Although the British finally persuaded the Portuguese to leave, Artigas turned his fellow landowners against the Spaniards and raised a gaucho army to besiege Montevideo.

The combined opposition of Spaniards, Portuguese, and the *porteños* forced Artigas and 3,000 followers into a dramatic retreat across the Uruguay River to Entre Ríos. There he quickly became the champion of the rural popular classes made up of mulatto and mestizo cowboys, small cattle raisers, and indigenous groups. In the politics of the region, Artigas represented federalism. He became the "protector" of the Federal League of the Río de la Plata, demanding equal status with Buenos Aires and retaining military and political autonomy within his region.

Federalism during the revolutionary wars rested firmly on a popular base. Many revolutionary military leaders understood federalism to be antithetical to old-fashioned Spanish authoritarianism. Those advocating federalism believed in decentralized political power, with local elites electing their own representatives. They envisioned a federal nation consisting of a weak executive and a powerful congress that would preserve the political prerogatives of the provinces. In the wars of independence, many local federalists also promoted social reforms in order to recruit volunteer combatants from the popular classes.

Wherever social authority had eroded to the extent that the popular classes were able to act on their own agenda, a popular caudillo such as Artigas emerged to represent their interests. The caudillo himself might have been a landowner, as was Artigas, but his followers determined the content of the federalist program. From 1813 to 1818, the popular followers of Artigas were very stout, indeed. Warfare had removed nearly all authority in the countryside. The gauchos who had been itinerant laborers during the late 18th century now inherited the land on which they had once worked. Small bands of men and women traveled in the backlands and helped themselves to cattle and horses. They dried a few hides to trade for tobacco, *yerba mate,* and *aguardiente,* the sugar brandy consumed by the popular classes of the region.

Artigas's control over these popular forces depended on his faithfulness to their agenda, and thus he enunciated a radical social program that included redistribution of the land. He proposed to take land from Spaniards and those Creoles who sided with Spaniards and redistribute it among "*pardos* [mulattoes], *zambos* [Afro-mestizos], and Indians." The banners of federalism also fluttered over the mounted gangs of *montoneros* from other provinces. All the federalist bands, to a certain extent, lived off pillage and their leaders adopted political programs of regional autonomy.

# THE LAND REFORMS
# OF ARTIGAS, 1815

As a popular military leader, José Gervasio Artigas had to renounce the property interests of his own class—for Artigas was a Creole landowner himself—in order to voice the demands of his followers. In the Río de la Plata, the free blacks, mulattos, and mestizos who made up the insurrectionary forces had come from the least privileged of colonial society. Therefore, they longed for a redistribution of one of the basic economic assets that had reinforced their low status: the ownership of land. Artigas addressed these concerns during the brief time he controlled Montevideo, the capital of the Banda Oriental in 1815. These attempts to transform rural workers into middle-class landowners never went into effect, because a Portuguese invasion from Brazil forced the popular forces of Artigas to vacate the territory known today as Uruguay. Nonetheless, the proposed reforms articulated some of the objectives of the popular classes during the long struggle for independence. The 1815 proposals of Artigas said in part:

> For now the Provincial Mayor and other officials under him will dedicate themselves to promoting vigorously the well-being of the population of the Campaign, for which they will inspect in each one of their respective Jurisdictions the available land, and the Subjects worthy of this act of grace, and with precaution, let the most miserable become the most privileged. Therefore, free Blacks, Sambos of this class, Indians, and poor Creoles, all can be favored with the good fortune of an estancia (cattle estate), if with their work and their honorable manhood, they advance their own happiness and that of the Province.
>
> . . . Poor widows with children will be likewise favored. Married people will be preferred over single citizens, and the latter over any foreigner. . .
>
> . . . Properties available for redistribution are all those of people who have fled to exile, of bad Europeans and worse Americans who so far have not been pardoned by the Chief of the Province so that they could possess their former Properties. . . .
>
> . . . The Government, the Provincial Mayor, and other subordinates will keep watch to make sure that the land recipients do not possess more than the designated size of land grant [1.5 × 2 leagues] . . .
>
> . . . The land recipient can neither alienate nor sell these lots nor contract any debt on them upon pain of nullification, until the formal regulation of the Province in which it will deliberate over what is advisable.

■

(Street 1959, 376–79)

The federalism of the revolutionary period contained its own contradictions of colonial origin. In all cases, the leaders were Creoles whose class and perspective were not the same as those of the followers. While the caudillo on the rise reflected the popular agenda, the caudillo who consolidated political power certainly returned to the colonial legacy of disciplining the popular classes and governing by autocratic rather than democratic means. These popular leaders ultimately brought a semblance of order out of the chaos of the revolutionary period by returning to these legacies of social control; however, José Gervasio Artigas was not to be one of them. He lost the political struggle before he was able to consolidate sufficient power.

The challenge of the *artiguistas* to Buenos Aires hegemony rose significantly when they liberated Montevideo from the Spaniards in 1815, ostensibly gaining political autonomy for the *orientales*. It was not to last. The Portuguese from Brazil returned in 1816, drove Artigas back across the Uruguay River, and blockaded Buenos Aires.

Other popular caudillos, in the meantime, were operating in the interior provinces of Argentina. Francisco Ramírez became the strongman of Córdoba; Facundo Quiroga operated in La Rioja; Martín Güemes protected the autonomy of Salta; and eventually Ramírez supplanted Artigas in Entre Ríos. Because some of his erstwhile federalist allies had turned against him, notably Ramírez, the defeated Artigas requested sanctuary in Paraguay. Caudillo José Gaspar Rodríguez de Francia, who had successfully consolidated power in Paraguay in 1813, wanted no problems with the caudillos of the neighboring provinces, so he forced Artigas to retire permanently from politics. Artigas, who lived out his days in Paraguay, is considered the father of Uruguayan independence, but Uruguay would not actually gain its independence until 1828, when Great Britain, the biggest trading partner of both Brazil and Buenos Aires, convinced these two powers to end their competition over the old colonial buffer zone known as the Banda Oriental.

Although independence of the Argentine region that formed the heartland of the former viceroyalty was assured in 1816 when a congress at Tucumán proclaimed it, the political system—federalist or centralist—that this region would adopt remained uncertain. The centralists formed an entity known as the United Provinces of the Río de la Plata and attempted to rule over these provinces from Buenos Aires, but the surviving federalist caudillos ran their own provinces. This version of local autonomy, of course, departed starkly from the centralizing program of the Bourbon reforms, but local autonomy in the Southern Cone had deeper roots, going back to the formative 17th century.

## The Consolidation of Independence

No matter that the federalist caudillos and their popular followers had destroyed the colonial political order, they had not been able to consolidate South America's independence. This challenge remained the task of two leaders who developed rather more national—even supranational—perspectives on eliminating Spanish rule. Both of these men were professional soldiers who commanded the loyalties of local caudillos in the course of determining the outcome of the revolution on a continental scale.

The two liberators of South America were José de San Martín and Simón Bolívar, although neither of these leaders represented the popular revolution. If anything, they attempted to tame the popular revolution in order to finally eliminate all remaining vestiges of Spanish power in the Americas. They were also visionaries. Each devised plans for the governments and social relationship that they hoped would follow independence; however, San Martín and Bolívar proved more successful at winning independence than at charting the future tranquility of the American nations. Each ended his career in bitter disillusionment.

### San Martín in Peru

In 1812, José de San Martín returned to the land of his birth, Argentina, after a career as an army officer fighting in Spain against the French occupation. His father had also been a career officer in the colonies, stationed at Yapeyú on the Uruguay River, where San Martín was born. On his return from Europe, San Martín offered his services to the various governments at Buenos Aires and engaged in the political intrigue of the old viceregal capital. He reorganized the *porteño* army, then took command of the patriot forces in the interior. In 1816, he and his army defeated a loyalist invasion sent across the Andes from Lima.

San Martín identified Lima as the key to securing independence in South America, for the viceroy in this royalist stronghold had sent military expeditions to put down rebellions in Ecuador, Bolivia, and Chile, as well as in Argentina. Not even Argentina would be secure in its newly declared independence so long as Spanish forces remained in Lima. He decided that the surest way to eliminate this Spanish bastion was through Chile; therefore, he established headquarters at Mendoza, where San Martín trained an expeditionary army composed of Argentines and Chilean exiles.

The majority of his force, especially the foot soldiers, consisted of persons of color. San Martín requisitioned slaves from the local gentry,

*José de San Martín, the great Argentine general who led the independence movement in the Southern Cone* (Théodore Gericault, c. 1819)

giving them their freedom on condition that they fight for the cause of independence. Eventually, 1,500 slaves entered his army. Under his command, the blacks, mulattoes, and mestizos formed a disciplined fighting force and did not engage in the sort of pillage that characterized other military units of the period. Exiled Chilean patriots led by Bernardo O'Higgins contributed another important element to this expeditionary force.

General San Martín executed a great military feat in safely leading his 5,000 troops across the Andes Mountains. He misled the royalists as to his route and reassembled three columns of his troops in time to defeat a divided Spanish force (led by General Marcó del Pont, brother of the Spanish merchant exiled from Buenos Aires) at Chacabuco in February 1817. His troops then liberated the Chilean capital of Santiago. Two more battles ensued, and San Martín decisively defeated the remaining Spanish forces at Maipo in April. With Chile liberated and now ruled firmly but not ruthlessly by O'Higgins, San Martín laid the strategy for the next continental move. He hired a British admiral, Lord Cochrane, to organize a patriot navy for the expedition. San Martín formed up a new army, now of Chileans, Argentines, and Peruvian patriots, but was without a Peruvian leader of the stature of O'Higgins in Chile. Again, slaves enlisted in his army and were subjected to military discipline in exchange for their eventual freedom. Chile levied special taxes to support the new patriot army, just as the citizens of Mendoza had supported the liberation of Chile. In 1820, 23 ships carrying a patriot army of 4,500 soldiers set sail for Lima.

The campaign in Peru did not unfold according to plan, however. San Martín disembarked his troops at Pisco, 125 miles south of Lima, and sent the fleet on to blockade the port of Callao. His patriot column then marched north, circling around the viceregal capital of Lima and setting up a headquarters at Huacho. San Martín's presence sparked guerrilla activities in the sierra, but the Creole aristocracy of Lima, on whom the Argentine general had relied for some demonstration of support, did nothing. Rather than confront San Martín in battle, the Spanish forces proceeded to negotiate. Finally, in 1821, they evacuated Lima and relocated to the highlands as San Martín entered Lima. The Creoles professed to be pleased but were also dismayed that the bandits and brigands, many of them free blacks and runaway slaves, who had made travel outside the capital so perilous were now joining San Martín's patriot troops.

### Bolívar in Peru

In the absence of a united Creole government, San Martín had to accept political leadership. The citizens of Lima may have been motivated more by public security than by making sacrifices for the liberation of Peru. They developed a widespread fear of the troops of San Martín. According to an English observer, "It was not only of the slaves and of the mob that people were afraid, but with more reason of the multitude of armed Indians surrounding the city, who, although under the orders of San Martín's officers, were savage and undisciplined troops" (Lynch 1987, 68). It was not lost on the local landowners that their own control of the slaves was undermined by the fact that most of San Martín's troops were former African slaves as well as free blacks. Moreover, San Martín levied special taxes to support his troops, which made him unpopular with the residents of Lima, the *limeños*.

San Martín's problems were numerous. The general hesitated to risk his army in confronting the enemy, who could gather twice the number of troops as he could. He was also receiving little assistance from the Peruvians. Moreover, as provisional governor, he alienated many Peruvian Creoles by enlisting their slaves into military service, decreeing a law that freed the children born to slaves, and outlawing Indian tribute and forced labor. The Creoles would not rise to his revolution, and by 1822, San Martín was ready to look for another solution. The arrival of General Simón Bolívar, fresh from liberating Colombia, Venezuela, and Ecuador, gave him the opportunity. In February 1822, San Martín sailed to interview Bolívar in Guayaquil, Ecuador.

While a stalemate confronted San Martín in Peru, Simón Bolívar was completing a series of stunning victories against royalist forces in northern South America. Bolívar had suffered all the vicissitudes of the independence movement. In his native Venezuela, he had been defeated in 1812 when the first patriot rebellion succumbed to internal dissent, not unlike that of distant Buenos Aires. Similar movements by other patriot factions also failed in Colombia and Ecuador. Following a period of exile, Bolívar returned to Venezuela in 1816. Three years later, he engineered his first major triumph in capturing the viceregal capital of Bogotá with a combined force of Venezuelan and Colombian patriots. He then returned to liberate Caracas from Spanish forces. Like San Martín, Bolívar had recruited soldiers from the popular classes by promising social reforms, such as an end to Indian tribute and freedom for slaves who enrolled in his army. Such strategies enabled Bolívar to liberate Ecuador from the royalists in 1821. Fresh from these victories, Bolívar traveled to Guayaquil to meet San Martín, a man he considered his rival.

San Martín, however, had decided that it was necessary to combine his own forces with those of Bolívar. When San Martín met Bolívar in Guayaquil, he was bogged down and discredited in Peru, and Bolívar had just triumphed in Ecuador. Bolívar had the upper hand in the negotiations and was not willing to share command with anyone else. The interviews between the two liberators were less than cordial. Abject and disillusioned, General San Martín turned over his forces to Bolívar and retired. San Martín traveled through Santiago, crossed the

# SAN MARTÍN'S FAREWELL LETTER TO SIMÓN BOLÍVAR

Unfortunately, I am fully convinced either that you did not believe that the offer which I made to serve under your orders was sincere, or else that you felt that my presence in your army would be an impediment to your success. Permit me to say that the two reasons which you expressed to me: first, that your delicacy would not permit you to command me; and, second, that even if this difficulty were overcome, you were certain that the Congress of Colombia would not consent to your departure from that republic, do not appear plausible to me. The first reason refutes itself. In respect to the second reason, I am strongly of the opinion that the slightest suggestion from you to the Congress of Colombia would be received with unanimous approval, provided that it was concerned with the cooperation of yourself and your army in the struggle in which we are engaged.

. . . I am convinced that the prolongation of the war will cause the ruin of her people; hence it is a sacred duty of those men to whom America's destinies are confided to prevent the continuation of great evils.

. . . I shall embark for Chile, for I am convinced that my presence is the only obstacle which prevents you from marching to Peru with your army.

■

*(Harrison 1943, 155–56) (Levene 1950, 251)*

---

Andes, and departed immediately from Buenos Aires in 1824 for a self-imposed political exile in France.

Not all Peruvian elites were happy at the prospect of yet another foreign army coming to "liberate" them. When he finally entered Peru with an army in 1824, Bolívar confronted the royalist forces in the highlands at Junín and then at Ayacucho. Bolívar routed them in a famous cavalry battle in which his Venezuelan, Argentine, and Chilean horsemen defeated the royalists. The Creoles of the high Andes won their independence in 1825 when Bolívar's army beat the royalists in the last battle of the wars of independence, at Tumusla, Bolivia; Peruvian independence was assured in January 1826 when the last Spanish forces left. After 16 long and destructive years, the era of civil war in the former colonies of Spain had come to an end. The grateful patriots of Bolivia named their new nation for the Venezuelan-born liberator, who promptly wrote for them a constitution. The new nation severed its ties to the former viceregal capital of Buenos Aires.

The problem of governing Peru and Bolivia, therefore, now thrust itself on Bolívar, who responded with characteristic confidence that his wisdom could fashion the perfect constitution for the new governments. He had long ago shed the liberal ideas of his youth and had come to design constitutions that featured strong executive powers (for example, a hereditary president in Bolivia), aristocratic congresses, and moralistic judiciaries. However, as a troop commander, he recognized the sacrifices and motivations of his mostly nonwhite troops, so his constitutions outlawed slavery and ended Indian tribute, recognizing the political equality of all Americans even though countenancing the inequality of their education and property holdings. (Once the Great Liberator returned to Colombia, however, his Peruvian associates rejected the complete end to slavery and the new Bolivian rulers reimposed Indian tributes.)

President Bolívar found that, daunting as it was, the liberation of South America had been an easier task that governing it. As president of Gran Colombia—a hybrid nation of Venezuela, Colombia, and Ecuador—he ruled from the old viceroy's palace in Bogotá. Late in 1826, his former comrades in arms rebelled and established Venezuela as its own independent nation. Ecuador fell away, too. Then, Bolívar narrowly escaped an assassination attempt in Colombia. Bitter and sick of body as well as heart, Bolívar renounced his shattered presidency in 1830 and traveled to the coast to follow San Martín into European retirement. He took to bed in Santa Marta, Colombia, and shortly before dying, penned his final epitaph to the independence of Latin America. His reference to the social causes of instability serves as a testament to the racial and ethnic inequalities that had been nurtured during colonial rule. "America is ungovernable," Bolívar wrote. "The only thing to do in America is to emigrate" (Groot 1893, V: 368).

Alone among South America's two liberators, José de San Martín survived to survey his handiwork—though from afar. He lived out his days in Paris, resigned that neither he nor anyone else could have prevented the political disintegration of Spanish America. He died in 1850 as the political turmoil in his native land continued. The former leader of the popular revolution, José Gervasio Artigas, also died that same year in his Paraguayan exile. The titans of independence by then had all passed from the scene, but Argentina was still far from forming a nation.

# 5

# AGRARIAN EXPANSION AND NATION BUILDING, 1820–1880

In 1816, representatives from all the Argentine provinces assembled in Tucumán and declared themselves independent of Spain, forming a nation they called the United Provinces of the River Plate; however, peace and tranquility did not return to the war-ravaged region. The hastily written constitution for Argentina established a national congress, states' rights, an anemic executive branch (with a "director" at its helm) and an even weaker judiciary. Everyone ignored it.

Instead, the revolutionary-era caudillos organized their own militias and ruled the provinces with iron fists. Each provincial strongman distrusted his counterparts in the neighboring provinces and made and broke alliances in numerous military actions against his neighbors. These authoritarian leaders brooked no opposition and preferred to maintain the neutrality at least of the elite families, from whom many of them had come. But they were not above intimidating the privileged few to stay in power—all in a selfish and counterproductive effort to save the "order of society." An electoral process began to operate but would not gain legitimacy until the end of the 19th century and then would be accompanied by vote manipulation. Under these circumstances, the political life of the Argentine nation did not begin auspiciously.

Argentines succeeded, nevertheless, in laying the foundations for constructing a modern nation. They reoriented the region's economy away from the defunct mines of Bolivia toward an Atlantic trade in a variety of ranch products. Expanding trade in Argentine hides and wool underwrote frontier expansion, integration into the world economy, and a significant rise in productivity. The economic growth ultimately contributed to a political rapprochement among the provinces. By

1853, Argentina acquired a constitution more consistent with its political realities, and the fighting of two wars, one against Paraguay and the other a final battle with the indigenous peoples, forged a national army that finally eclipsed the disruptive local militias.

In its arduous process of economic growth and political unification, Argentina also began to develop opportunities for its growing population. However, the country could not shake its colonial mentality while deciding how to share the opportunities that economic growth and nation building presented. The politicians continued to put public trust behind personal gain for themselves and their political insiders. Expansion of settlements on the frontier solidified the power of a landed elite that remained socially conservative despite its economic dynamism. The economic boom, therefore, went hand-in-hand with an effective repression that curtailed the economic opportunities of the rural residents of color—mestizos, mulattoes, and blacks. Immigrant Europeans continued to enjoy greater social mobility than did native-born workers. Neocolonial social practices did not diminish in the postrevolutionary period.

## Disunity and Caudillo-Style Politics

Buenos Aires sought to claim its revolutionary and economic birthright in dominating the rest of the disunited provinces. Those who headed the government at the capital pretended to speak for the nation and utilized its commercial position to reinforce this pretension. They decreed repeatedly that all trade with Europe was to pass through Buenos Aires, setting the small *porteño* navy to regulate trade on the Paraná and Uruguay Rivers. To the provincials, it seemed that Buenos Aires in the early 19th century was treating them as the Spanish Crown had once treated colonial Buenos Aires.

Moreover, the politicians of the port city did not agree among themselves and conspired against one another. The political maelstrom in Buenos Aires forced every single head of government out of office well before his official term expired. Most ruled with emergency, extraconstitutional powers under states of siege. The revolutionary militia leader Juan Martín de Pueyrredón left office as director of the United Provinces of the River Plate early in 1819 and was succeeded by José Rondeau, who lost his position the following year after losing the battle of Pavón to the combined forces of Entre Ríos and Santa Fe. The two caudillo leaders who defeated Rondeau—Francisco Ramírez and Estanislao López—had a falling out in 1821, and López killed Ramírez.

The only nonmilitary figure of the era, Bernardino Rivadavia, claimed the directorship of the United Provinces in 1826. He ambitiously enacted numerous "reform" laws totally out of cadence with the political rhythm of the country, annoyed the caudillo governors of the interior, alienated the landowners of his own home province of Buenos Aires, and resigned his office in less than two years.

# THE ORIGINS OF AN ARGENTINE SAINT: LA DIFUNTA CORREA

The incessant civil disturbances during the decades that followed Argentine independence were devastating for the people and the country, and the troubled times gave rise to Argentina's popular patron saint. As the Mexicans have their Virgin of Guadalupe, Argentines today have their mother figure, la Difunta Correa, (the deceased woman Correa). Neither the Vatican nor the Argentine Catholic Church officially recognizes la Difunta, but that does not prevent an estimated 600,000 devotees from visiting her remote shrine in the Andean foothills of La Rioja province every year.

Señora Deolinda Correa was a victim of the interminable civil wars of the first half of the 19th century. Sometime in the 1840s, Correa was carrying her infant son as she followed her husband's military unit crossing the barren desert of western Argentina. Exhausted and hungry, she died of heat stroke along the trail. Legend has it that muleteers later found her body, with her son still alive, suckling at her breast. The scene was interpreted to represent the miracle of motherly love, and the legend spread by word of mouth throughout the region. Much later, in 1895, some herdsmen lost their cattle in a dust storm and appealed to la Difunta for assistance. The herd miraculously reappeared the next day, and in appreciation, the cattlemen built a monument on the hill where her remains were buried.

Today, all across Argentina, travelers and truck drivers stop by little roadside shrines to pay homage to la Difunta, light a candle, and ask for help. Those who seek special favors—health for a loved one, success at university examinations, a new vehicle—will visit the original shrine nestled on a foothill of the Andean mountains, where centuries before, the indigenous peoples of these parts had prayed at similar shrines to Pachamama, the goddess Mother Earth.

This exhausting list of coups, civil hostilities, political unrest, and feckless leaders held true for every province of Argentina in the 1820s. Suffice it to say that 19th century caudillo-style politics became identified with unstable political leadership, assassinations, coups and countercoups, civil unrest, intimidation of critics, and the flouting of the constitution. It has endured and is practiced even today. Most Argentine citizens can recount numerous instances of caudillo-style politics during the last quarter of the 20th century.

No one escaped the repercussions of revolution and civil war in the Río de la Plata. The military impressment recruited hundreds of young men of the popular classes in the cities and countryside. Deserters turned to banditry, preying on cattle herds and plaguing the commercial routes, or they went to live among the Indians. Gaucho armies laid siege to Montevideo and invaded Paraguay and Bolivia. Once the loyalist forces retreated, armed factions turned on one another as patriot politicians sought advantage. Long subject to Hispanic incursion, the Pampas Indians took advantage of the confusion and raided rural settlements and cart trains. Merchants had to pay forced loans and extraordinary taxes, landowners lost cattle, rural women were kidnapped by Indians, and urban women saw their men taken into the militias.

In 1825, Buenos Aires began a protracted war in the Banda Oriental with the empire of Brazil, which had proclaimed its independence from Portugal in 1822. More military impressment, desertions, and banditry followed. Only the emergence of Juan Manuel de Rosas as the governor of Buenos Aires stanched somewhat the political instability of the first half of the 19th century. However, Rosas controlled only his home province and had to perfect rather than depart from caudillo-style politics in order to remain in power for 20 years.

It is little wonder that the once-bustling colonial economy of the Río de la Plata lay in ruin. The Bolivians stopped working the rich mines of Potosí that had been the engine of transport and production in the interior provinces and of commerce at Buenos Aires. Caudillos with their personal mounted armies took over provincial governments, taxed their enemies, and set up customs houses on provincial borders. In the interior, overland trade came to a halt and the river trades declined dramatically. In 1840, one Tucumán resident reflected that the previous three decades had been filled with nothing but "disasters and misfortunes." "After the anarchy of so many years, after the sacrifices that these peoples [of the interior provinces] were obliged to make in the wars," he wrote, "they have remained submerged in the most dreadful misery, and they need many years of peace and tranquility in order to recuperate their lives" (Szuchman and Brown 1994, 241). It must have seemed to many an Argentine that, in the revolutionary and civil wars, the long-term reward of nationhood was economic privation.

## International Trade in Buenos Aires

One area of the new nation was better situated than others to recover quickly from the economic and social dislocation attending the aftermath of revolution. The port city of Buenos Aires and its prairie hinterlands to the south and west represented a haven from the prolonged economic decay. Although the riparian provinces and even the landlocked interior of Córdoba and Tucumán eventually participated in the new foreign trade of the Río de la Plata estuary, Buenos Aires province reaped most of the benefits.

In the late 18th century, the cattle industry had further developed in commercial intensity in the Banda Oriental (present-day Uruguay). The East Bank was well watered, more densely populated, and more protected from marauding Indians than the hinterland of Buenos Aires. Montevideo and Colonia became important emporiums for the collection of export hides. Large estates along the shoreline specialized in the domestication of cattle and produced large quantities of hides for export. The first *saladeros* began processing cattle hides and salted beef for

A saladero *for processing hides and salted meat. Such crude enterprises supplied what* became important products for Argentina's international trade. Most of the work was done by itinerant gauchos. (Leon Pallière, 1858)

export. Paraguayan cowboys, many of them Guaraní Indians expert at handling horse and lasso, left their women and families in Paraguay and wandered through the Banda Oriental working at a succession of jobs herding cattle. The Banda Oriental, however, suffered the ravages of the revolution to a greater extent than Buenos Aires. The Argentine-Brazilian wars further arrested the recovery of the pastoral economy of this fertile but tragic land. Thus, in the first half of the 19th century, Buenos Aires province had few competitors in producing cattle.

Buenos Aires's phenomenal commercial growth was part and parcel of 19th-century industrialism in Europe because the city served as the hub for one of the world's most important suppliers of pastoral raw materials. Port operations remained basic and unimproved, yet oceanic ships in increasing numbers risked the hazardous journey up the shallow estuary. The export of goods produced on the ranches of the hinterlands likewise increased, adding to a commercial prosperity that defied even the region's political instability and four foreign blockades of the port. The first half of the 19th century also witnessed the usurpation of the import-export trade by non-Spanish, especially British, merchants who had important connections in industrial markets. They assumed the risks and reaped the profits of the era's commerce.

It would be erroneous, however, to view Buenos Aires merely as a commercial submetropolis whose trade was dominated by England or even by industrial markets. True, the prosperity of the entire region

| Destination of Ships Leaving the Port of Buenos Aires, 1849–1851 | | | |
|---|---|---|---|
| Destination | No. of Ships | Tonnage | Percent of Tonnage |
| Great Britain | 322 | 71,140 | 22.8 |
| United States | 253 | 67,589 | 21.6 |
| Cuba | 205 | 41,107 | 13.2 |
| German states | 173 | 37,526 | 12.0 |
| Brazil | 207 | 35,320 | 11.3 |
| France | 135 | 28,548 | 9.1 |
| Italy | 75 | 15,622 | 5.0 |
| Spain | 56 | 15,700 | 5.0 |
| Source: Juan Carlos Nicolau (Unp. Ms., table II) and Parish (1852, 355) | | | |

depended on foreign trade, and the major portion of that trade went to industrial nations of the North Atlantic. Yet, important shares of Buenos Aires's exports went to nonindustrial nations as well: Brazil, Cuba, Italy, and Spain. After an initial period of British shipping pre-eminence up to the 1830s, Great Britain lost its dominance of the carrying trades out of Buenos Aires to the vessels of other nations. Judging from the destinations of the ships clearing the port of Buenos Aires from 1849 to 1851, the pastoral products of the region were going to a diversified set of customers.

By today's shipping standards, the port of Buenos Aires was a miserable place to load and unload the freight of international commerce. Sailing vessels of 150 to 300 tons had to venture almost 190 miles up to the city by tacking back and forth across the sandbars of the estuary. The trip from Liverpool took about 70 days and from New York about 80 days. Approaching the port, foreign sailors sighted the two-story, stucco dwellings that formed the city's skyline, punctuated occasionally by church spires, stretching out for a mile and a quarter along the banks. Black and mulatto washerwomen, the servants and slaves of the finer *porteño* households, daily lined the shores, scrubbing articles of clothing on the rocks. The first vista of Buenos Aires was not imposing.

Loading and unloading the ships appeared as unimpressive as the skyline. Shallow waters prevented the larger wooden sailing vessels from anchoring closer than $3^1/_2$ miles from shore. Sailors had to transfer passengers and freight to and from sailing lighters, which carried them across the shoals. Passengers and freight were then transferred from sailing lighters to horse-drawn carts, which had been pulled a third of a mile into the water. Each cart had wooden wheels nearly 13 feet high to keep the cart bed off the water. As described by travelers, the whole port presented a scene of bedlam: "The sand-flat, and water beyond it, was covered with carts . . . conveying goods to and from the ships in the roads, with Gauchos riding about with lassos, made of strips of hide plaited, tied to their horses' girths, to help carts requiring an extra tug" (Videl 1820, 61–62).

Buenos Aires in this era was atypical in that it did not have a monocultural export economy that depended on the export of just one or two staple products. Cattle hides dominated trade throughout the entire period, but they lost their primacy to raw wool as the principal export at the close of the 1850s. Great Britain still took great portions of tallow, horsehides, and bones. The United States, the German states, and France became good customers for Argentine raw wools and salted hides. France and North America imported most of the region's sheepskins, while all of the salted beef produced in the Río de la Plata found markets in Cuba and Brazil, where slaveholders bought Argentine beef to feed the growing slave populations.

Great Britain monopolized import markets early in the 19th century but gradually lost shares to products of other nations. It had once been said that most clothes worn by men and women in the streets of Buenos Aires had been manufactured in Manchester and Lancashire. British ironmongery, earthenwares, and cutlery predominated even among the rural population of the province. As mid-century approached, however, French ships arrived with fine clothing goods, perfumes, and wine, and Genoa and Cádiz sent out Italian and Spanish wines. From Hamburg came iron goods, gin, and stockings; Brazil supplied sugar. Yankee traders from Baltimore and Philadelphia came with lumber and with wheat flour, which the agricultural economy of Argentina did not yet produce in abundance because of a lack of manpower in the countryside.

Shortly after 1810, a group of non-Hispanic merchants with connections in North Atlantic markets supplanted the wealthy Spaniards and Creoles who had directed the import-export trade of colonial Buenos Aires. English merchant houses predominated but by no means excluded French, German, and American traders who resided in the Río de la Plata. Their advantage over the Argentine Creoles lay in their affiliation to markets abroad and their access to superior capital for the worldwide movement of goods. Unlike the Spanish merchants, such as Marcó del Pont a generation before, these foreigners lacked the commercial contact of kinfolk throughout the region and therefore depended on a secondary level of native *porteño* merchants to handle the merchandising in the backlands. *Estancia* production became an important investment outlet for native capital. Many families of colonial commercial origin put their funds into cattle raising. Similarly, native merchants took charge of assembling pastoral goods for export. Some foreign entrepreneurs succeeded in investing in rural production, particularly in introducing European sheep breeding to the Pampas.

Foreign investment had severe limits, however. Domestic transportation, retailing, processing, ranching, and farming expanded on relatively modest investments by Creoles and immigrants. Economic expansion in Buenos Aires justified investments of no grander scale, a lesson foreign investors soon learned. In 1824, a London investment bank, the House of Baring, floated a bond issue for £1 million, backed by the Rivadavia government. Politicians soon misappropriated the loan for the war against Brazil, and their successors saw little advantage even in paying the interest. It marked the first time that Argentina defaulted on foreign loans. Meanwhile, foreigners residing in the port and several *porteños* attempted to establish an investment bank in Argentina, the Banco de la Provincia de Buenos Aires. They responded to a European mania for reviving the old silver mines of the Andean region. Speculators in London invested heavily in two mining enterprises for the region, both of which collapsed in the 1826 financial panic. Soon thereafter, the Banco de la Provincia turned to issuing paper money, which quickly lost value and set off an inflationary spiral in Argentina. This financial debacle in the mid-1820s discouraged future international investment and restricted foreign management to the import-export trade, a few shops, and sheep ranches.

Foreign trade through the port of Buenos Aires periodically fell off as a result of four naval blockades by foreign powers within the first 40 years of independence. A squadron of the Spanish navy, stationed at Montevideo, maintained a blockade of Buenos Aires from 1811 to 1816. In the war over the Banda Oriental, a Brazilian fleet invested the port in 1827 and 1828. Ten years later, the French blockaded Buenos Aires. The British fleet enforced the final blockade, that of 1845–48, attempting to force the provincial government to open the Paraná River to international shipping. None of these blockades succeeded well. The British broke the earliest Spanish blockade and ignored the others. The Yankee shippers took pleasure at slipping through the later British blockade. "American vessels were weekly running past, breaking the blockade, and making fortunes for their owners," observed one foreign merchant, "while scarce an English one made the attempt" (Brand 1828, 34). Trade continued despite the diplomatic disagreements that accompanied political unrest in the region and resumed in greater measure following each naval blockade.

Buenos Aires was one of those remarkable economic success stories of early 19th century Latin America. Even while the civil strife continued in the interior, foreign trade at the port rose. Around 100 foreign ships put in at Buenos Aires each year in the 1810s. By the 1820s and 1830s, the average yearly numbers had increased to 280 vessels. Ship arrivals at Buenos Aires amounted to 452 per year in the 1840s and to 674 in the 1850s. River shipping to and from Buenos Aires also increased up to mid-century, despite the civil wars, river blockades, and foreign entanglements.

Markets for hides and cattle by-products flourished, and so did the cattle production of Buenos Aires. To meet the growing demands, a new processing industry began to develop at the port. *Saladeros,* hide and meat-salting plants, were established in the southern suburbs of Buenos

Aires. From the countryside, cowboys drove herds of cattle to these processing factories. By 1825, more than two score *saladeros* were slaughtering approximately 70,000 head of cattle a year at Buenos Aires. As trade expanded through the 1830s and 1840s, so did the industry. *Saladeros* at mid-century were processing more than 300,000 head of cattle, and horses, too, per year. These salting plants turned the slaughter of cattle into an efficient manufacturing process, but without dispensing with the traditional "technology" of cowboy, horse, lasso, and *facón,* as the long knife common to Argentina was called. "The whole sight [of the *saladero*] is horrible and revolting," observed Charles Darwin in the 1830s. "[T]he ground is almost made of bones; and the horses and riders are drenched with gore" (Darwin 1858, 104).

## Expansion of the Cattle *Estancia*

When finally blessed with a modicum of peace in the early 19th century, the colonial cattle ranch, or *estancia,* developed into a complex business enterprise. Production and marketing of pastoral products, in fact, supported the development of a diversified rural society. Farming, far from being squeezed off the land, actually expanded in relation to growth of the urban market of Buenos Aires. Commercial growth created some truly great estates in the countryside, but the large landed units, which initially pushed back the frontiers toward the south, were reduced in size and their ownership diffused as the demand for efficiency required the application of more capital and management than land. Improvements in Argentina's economy in the first half of the 19th century spawned a rural society on the Pampas surrounding Buenos Aires that grew vibrant, booming, and open to economic and social opportunity—though tempered by colonial-style discrimination.

The growing export trade in cattle hides, wool, salted meat, and tallow provided the catalyst for rural expansion. Population increase on the Pampas even outstripped growth of the city of Buenos Aires. While the number of urban residents yearly increased by 1.5 percent between 1820 and 1860, the population growth rate in the countryside reached 3.4 percent per annum. In 1822, Buenos Aires had more than 55,000 inhabitants and the rest of the province 63,000; in 1855, the city had grown to 90,000, and the countryside, to nearly 184,000 people. Nothing characterized this growth and diversification more than did the expanding range cattle business.

Prospective cattlemen initially acquired their land on the Pampas from the government of Buenos Aires province. As in colonial days, a simple declaration of vacant land (*tierras baldías*) sufficed for an individual to register a claim with authorities. In the 1820s, reform politicians led by Bernardino Rivadavia established a program known as emphyteusis, in which the state rented out frontier land rather than giving it to private owners. Under emphyteusis, the government allotted land in huge tracts, some as large as 30, 60, and 100 square leagues (a league equaled 3.54 miles), to individuals. The average grant varied between 5 and 10 leagues, and foreigners as well as native-born residents received grants. The collection of rents, however, proved nearly impossible, so when Juan Manuel de Rosas became governor, he sold the lands to the tenants, as well as political friends, on easy terms. Some paid in cattle and horses. Governor Rosas also made new land grants to soldiers participating in frontier wars against the Indians. With little capital to stock the land, the soldiers sold their small grants to speculators. The sheer abundance of virgin prairie, whose availability only the Indians contested, encouraged the granting of the original tracts in large chunks. At mid-century, frontier *estancias* far to the south of Buenos Aires measured from 22,000 acres to 74,000 acres.

From the beginning, the commercial growth gave rise to a vigorous market in private land sales. The value of land in the province rose according to the worth of its products. Land worth 15 centavos per hectare in 1800 sold for 3 gold pesos in 1837 and fetched 30 gold pesos by mid-century. (The gold peso was a notional measure of value and, in fact, did not exist in physical form. Most money actually changed hands in the form of inflated paper pesos, but because the value of the paper money fluctuated rapidly, usually declining, many businessmen made long-term arrangements in the stable medium of gold, which they designated in units of "gold pesos.")

Naturally, rising land values motivated owners of *estancias* to add improvements to their properties. *Estancieros* constructed wood corrals, ranchos for workers, sheds for storage and animals, oxcarts, residences for owners and majordomos, perhaps even a *pulpería* (country store), as well as digging ditches to protect fields of wheat and alfalfa, and planting orchards of fruit trees. Tenancy also became a more common arrangement between owner and producer.

As land became more intensively utilized, the scarcity of labor encouraged owners to maximize profits by renting out parcels of their *estancias* to a family who would cultivate the land themselves. Renting the land relieved the owner of having to raise crops or care for milk cows with expensive hired help. Foreigners were preferred as renters, just as they were desired as *pulperos* (shopkeepers). The owner could depend on them for stability, because the military drafts applied only to native-born males. Prejudice toward the uncouth, independent gaucho also played a role. As in colonial times, European immigrants moved into a middle-level social status denied to native-born mestizos and mulattoes. Inasmuch as farming earned the renter an income above subsistence, immigrants enjoyed the opportunity of eventually buying their own parcels, despite land's rising cost.

Argentina's cattle business in the 19th century necessitated production on large landed estates because traditional ranching techniques placed a ceiling on the efficiency of land use. But as production became more intensive, when land was converted from cattle to sheep and from sheep to crops, the rural estate decreased in size while increasing in efficiency. Landowners sold off portions of large estates or divided them among their children. This process of fractionalization of the originally large *estancias* continued throughout the early 19th century on the Pampas.

The boom in foreign trade made investment in cattle *estancias* quite profitable for Argentine businessmen. Old merchant families, eased out of export commerce by foreign traders, converted their assets to land and cattle. For example, in the 1820s, the Anchorena merchant clan shifted capital from overseas commerce to ranching, eventually creating the largest of all the cattle operations; by 1864, the Anchorenas owned more than 2.3 million acres of ranch land on the rich Pampas. Wealthy landowners lived in Buenos Aires, leaving daily ranch management in the hands of resident majordomos. In the port city, *estancieros* dealt directly with merchants who collected goods for export and with slaughterhouse owners who sought timely delivery of fattened steers. They were not disinterested absentee landlords but successful capitalists who linked the production of the countryside to domestic and export markets in the city.

Despite the visibility of wealthy ranchers, the small family ranch and family farm were by far the most common productive units on the Pampas. A majority of the ranchers lived on comparatively modest spreads, which they worked with the aid of family members and a few hired hands. The typical rural residential unit was a farm or small ranch with six to eight people: a man, his wife, their children, a *peón* (hired worker), an orphan, and perhaps a slave or a *liberto* (a child born to slaves after 1813 and considered chattel until age 21, when he or she became free). In addition, disparate sources seem to indicate a constant turnover of land tenure. Business failures, trade recessions, the effects of drought, and increasing costs of rural production provoked the sale and rental of numerous rural properties. Renting rural property offered newcomers, especially Europeans, the opportunity to operate ranches and farms in this era of growing markets.

Expanding foreign trade accounts for much of the profit margin in ranching, yet Argentine producers themselves had to streamline and rationalize cattle production. The major cost-saving breakthroughs for the cattle industry came in the marketing of livestock and livestock products. In the 1810s, as in colonial times, the *estanciero* butchered most of his own cattle and prepared the hides and tallow at the ranch. An account book for 1812 reveals that one rancher made only 12 percent of the year's revenues from the sale of live cattle—probably to the butchers who purveyed beef to the residents of Buenos Aires. By mid-century, however, any given *estanciero* sold a major part of his herd on-the-hoof to the port's stockyards and slaughterhouses. Cattle drivers delivered great herds of up to 800 head of cattle directly to *saladeros*. Because the meat-salting plants also produced tallow and grease, the cattleman had to provide steers and cows with "fat meat."

These changes in the final destination of his product contributed a significant efficiency to the cattleman's operations. No longer did he rely on the processing of hides and tallow on his own property or by his own increasingly expensive employees. The *estanciero* now garnered 70 percent of his revenues from the sale of live animals. Much of the costly processing of pastoral goods on the ranch was eliminated.

## Labor Conditions in the Countryside

Constant expansion of cattle and sheep production on the Pampas offered much economic and social opportunity for newcomers. An 1854 census reckoned that a quarter of the rural population of Buenos Aires province, then numbering more than 183,000 persons, consisted of newcomers. While native-born peons worked the cattle, industrious immigrants found jobs in sheepherding, construction, and petty merchandizing or as artisans. Newcomers seemed to find greatest opportunity in the agricultural zone close to Buenos Aires, where the infrastructure was more highly developed.

Besides economic opportunities in the expanding marketing system, the immigrant also found advancement as a renter or landowner. Large cattle ranchers were subdivided numerous times between 1820 and 1850 as the value of land and its products steadily rose. Each step in the process intensified land use and rural production on the Pampas. On the frontier, owners still held giant tracts and worked them as huge

| Rural Population in Buenos Aires Province, 1854 | | | |
|---|---|---|---|
| Origin | Men | Women | Total |
| Natives of Buenos Aires province | 39.8% | 34.8% | 74.6% |
| Migrants from interior provinces | 9.0 | 5.9 | 14.9 |
| Foreign-born immigrants | 7.6 | 2.9 | 10.5 |
| Total | 54.4% | 43.6% | 100 |
| Source: *Registro estadístico de Buenos Aires, 1854* (1855, table 9). | | | |

production units. Land closer to the expanding markets of Buenos Aires was subdivided, and the units of production became smaller. In district after district straddling the Salado River, the larger cattle estates of the early 19th century gave way to smaller, more intensively worked properties producing sheep and eventually cash crops. Usually, sons of *estancieros* and immigrant Europeans benefited from the spread of landownership. Native-born gauchos did not.

The structure of the *estancia* followed traditional Hispanic patrimonial organization. Although the owner of large properties lived in the city, he controlled life on the ranch, for example, making all arrangements for marketing the ranch's products in the city. The biggest *estancieros* in a particular sector of the countryside, especially in the sparsely settled frontier areas, effectively dominated the entire area through their monopolies of *pulperías* (rural stores) and transportation. The landowner's nominal control over the workers went a long way toward enforcing order in the rural hinterland. Still, this control was never complete.

A racial division of labor evolved on the Pampas. Native-born and migrant mestizos and mulattoes usually handled cattle. Immigrant whites went into sheep raising, farming, and merchandizing. Native-born males were susceptible to the military drafts, while the exempt foreign-born saved to buy land. The same kind of social process marginalized people of color in the city of Buenos Aires, where immigrants also enjoyed the advantages of upward mobility. Most artisans and shopkeepers in the capital were foreign-born; most household servants were native-born Argentines of color.

Manpower in the Argentine hinterland was always scarce in the 19th century. *Estancieros* complained of how levies for the provincial militia drained the labor pool of gauchos. Labor shortages meant that

An early 19th-century scene of cattle branding on an Argentine estancia, or cattle ranch, in Corrientes province. The workforce on such ranches was made up of gauchos and indigenous laborers, both of whom are shown here. (Alcides D'Orbigny, 1827, courtesy of Emece Editores)

landowners had to put off branding and other chores. As late as 1846, large numbers of cattle without brands wandered through the fenceless prairies. "[T]he land all around here is very fertile, and ready for the plough," observed a traveler at mid-century, "but where the population is not sufficient to care for the cattle, they [sic] cannot be expected to attend to the labor of agriculture." (MacCann 1853, I:62) In times of crisis, such as the 1830 drought, cattlemen were unable to turn dying cattle into dried meat and hides or to move the herds to less desiccated pastures. Peons (any workers employed by a rancher or a farmer, including gauchos) made themselves scarce and expensive. In fact, the ranch managers found that available peons held out for higher wages in the rancher's time of need. As another British traveler concluded, "Resources of the country are altogether neglected for want of an indus-trious population." (Parish 1852, 256)

Nonetheless, the intensification of land use on the Pampas does not seem to have eliminated—indeed, it enhanced—the worker's ability to move from job to job, though not necessarily up the social ladder. Labor scarcity was endemic. Recruitment into the militias, the end of the slave trade, and the free birth laws had depleted the numbers of slaves in Buenos Aires province. For the most part, the men in the coun-tryside were native-born of mainly mixed blood. All called themselves *blancos* (whites), although many had a swarthy skin color. Some ranches also had many mulatto and black workers (*pardos* and *morenos,* respectively). But the elites considered these persons of color fit only for wage labor. Lack of even a rudimentary education prevented them from rising to the ranks of foremen, and social prejudices closed off opportunities to rent land or to run a country store.

The labor shortage also created opportunities for immigrant workers. They took jobs that self-respecting gauchos would not do, such as digging ditches to protect orchards and gardens from grazing cattle. Irish and English immigrants worked for British sheep ranchers. English immigrants became adept at digging wells and constructing watering holes for cattle. Often they charged—and received—more than the landowners wanted to pay. Employers favored foreigners, especially literate Spaniards, as *pulperos,* operators of country stores. They were thought to be able to prevent the natives from running up their bills and to be immune to the latter's "weakness" for liquor and gambling. Immigrants had opportunities to save money and acquire property by first working as artisans and farmers. "I have often known poor [immigrant] men to make one hundred pounds a year each, in making ditches alone," remarked a foreign traveler. "In a country like this, where there are no stones, a large number of labourers must find employment at work of this kind. . . ." (MacCann 1853, I:227–28)

Seasonal work harvesting grain, branding cattle, and shearing sheep was abundant, in part because the native-born worker refused to give his services full time. A continuous stream of men and women came to the Pampas from interior provinces, even as far away as Paraguay, to accomplish this part-time work. During cattle roundups and sheep shearing, the rancher obtained labor from the nearby rural communities, but shortages often forced sheep ranchers to hire women and children, usually native-born locals and *provincianos* (migrants from the interior), for shearing. One British sheepraiser paid his workers 25 paper pesos per day plus food; a native-born laborer who hired himself out with a string of his own horses could get 20 to 25 pesos per day in cattle-branding season. The high pay encouraged some wandering peons to steal horses in order to gain this degree of independence. To attract workers, some *estancieros* were even willing to advance salaries and provide them ample credit at the *pulpería.*

Public authorities enacted vagrancy laws intended to discipline workers by requiring that rural residents carry employment papers signed by their bosses. Rural constables could stop passersby to inspect their papers. Those without papers could be considered vagrants and forced into public works or the armed services. Despite the increasing labor demands, the militia recruitments, and the vagrancy laws of the first half of the 19th century, adult males working as hired hands may have been able to preserve some measure of dignity in the countryside.

The perpetual labor shortage in this era of expansion favored the worker. His real wages rose from $7\frac{1}{2}$ gold pesos per month in 1804 to 12 pesos in 1864. Permanent labor, as opposed to seasonal workers, actually may have been quite stable, and satisfactory relationships between *peón* and *patrón* often passed from one generation to the next. Profit sharing was not unknown, especially among the foreign-born shepherds, who earned up to one-half of the sale of wool, grease, and sheepskins. Furthermore, the resident peon supported his family on his employer's estate, where he had a hut, rations of beef, and a small garden plot. For instance, a farm located close to Buenos Aires might support approximately 30 people, including the wives and children of the workers. Itinerant laborers finding seasonal work on this same farm as carpenters, brick makers, tree planters, fence makers, wool shearers, and harvesters numbered approximately 40 people per year. Not only were actual labor conditions in the countryside more personal and satisfying to the peon than the harsh laws suggest, but *estancia* work supported large numbers of rural tradesmen and artisans as well.

In fact, much evidence exists as to the inability of the landowners to transform the native-born worker into a dependent, hardworking, and stable peon. Workers had a long tradition in the countryside of escaping labor discipline. They tended to take the day off whenever they felt like it. Already, the gauchos had gained rights to leisure time on the numerous fiesta days. Employers needed permission from the police to get them to work during a festival. Moreover, the employer frequently had to put up with a lack of respect among his peons. They could and did insult the owners and their foremen.

The work habits of the native-born laborer apparently did not improve much with the growth of the provincial economy. Most refused to perform any work on foot, such as plowing, ditch digging, gardening, or repair work. And apparently, native-born workers could not be left alone without strict supervision. Each *estanciero* had to be involved full time in the work of his ranch and in the management of his men in order "to escape pillage." While the successful rancher may have lived in town, "he must still pass a considerable part of his time on his estate," one traveler observed, "to superintend personally the operations of buying and selling; for as those transactions take place generally between persons who know nothing of the arts of writing and account keeping, unless the payments come direct into the hands of the principal himself, sad mistakes are too likely to occur" (Beaumont 1828, 63–64). Clearly, if the employer wanted diligence from his employees, he had to be there to enforce it. Otherwise, the peons took advantage of him, gaining a reputation for procrastination, and as another foreign traveler observed, "a life of a procrastinator is an everlasting tomorrow" (MacCann 1853, I:156). In the eyes of the employer, it was as if the peons purposely disobeyed their superiors who, anyway, disdained the customs and skin color of the lower class.

Culturally, the work offered familiar social occasions steeped in the gaucho's own traditions. The cattle roundup on large *estancias* attracted as many as 30 itinerant peons and their strings of horses. Between lassoing, branding, and castrating the cattle, there would be beef roasts, singing and guitar playing, smoking and storytelling, horseplay, and mock or real knife fights. As long as he was free to move about, the gaucho never felt out of his element.

The restrictive laws and militia recruitment, more arbitrary than systematic in their enforcement, never succeeded in reducing the workers' mobility. Short-term work contracts still seemed very much the norm. The horseman would work for three or four months, then ask for his pay so he could move on. Many *estancieros* attempted to encourage a more permanent labor force by raising the wages of those who stayed six months or longer; nevertheless, peons had a habit of leaving their work without notice. Given the scarcity of labor, the worker could always find another job. Unable to control the native-born rural working class, the elite disparaged their culture as "uncivilized" and "barbaric."

No doubt, the political problems and the arbitrary exercise of authority provided some check to the complete freedom of the peon. Landowners took the passbook system seriously enough to make sure that their foremen and *provinciano* employees were registered with the local authorities. The police of Buenos Aires apprehended some workers who lacked the proper documents, and military press gangs were particularly active on the frontiers during times of political stress. But the government only had the ability in the countryside to be arbitrary, to enforce the vagrancy laws here and there. It could not be systematic, for it lacked resources and cooperation from the powerful landowners.

Although employers attempted to increase the efficiency and the rhythm of work, the peons turned the scarcity of labor to their advantage. They successfully demanded higher pay, moved from job to job,

# THE ELITE VIEW OF THE RURAL FOLK, 1868

[The country folk] belong to two different races, the Spanish and the native; the combinations of which form a series of imperceptible gradations. The pure Spanish race predominates in the rural districts of Cordova and San Luis, where it is common to meet young shepherdesses fair and rosy, and as beautiful as the belles of a capital could wish to be. In Santiago del Estero, the bulk of the rural population still speaks the Quichua dialect, which plainly shows its Indian origin.... The Negro race, by this time nearly extinct (except in Buenos Aires), has left, in its zambos and mulattoes, a link which connects civilized man with the denizen of the woods....

With these reservations, a homogeneous whole has resulted from the fusion of the three above-named families. It is characterized by love of idleness and incapacity for industry, except when education and the exigencies of social position succeed in spurring it out of its customary pace. To a great extent, this unfortunate result is owing to the incorporation of the native tribes, effected by the process of colonization. The American aborigines live in idleness, and show themselves incapable, even under compulsion, of hard and protracted labor. This suggested the idea of introducing Negroes into America, which has produced such fatal results. But the Spanish race has not shown itself more energetic than the aborigines, when it has been left to its own instincts in the wilds of America....

... All civilization, whether native, Spanish, or European, centers in the cities, where are to be found the manufactories, the shops, the schools and colleges, and other characteristics of civilized nations. Elegance of style, articles of luxury, dress-coats, and frock-coats, with other European garments, occupy their appropriate place in these towns.

... The town inhabited by natives of the country[side], presents a picture entirely the reverse. There, dirty and ragged children live, with a menagerie of dogs; there, men lie about in utter idleness; neglect and poverty prevail everywhere; a table and some baskets are the only furniture of wretched huts remarkable for their general aspect of barbarism and carelessness.

■

*(Sarmiento 1974, 10–11, 13)*

and flouted the vagrancy and impressment laws. Landowners were not able to profit at the expense of the workers, only from the strong demand for pastoral products. The structure of the *estancia*, after all, proved flexible enough. It served as the chief mode of frontier expansion despite the scarcity of labor and lack of significant technological improvements in pastoral production.

## Reorientation of Trade in the Interior

The economic florescence of the province of Buenos Aires did not reach the interior provinces in equal measure. No sooner was independence from Spanish colonial rule achieved than provincial military chieftains quarrelled among themselves, and the conflicts often halted commerce and scattered cattle herds and rural residents alike. From 1810 to 1820, the colonial cart trades between Buenos Aires and Salta nearly ceased, and river commerce in the Paraná River Basin as far as Paraguay was interrupted. Meanwhile, Potosí's mines had declined rapidly after two and one-half centuries of yielding the richest silver ores in the world. No longer could the towns and provinces of the interior depend on the prosperous carrying trades between Potosí and Buenos Aires.

Potosí's mining industry did not survive the wars of independence. The silver content of the ore had been deteriorating rapidly at the end of the colonial period, and workers and entrepreneurs abandoned most of the mines during the decade and a half of warfare and uncertainty. As the former center of the colonial mule fairs, Salta had difficulty adjusting to its new position at the end of the Buenos Aires commercial lifeline rather than at the center of trade between the Río de la Plata and Bolivia. The impact of Potosí's decline reached Tucumán and Córdoba. There, *estancieros* who once prospered on the mule trade found that the value of their land in the 1820s had dropped by 85 percent.

Initially, the new international trade that underwrote the economic expansion of Buenos Aires tended to undermine the internal trade of the Río de la Plata. Cheap imports drove Córdoba's textiles, Tucumán's timber and sugar, and Mendoza's wines off the Buenos Aires market. Overland freight hauling via mule and oxcart from the interior, in the absence of Potosí's silver, simply could not compete with the more cost-efficient shipping of consumer goods from Europe. The economic life of the interior in 1820 seemed depressed beyond remedy.

The interior provinces did not begin the long recovery from their economic depression until the 1830s, on the strength of the new Atlantic commerce of Buenos Aires. Growth of the pastoral trade at the port opened up alternative markets for the productive capacity of the interior that had served Potosí for so long. Recovery was stronger in those provinces closest to Buenos Aires. The riparian provinces of Santa Fe, Entre Ríos, and Corrientes increased production of cattle-related goods sent aboard riverboats for sale in Buenos Aires. Córdoba, Santiago del Estero, and Catamarca managed to sell ponchos to the expanding population of Buenos Aires province. Domestic brandy from Mendoza, a favorite of the popular classes, made a comeback on the Buenos Aires marketplace.

But the depression persisted deep in the interior provinces because the technology of the day could not sustain the new long-distance trade in pastoral products. Silver had been a high-value, low-volume product that could profitably be transported overland on the long trip from Bolivia to the Río de la Plata estuary. But the bulky dried cowhide in Salta, lying more than three months' journey by oxcart over more than 1,240 miles from Buenos Aires, could not compete with hides produced closer to the port. Many ranchers in the western provinces drove their cattle across the Andes for sale in Chile.

The political unrest among the caudillos of the interior did not help matters. "The country people, by the duration of a system of robbery and pillage, have become demoralized," observed one traveler in the 1820s. "In one place was Ramirez, with the troops of Entre Rios, or, as they are termed in abhorrence, the Mounteneros [sic]; in another was Carrera, with the troops of no place at all, but with all the vagabonds who preferred a life of rapine to any other" (Hibbert 1824, 65–66). Interprovincial trade met additional obstacles in the form of internal customs duties. Each provincial government set up customs agents at the borders to collect taxes on the freight produced in neighboring provinces.

Despite all these drawbacks, the provinces of the interior did indeed experience a commercial renaissance beginning in the 1830s. Access to the Paraná and Uruguay Rivers enabled the riparian provinces of Santa Fe, Corrientes, and Entre Ríos to successfully integrate into their economies the export commerce in livestock products. Some oceangoing vessels arrived at river ports to load hides and wool. The export trade even sustained meat- and hide-salting factories in Entre Ríos. Corrientes and Santa Fe more commonly sent hides and wool to Buenos Aires on smaller boats. The river port city of Rosario began to prosper as an intermediary in the trade overland from Córdoba, as goods were transferred to riverboats for the journey down to the estuary.

Córdoba too recovered some of its commercial importance by mid-century as the link between the western Andean provinces and Buenos

Aires. It became the key transfer point for trade in native handmade textiles, especially the ponchos and *chiripás* (bulky cotton trousers) favored by the country folk of the Pampas. Córdoba cattle hides and wool also traveled overland to enter into European trade.

Like those of many Andean provinces, Mendoza's economy recovered in lethargic fashion. Its irrigation ditches directed the Andean snowmelt onto the orchards, vineyards, and wheat fields surrounding the city. The local wine did not yet compare to European wines, so cultivators converted most Mendozan grapes into brandy or raisins. Mendoza sent wheat and flour to the consumers of Buenos Aires, whose *estancias* did not produce grain in bulk until the end of the 19th century. Even raw wool from the neighboring San Luis province entered trade to Buenos Aires.

Economic recovery of the interprovincial trade meant the continued increase of the population of the interior. Argentina's populace was growing by around 2.5 percent per annum. Although the number of Argentines rose from 406,000 in 1810 to 1 million in 1860, the country was still underpopulated; in fact, its population at the time was only equal to that of the island of Cuba. Buenos Aires and the riparian provinces, because they were destinations of foreign immigration and domestic migration, accounted for most of Argentina's population growth.

By comparison, the interior provinces suffered from outmigration. Every cart train headed for the port contained migrant workers, more of them men than women. The towns of the interior, thus, had more women in residence than men. La Rioja in 1855 had only 88 men to every 100 women, whereas the ratio was reversed in the littoral provinces. The male-female ratios were skewed in another fashion in the 19th century: More men than women resided in the rough-and-tumble countryside of the Río de la Plata. Females predominated among residents in the safer towns and cities.

Yet, all in all, the provinces of the interior in the 19th century successfully converted their economies away from Bolivian silver mines toward the Atlantic markets. Their populations expanded by a respectable 2 percent per year, despite sending out numbers of migrant workers for the littoral provinces. Nonetheless, the age-old horse and ox technology in the transport trades limited the extent of the interior's prosperity and growth compared to that of Buenos Aires and, to a lesser extent, the river provinces. Only toward the end of the century, with the arrival of the railway, would this relative lethargy reverse itself.

## Rosas, Restorer of the Laws

One politician stands out in this period. Juan Manuel de Rosas reigned over Buenos Aires province as governor and virtual dictator from 1829 to 1852, and his province's commercial importance aided him in directing the fate of the interior provinces as well, even if he did not rule them. As a federalist politician, Rosas supported states' rights over a strong central Argentine government. Rosas and his own social class of Buenos Aires *estancieros* benefited from relative free trade to a greater extent than the landowners of other provinces. Governor Rosas collected port revenues for his own province, reserving a major share for his militia forces.

Rosas played the trump card of antiforeign nationalism, no small trick in a country that depended on foreign trade, and appealed blatantly to the popular classes, taking on the rural gauchos and the urban blacks as his constituents. Being a successful livestock businessman as well as frontier defender against Indian attacks endeared him to *estancieros* and gauchos alike. Nonetheless, he acted as a populist politician in order to preserve and reinforce—not to change—the colonial social order so threatened by political anarchy and lawlessness. It was for a reason that he called himself the "Restorer of the Laws."

Rosas was born into the Creole landowning class of Buenos Aires province toward the end of the colonial period. As such, he was the poor cousin of the wealthy merchant class of the port city. Rosas participated neither in the politics nor in the battles of independence. He did, however, benefit from the new international trade in Buenos Aires of the postindependence period. He expanded cattle production on his family's ranch and started a salting plant in Buenos Aires in the 1820s that profited from the rising market for hides and meat. His business acumen earned him the appointment as manager of the estates of his wealthy cousins, the Anchorenas.

Advancement of the frontier line past the Salado River nearly to Bahía Blanca destined Rosas to become an Indian fighter as well. Rosas resented those "incompetent" city politicians whose bickering weakened the provincial government and prevented a coordinated defense against Indian raids in the 1820s. The gaucho herdsmen of his own and the Anchorena *estancias* formed his frontier fighting forces, the famed Colorados del Monte, or "Red Rangers." As their employer and commander, Rosas styled himself the consummate gaucho leader. He was able to ride, rope, and wield the *facón* with the best of his men. Rosas dressed like them and spoke like them—on purpose. "Previous governments had acted very well towards educated people, but they

*Illustrating the high regard—or fear—some elements of Argentine society felt for him, a por-trait of General Juan Manuel de Rosas adorned the bedroom wall of this woman of the elite Buenos Aires class. Rosas, a Creole of the landowning class, was the most successful of Argentina's 19th-century strongmen, known particularly for bringing stability to economic and political life and for leading his guacho warriors against the indigenous tribes of the Pampas.* (Getano Descalzi, 1845, courtesy of Emece Editores)

despised the lower classes," Rosas later wrote. "So . . . I thought it very important to gain a decisive influence over this class in order to control it and direct it" (Lynch 1981, 109).

It was during the crisis of 1829, following the rebellion of unpaid *porteño* troops returning from the war against Brazil in Uruguay and the assassination of interim Buenos Aires governor Manuel Dorrego, that General Rosas marched triumphantly into Buenos Aires. A grateful and relieved elite appointed him governor with emergency powers. He resigned in 1833 after a successful term as governor and led his troops on a campaign to pacify the Indians. His campaign contained typically diplomatic and military elements. Those indigenous groups who opposed him felt the lance tips of his gaucho cavalry, but Rosas also cultivated alliances with certain Indian caciques. In return for an end to frontier raids, Rosas offered to distribute horses, cattle, tobacco, and *yerba mate* to these indigenous leaders. He obligated the treasury of the provincial government to pay for this tribute. The *porteño* political elite thereupon reappointed Rosas as governor in 1835—this time with dictatorial powers.

Though the slave trade had ended during the revolution, slavery itself did not. The agrarian expansion of the 1820s gave additional rationale for its continued existence. In the labor-scarce Pampas, Rosas himself had purchased slaves in Córdoba to work his own *estancias.* Blacks and mulattoes comprised nearly half of his ranch workers in 1830. Moreover, the port itself had a population composed of one-quarter Afro-Argentines. They worked mostly as free men and women in household service, unskilled jobs, the marketplaces, and other menial occupations. Rosas viewed them as useful political supporters if not his social equals. His wife, Encarnación, and daughter, Manuela, became patronesses of the blacks of Buenos Aires. They attended Afro-Argentine festivals, distributed gifts to the faithful, and sought information from the servants of Rosas's political rivals. Rosas enlisted blacks in the provincial military and police forces. Afro-Argentines responded to this favor and attention with political support. At their dances and parties they shouted, "Long live our Father Rosas, the best governor of them all" (Szuchman and Brown 1994, 223).

Rosas was also responsible for developing state terrorism in Argentina. Not only did he take advantage of political unrest to secure dictatorial powers, but he also organized a secret police force known as the Mazorca. Opponents called it the "más horca," a play on words that translates to "more hanging." Rosas kept the Mazorca, a group of political thugs of working-class origin, to intimidate opponents and to

# GOVERNOR JUAN MANUEL DE ROSAS JUSTIFIES HIS CAMPAIGN OF STATE TERROR

Señor Dorrego was shot at Navarro by the unitarians. General Villafaña, companion of General Quiroga, was killed by the same people on his journey from Chile to Mendoza. General Latorre was put to the lance after surrender and imprisonment in Salta, without being allowed a last minute to prepare himself. The same fate befell Colonel Aguilera. General Quiroga had his throat cut on 16 February last [1834] on his return journey eighteen leagues before reaching Córdoba. Colonel José Santos Ortiz suffered the same fate, as did all sixteen of the party, the only ones to escape being a courier and an orderly who fled through the mountain fastnesses. So! Have I understood or not the true state of the country? But even this is not enough for the men of enlightenment and principles. . . .

You have known me for many years and know that I am not blood-thirsty, and I have proved this during the time of my government. Who in my position would have been so economical in shedding blood? And whose have I shed? Not a drop apart from what may be considered normal routine. To order this or the other villain to be shot is common in all parts of the world and passes without notice, for society could not survive otherwise. . . .

The law which gave me authority is the law which ordered Montero to be killed. It will be said that I abused the power. If this is so, it will be my error but not a crime to cause me remorse. Because when I was given this hateful extraordinary power I was given it not on condition that I always had to be right but to act with complete freedom, according to my judgement, and to act without restrictions, for the sole object of saving the dying country.

■

*(Lynch 1981, 208–9, 220, 221)*

punish those who might challenge his rule. Indeed, their brutal work did result in the murders of approximately 2,000 people during the more than two decades that Rosas served as governor. Beheading and the prominent display of the severed heads became a favored tactic of the Mazorca. Members of Rosas's secret police operated with total immunity; no one ever answered for the torture and death of opponents to the regime. Rosas justified using state terror on the grounds that he was saving the nation.

The terror did bring about political security for the young nation for the first time since the outbreak of the War of Independence, but it also resulted in the exile of some of Argentina's brightest statesmen and literary figures. While in exile, future president Domingo F. Sarmiento traveled in Chile and the United States. The jurist and economist Juan Bautista Alberdi came to know Montevideo, Santiago, and Paris before he returned from exile to write a new constitution for Argentina. The exiled writer Esteban Echeverría likened the state terror under Rosas to the dregs of society having come to power: "[T]he butchers of the slaughterhouse were the apostles who propagated the *rosista* federation at the point of a dagger. . . . [T]hey labeled as [an opponent] anyone who was not a decapitator, a butcher, a savage, or a thief; anyone who was a decent man, with his heart in the right place, any enlightened patriot who promoted knowledge and freedom; and . . . it can be clearly seen that the source of the federation could be found in the slaughterhouse itself" (Ross and McGann 1982, 57).

Although Rosas was not above exploiting race and class antagonisms, he did not set about reforming the social order. Never did he suggest the redistribution of land, as did the federalist José Gervasio Artigas; nor did Rosas renounce the need to discipline the popular classes that supported him. He favored the ranching interests of the emerging elite of *estancieros,* to which he belonged. Rosas permitted trade with all countries wishing to purchase Argentine ranch products and upheld the private property rights of the well-to-do. The governor gave his staunchest friends lucrative government contracts to supply the troops and to provide horses and cattle to his Indian allies beyond the frontier. Above all, Governor Rosas wished to reestablish order, rule as a dictator, and intimidate political opponents from his own class. But he could not rule a nation with these policies.

## The Interior Fights Back

The other provinces, as well as the republics of Uruguay and Paraguay, did not approve of what appeared to them to be Rosas's selfish, pro–Buenos Aires policies. He used the wealth and military forces of his home province to intervene in the internal politics of neighboring ones. For much of the 1840s, Rosas lent his forces to one Uruguayan faction that laid siege to a rival party in Montevideo. The governor of Buenos

Aires also prevented direct foreign trade on the Paraná and Uruguay Rivers. In this, he alienated the local elites of the riparian provinces and the French and British governments, provoking the latter to send fleets to blockade the port of Buenos Aires in 1838 and 1848 in a vain attempt to open trade in the Paraná River basin. Rosas also kept Paraguay isolated and punished foreign merchants who wanted to open trade to Asunción. Ultimately, these narrow policies led to his downfall.

Justo José de Urquiza of Entre Ríos succeeded in uniting provincial opponents to topple Rosas. General Urquiza was, in fact, a caudillo very much in the mold of Rosas. He owned extensive cattle-grazing *estancias* in Entre Ríos, established meat-salting plants (*saladeros*) to process cattle products for export, commanded a powerful army of gaucho ranch hands, and made himself governor of his province. In January 1852, Governor Urquiza led a powerful gaucho army into Buenos Aires province and defeated Rosas's provincial forces at the battle of Caseros. Rosas, who had often wrapped himself in the cloak of nationalism and defiance of foreign powers, thereupon boarded a British ship and fled to exile in England.

While *porteño* opposition soon drove Urquiza, the new director of the United Provinces of Argentina, from Buenos Aires, he succeeded in laying the foundation for the modern Argentine nation. Urquiza convened a congress in 1853 to ratify a new constitution. In the liberal tradition, this constitution outlawed slavery once and for all, and it became legal to engage in direct foreign trade on the Paraná and Uruguay Rivers.

While its commercial provisions benefited provincial interests, the constitution rejected the loose federalism of the recent past in favor of a strong executive power. The constitution contained a provision for its own suspension in a so-called state of siege. It also gave the president power of *intervención,* the right of the federal executive to intervene in provincial governmental affairs in times of local political turmoil. In the future, these constitutional provisions enabled national leaders to reduce the autonomy of the governors. The federal construct of the United Provinces of Argentina gave way to the new Republic of Argentina.

Constitutional architect Juan Bautista Alberdi devised a new policy to remedy the problem of labor scarcity. He incorporated constitutional features that encouraged European immigration as well as foreign investment. Foreigners were free to practice their own religions in Argentina, were exempt from military draft, and could freely remit

# JUAN BAUTISTA ALBERDI'S ECONOMIC BLUEPRINT FOR A PROSPEROUS ARGENTINA, 1853–1884

O*n government:* "Government represents consumption, not production." "There is no worse agriculturist, merchant, or manufacturer than government."

*On immigration:* "Every European who comes to our shores will bring us more civilization in his habits, which later will be communicated to our inhabitants, than numerous philosophy books could. The perfection that one cannot see, touch, or grasp is not well understood. A hardworking man is the most edifying catechism."

*On foreign trade:* "To disdain the countryside and treat it as brutish because it produces only raw materials is proper to an idiotic and suicidal charlatanism that does not take into account that raw material is the entire means by which South America can acquire and enjoy the manufactured products that commerce with Europe scatters about in its cities that lack machines and factories."

*On individual rights:* "There is neither security nor confidence in the promises of a merchant whose person can be assaulted in an instant and flung into prison or exiled.... It is impossible to conceive of rural, agricultural, or mining production where men can be carried away from their labors in order to form the ranks of the army."

*On building railways:* "In this way, [U.S. engineer William] Wheelwright wanted to deliver the locomotive of civilization not only to Córdoba but also to La Rioja, to bring the minerals of the Famatina [mines in the Argentine Andes] to the ports of the Río de la Plata, to pass his locomotives of iron over the Andes that San Martín crossed with light artillery pieces, to give the western Argentine provinces as their own the ports and markets of the Pacific Ocean, to make of the Argentine soil the royal road of intercourse between Asia and Europe, to unite Chile with the Argentine Republic by chains of gold more durable than all the bonds of diplomacy."

■

*(Brown 1993, 61–74)*

profits. He and several other 19th-century liberals promoted European immigration as the solution to Argentina's legendary problem of underpopulation. They reasoned that European workers were superior to African, Paraguayan, or Bolivian workers and should be encouraged to come to develop Argentina's agricultural resources. Alberdi became famous for his dictum "To govern is to populate."

As an exile during the reign of Rosas, Alberdi had witnessed the power of railways in Europe and envisioned a vast network for Argentina. He saw them as a way to settle "the desert," a euphemism for the southern Pampas and Patagonian regions still under indigenous control. Alberdi also foresaw the benefits of a transcontinental railway between Buenos Aires on the Atlantic coast and Valparaíso, Chile, on the Pacific. Portions of his dream would come to fruition. Railways and immigration would indeed transform Argentina, and the constitution he fashioned remained the blueprint for nation building in the late 19th century and still endures as the law of the land.

Nation building, however, was not accomplished merely with the writing of a new constitution. The provinces still retained their own militia forces, although the *porteño* troops remained the most powerful in the region. The post-Rosas politicians of Buenos Aires would not willingly give up their control of money, commerce, and collection of customs duties. They drove Urquiza from the capital in 1854, lost the battle of Cepeda against the president of the republic in 1859, but won the battle of Pavón two years later. Urquiza subsequently retired to his private business affairs, and the *porteño* political leader General Bartolomé Mitre became president of Argentina. National unification was still a work in progress, and two wars soon assisted the project.

## War with Paraguay

The national army created on paper by the 1853 constitution in reality hardly existed when, in 1865, an international conflict broke out in Paraguay. At the time, Francisco Solano López was Paraguay's third autocrat, succeeding the nation's founder, José Gaspar Rodríguez de Francia (who died in 1850), and Carlos Antonio López, Solano López's father (who died in 1862). Solano López inherited leadership of a government that, because of its long isolation, had gained monopoly control of foreign trade in *yerba mate* and tobacco and owned extensive herds of cattle and horses. A large peasantry of mestizos and native Guaraní sustained themselves on small holdings, in service to the state's ranches, or in the military. Paraguay's rulers seemed to have successfully institutionalized the mentality of the Jesuit colonial missions. The national treasury kept the president and his sycophants in power while also supporting the largest military force in the region: 28,000 regular soldiers and 40,000 reservists.

The war began over border tensions arising from Brazil's development of its southernmost territories, which bordered Uruguay, Argentina, and Paraguay. The Paraná River remained Brazil's fastest route of communication between the capital of Rio de Janeiro and the interior state of Mato Grosso. In late 1864, the Paraguayans intercepted and held a Brazilian gunboat taking the new Mato Grosso governor to his post via the Paraguay River; in response, the political authorities in Rio de Janeiro declared war. A supremely confident Solano López decided to strike Brazil with a Paraguayan invasion through the Argentine territory of Misiones. When Argentina objected to this incursion, Solano López invaded the state of Corrientes, too. Argentina declared war. Ultimately, Uruguay joined Brazil and Argentina in the War of the Triple Alliance against Paraguay, which lasted from 1865 to 1870.

Although the triple alliance would appear to make the war lopsided and unequal, none of the three allies was prepared. Individual provinces in Brazil and Argentina were loath to send their own militias to Paraguay, and the troops of Solano López acquitted themselves well in the first battles. In the last two years of the war, the Paraguayans had the advantage of fighting on home territory, too. They fought valiantly, aided and abetted in national defense by Paraguayan women, and supported Solano López in fighting on until death. In the end, however, the triple alliance prevailed and occupied Paraguay. The Paraguayan population was ravaged by the five-year war: Only 230,000 citizens survived from a prewar population of more than 400,000. By war's end, women outnumbered men by a ratio of 14 to one.

To defeat such a foe, President Bartolomé Mitre of Argentina had to mobilize his country on a massive scale. He instituted a national draft in order to build up the weak army. Eventually, he fielded an army of 28,000 men, which he personally led in battle; however, provincial revolts against the draft and against direction from Buenos Aires preoccupied the new Argentine army. A professional officer corps developed and attracted members of the shopkeeping middle classes and the rural gentry, especially from the interior provinces. Working-class men of color formed the bulk of the conscripts. Immigrants were exempt from military duty. The war became so unpopular in the western provinces that Salta attempted to secede from the republic.

Landowning, political, and merchant elites remained aloof from military services, except in their provisioning. The support of such a large army in the field created business opportunities that, in traditional fashion, were restricted to the friends and supporters of President Mitre. His political group, the Liberal Party, came to be known as "the party of the purveyors." They monopolized the fattest contracts to sell cattle and horses to the army and to purchase arms and equipment from abroad.

The war against Paraguay enabled the government of Argentina to consolidate political control over the nation's previously autonomous provinces. Moreover, the new Argentine army would become an active progenitor of additional national unification and would help realize the intent of the Constitution of 1853. Buenos Aires still posed an obstacle to nation building. The powerful and wealthy elites of the ostensible capital of the republic refused to give up control of their substantial foreign trade to the national government. Domingo F. Sarmiento succeeded Mitre as president in 1868, but this worldly native of San Juan could not overcome *porteño* protectionism of its commercial powers and customs revenues. The *porteños* easily defeated Sarmiento's attempt to establish agricultural colonies of immigrant farmers in Buenos Aires province. The army eventually provided political resolution after forging itself in a second battle, this one the last chapter of the three-century-old struggle with the native peoples of Argentina.

## The "Indian Problem"

As in colonial days, relations between settlers and the indigenous peoples in the 19th century alternated between peaceful trade and sanguinary hostilities. When Charles Darwin passed through the province in 1832, he noted that frontier landowners fortified their ranch houses due to the constant danger of Indian raids. Indian depredations increased when drought threatened the wild cattle and horses on which the natives subsisted and also when provincial militia forces were engaging in conflicts elsewhere. Mounted warriors armed with bolas and lances descended on isolated ranches, killed peons, stole herds of cattle and horses, and kidnapped women and children. Yet peaceful groups of Indians always lived among the cattle *estancias,* tolerated even if not respected by the country folk.

Extensive trade had developed between the Hispanic and indigenous peoples of the Río de la Plata over the centuries. Indian groups grew accustomed to Creole products such as hardwares, horses, cattle, tobacco, and *aguardiente,* which became life "necessities." At frontier forts and rural *pulperías,* they exchanged these items for indigenous goods useful to Western society: guanaco skins, ostrich feathers, plaited leather goods, and ponchos. Yet, there existed no exchange for the commodity that the Hispanic Argentines most coveted—the land itself.

The expanding *estanciero* class of the 19th century wished to turn the seminomadic Indians into "good peons." The landowners were unsuccessful. Prairie hunters were indifferent agricultural workers. Frontier officials gave landowners and their foremen the authority to punish peaceful Indians as if they were children. In order to deal with hostile natives, the government maintained militia outposts on the expanding frontiers, and Governor Rosas regularized a colonial policy of requisitioning horses and cattle from the *estancieros* as a ration for the Indians, who grew partial to the taste of mare's meat. By mid-century, ranches and frontier towns enjoyed relative security.

But Indian raids occurred once again during the war with Paraguay. Thereafter, the prospect of immigrants replacing the indigenous people as the future workers on the Pampas motivated the national government to resolve the "Indian problem" through extermination. The national army provided the means. Rather than each frontier province dealing haphazardly with the indigenous peoples, the job now fell to a

*Throughout the middle part of the 19th century, indigenous tribes continued to raid Argentine estancias and cart trains, as shown here. It was not until 1879 that the raiders were quelled by a campaign of overwhelming force. (Albérico Isola, 1844, courtesy Emece Editores)*

national army forged in the crucible of the Paraguayan war. General Julio A. Roca's "Conquest of the Desert" in 1879, finally deprived the indigenous peoples of the last vestiges of their separate autonomy, after 300 years of European effort. Though born and reared in the interior, General Roca was not a provincial caudillo. He had advanced through the ranks during the War of the Triple Alliance and took on a national perspective rather than that of his native Tucumán.

Meanwhile, however, native groups on the southern prairies had not been idle, merely awaiting developments in Hispanic society. Provided with tribute by Governor Rosas, they had formed ever tighter political alliances among themselves and engaged in more extensive frontier commerce. Their military capabilities had also strengthened as a result. The leadership of the recently arrived Araucanians expanded to all Pampas and Patagonian groups as they integrated through intermarriage. Indigenous leaders offered their daughters as wives to establish alliances within the indigenous society. The distribution of horses and cattle facilitated the exchange of brides between allied Indian clans.

Prominent political and military leaders emerged as a result of this unification process. Llanquetruz gained fame as leader of the Ranqueles in what is today the province of La Pampa. His group attracted gauchos who sought to escape recruitment into the militias. Among the Voroganos, Calfucurá assumed leadership after assassinating a chieftain who had favored peaceful relations with the Hispanics. He then consolidated his political control of the area around the salt flats of Salinas Grandes. Sayhueque rallied support among the Araucanian villages in present-day Neuquén. These and other leaders assembled, through marriage and exchange of goods, the scattered bands of the Pampas.

Annuities from Governor Rosas sustained these groups, but they were also increasingly engaged in frontier commerce. This trade with Hispanic society proved to be a strong motive to continue peaceful frontier relations. "Our contact with the Christians in the past few years has produced *yerba*, sugar, biscuit, flour, and other luxury articles that were unknown to us before, but which have now become necessary," Sayhueque reportedly said. "If we make war on whites, we would not have a market for our ponchos, hides, feathers, etc., and, consequently, it is in our interest to remain on good terms with them" (Szuchman and Brown 1994, 119).

The fall of Rosas ended the flow of tribute and annuities across the frontier. In this new atmosphere, many Indian groups shifted their allegiance from the peaceful chieftains to the great military leader of the

Pampas Indians, Namúncura. From 1852 to 1879, the Indian raids resumed in earnest. They took cattle and horses by the thousands from isolated frontier ranches on the Pampas, then indigenous horsemen herded them to sell (illegally) in Mendoza and San Juan. Other native drivers moved cattle herds up the Río Negro valley and over the southern Andean passes into Chile. Their participation in commerce produced a labor shortage in the Indian economy as severe as that on the *estancias*.

The need for labor prompted the Indians to raid for *cautivas,* captive women and children who were to perform menial work. One such Indian expedition in 1876 came to within 185 miles of Buenos Aires and resulted in the loss of 300,000 cattle and 500 captives. These non-Indian captives were rural residents, most of them illiterate Spanish-

# TREATMENT OF *CAUTIVAS* AMONG THE RANQUELES, 1870

[ **C** ]aptives are regarded as things among the Indians. You can well imagine their condition. They are the saddest, the most unfortunate of all. Adult or adolescent, young boy or young girl, black or white—it makes no difference. It is the same for all of them until they can win the complete trust of the Indians and ingratiate themselves. Their first days in captivity are a true *via cruces.* They must wash, cook, cut firewood in the woods with their own hands, build corrals, break in colts, take care of the cattle, and serve the brutal pleasures of concupiscence.

Woe to those who resist!

. . . It often happens that the Indians will feel sorry for the new captives and protect them from the older ones and from the Indian women. Yet, this too only worsens the situation unless they take them as concubines.

A certain captive, whose life I was looking into, answered one of my questions as follows: "Before, when the Indian desired me, things went very badly for me, because the other captives and Indian women mortified me terribly. They would lay their hands on me in the hills and beat me. Now that the Indian doesn't want me any more, everything is all right. They are all my good friends."

Simple words that sum up the existence of the captive woman.

■

*(Mansilla 1997, 224–25)*

speaking people of mixed ancestry. Men did not make pliant captives and were instead put to death. Many accounts testify that the indigenous peoples incorporated the non-Indians into their groups as virtual slaves. The women were given as brides to warriors with whom they brought up a new generation resistant to losing more frontier territory to the cattle and sheep ranches. Some of the *cautivas* declined to escape and avoided "liberation" because they did not want to abandon the children to whom they had given birth.

General Roca and the national army resolved the centuries-old frontier conflict in 1879. Technology contributed to Roca's rapid success. In his Conquest of the Desert, he armed his soldiers with imported repeating rifles and used telegraph lines to communicate orders to five separate military columns. These columns departed from Buenos Aires, Córdoba, San Luis, and Mendoza in a pincer movement converging on the Río Negro. The cavalry forces quickly scattered or exterminated the Tehuelche, Pampas, and Araucanian villagers. Then Roca closed the southern Andean passes and garrisoned them with army soldiers. The surviving Indians went to live under government supervision on special reservations; the liberated *cautivas* reentered Creole society as servants in Spanish-speaking households.

Once indigenous resistance was broken, land became available for settlement in the southern Pampas and the entire Patagonia. The rich and powerful and the politically connected once again claimed the lion's share of the booty. As much as 21 million acres of frontier land now passed into the possession of just 381 people.

## The Crucible

While the interior provinces stagnated or moved ahead slowly, the rural economy of Buenos Aires bounded ahead confidently, absorbing Indian raids, occasional uprisings, political divisions, and a chronic labor shortage. Landholdings were large, a fact accounted for by the tradition-bound production methods of the day, yet landed units became reduced in size and their ownership diffused. Stimulated by the cattle industry's need for an expanding rural infrastructure, Pampas society displayed increasing complexity in its structure. Most country folk worked on the land as proprietors, renters, or hired hands. Natives, migrants, and foreigners found opportunities as artisans and in commerce and transportation. Much of the opportunity and diversity of rural society can be attributed directly to the development of the Pampas as producer for the external market.

Meanwhile, the economic and social transformation of Buenos Aires province aggravated its separation from the provinces of the interior. By the 1830s, the trend was clear. Trade at the port of Buenos Aires was the single most important economic growth factor in the entire region. The province became the most populous and the wealthiest. Its politicians and state government became the first among provincial equals. As the so-called United Provinces of the River Plate restructured itself following the War of Independence, Buenos Aires province assumed the region's economic, social, and political leadership, which thereafter it would never relinquish.

Other inequities of postrevolutionary Argentina had their roots in the colonial social order. While the native-born working class salvaged a degree of autonomy and independence in the era of economic resurgence, it clearly did not enjoy social mobility. Expanding rural society tended toward the elimination of the prairie Indians. Economic growth also was shared unequally. The biggest landowners, themselves scions of colonial Spanish merchants, favored European immigrants in subordinate positions as renters and petty merchants. Native-born people of color—be they mestizos, blacks, or mulattoes—found opportunities galore, but at the bottom of the rural social ladder. They worked in the *saladeros* and on ranches, doing the shearing, harvesting, and branding; driving cattle; and conducting oxcarts. They chose to exercise a measure of personal freedom in the developing but rigidly stratified rural society. Native-born people of color moved from job to job and searched for higher wages and leisure in defiance of the laws and contrary to the wishes of the landowners. Postrevolutionary rural society of Buenos Aires province was vibrant and far from egalitarian.

Argentines had nonetheless begun the process of national consolidation. With the fall of Rosas in Buenos Aires, the interior provinces led the way toward a new constitution and the negotiation of the responsibilities and benefits of nationhood. Ultimately, the war against Paraguay and then the final battle against Indian resistance on the frontier gave new urgency to a stronger nation-state. In this crucible arose a new political leader, a military man, to be sure, but one of a national army rather than a provincial militia. General Julio A. Roca had risen through the officers' ranks during the War of the Triple Alliance and then commanded the army to a quick victory over the indigenous peoples.

Roca resolved to convert his military prestige into political power and to use his army leadership to remedy the remaining item on the political agenda of nation building. That item was the status of Buenos Aires.

# 6

# THE LIBERAL AGE, 1880–1916

The year 1880 marked the beginning of an unprecedented period of "peace and administration" in Argentina. The accession of General Julio A. Roca to the presidency that year ended seven decades of political turmoil that had prevented national consolidation. Rule by the elitist "Generation of Eighty," the clique of landowners and politicians who came to power with Roca, provided the necessary political stability to accelerate modern economic development. The nation-state was firmly under the control of the PAN (Partido Autonomista Nacional, or National Autonomist Party), a political vehicle of the landowners. The PAN assured orderly presidential succession until 1916, followed by a peaceful broadening of political participation up to 1930. Restricted suffrage and official electoral lists became the rule under the Generation of Eighty, and promotion of the import-export economy, the policy.

Indeed, the liberal age is known for its economic transition. Argentina became a modern nation based on exports of agricultural products and imports of European technology, capital, entrepreneurship, and labor. The country capitalized on its comparative advantage in producing beef, wheat, mutton, and wool for international markets. Cities grew, the land was populated, and railways were built just as Juan Bautista Alberdi and Domingo F. Sarmiento had envisioned. At no other historical period did the country change so much and experience such a long period of economic development, but to the benefit of whom?

The Argentine oligarchs who initiated this national unity chose to limit the social impact of economic expansion. They never entertained any conception that material improvement was supposed to alter the social and political values with which they were comfortable, but it did. The immigration they invited to remedy the chronic labor shortage created a rambunctious working class as well as an expectant middle class. Eventually, the demands for participation in national affairs forced the oligarchs to open the political system to a more democratic voting system. It was to cost the elites their political supremacy, though not their wealth.

Liberalism refers to an ideological program that dominated two generations of oligarchs and politicians who consolidated national power and ruled from 1880 to 1916 and a more socially diverse group of politicians from 1916 to 1930. In broad terms, their brand of liberalism stood for economic progress, open trade and open markets, foreign investment, and a strong central government. The Argentine brand of liberalism, which today might be called conservative economics in some countries, should not be confused with broadening political participation and instituting social reforms. For the most part, this was a regime of the elites and for the elites.

But the oligarchs could not hold back the tide of social and political change at the same time that they benefited from economic transformation and expansion. In Argentina, economic modernization meant immigration, the formation of a middle class, and the mobilization of labor. The landed oligarchy that benefited most from the liberal age was forced to make significant concessions to the new political and social forces their self-serving economic policies had generated. Nonetheless, no period of Argentina's history before or since has equaled the liberal age for political stability and material growth.

## Roca and the Generation of Eighty

First and foremost, Argentine politicians had to settle the festering issue of the status of Buenos Aires. *Porteños* in the 1870s retained their control over trade at the port, took charge of collecting customs duties there, and sustained their prerogatives with the largest provincial militia of the republic. Presidents Domingo F. Sarmiento and Nicolás Avellaneda, both from the provinces, governed from the national capital in the 1870s almost as guests of the Buenos Aires provincial governor. Finally, General Roca's defeat of a *porteño* in the presidential election of 1880 helped to settle the issue of federalization. When the *porteño* militia revolted at the prospect of yet another *provinciano* president, General Roca, with the support of the federal army, crushed the rebellion.

President Roca then "federalized" the city and port of Buenos Aires by placing them under direct rule of the central government and forcing the governor of Buenos Aires to relocate the province's capital to the city of La Plata. Not only did the federal government assume full control of customs revenues, but it also abolished all state militias, including that of Buenos Aires. In these final acts of nation building, General Roca and his political allies enjoyed the full support of the federal army. The Republic of Argentina finally had become a nation in fact as well as name.

While basing its political hegemony on the most technologically innovative economy in Latin America, the Generation of Eighty also honored political traditions such as patronage. There would be no meritocracy in national politics. Roca's PAN functioned not as a party with a definitive political program but rather as an organization of public officials wanting to perpetuate their own power. Informal alliances continued to win out over electoral legitimacy and the rule of law. The genius of the PAN lay in the ability of Roca and his collaborators to forge political alliances supported by electoral manipulation among the provincial oligarchs. "Political force," said Roca, "lies in knowing how

## AN INTELLECTUAL'S DESCRIPTION OF THE GENERATION OF EIGHTY

The governing elements [of the nation] are recruited from a class of citizens which, if it does not properly constitute a caste, nonetheless forms a directing class. . . . This class corresponds approximately to the highest social stratum, formed by the members of the traditional families, by the rich, and by the educated ("hombres ilustrados"). The members of this class maintain among themselves more or less tight social and economic relations and, as is natural, share common sentiments and opinions.

. . . Without this common code there would not exist that interchange of services and favors which they reciprocally lend without distinction of party politics. It is this moral code of the directing class which the citizens designated for the different government positions carry into the public administration, whence they manage the interests of the country.

■

*José Nicolás Matienzo, El gobierno representativo federal en la República Argentina (McGann 1957, 33)*

to play the lion and the fox at the same instant." He called his political program one of "peace and administration" (McGann 1957, 27, 32).

Did political compromise replace factionalism? Rebellions actually continued among the competitors for power, as factions in the provinces sought outside intervention from federal authorities to destroy their local enemies. Although federalized and professionalized, the national army did not retreat far from politics. Civilians continued to influence promotions and to manipulate the officer corps for their own political gain. Opponents of the dominant PAN used obstructionism and rebellion where they could. They plotted revolts in the political crises of 1890, 1893, and 1905 by suborning the loyalty of army officers bearing the brunt of government repression as well. *La política criolla* (old-style Creole—that is, caudillo—tactics) survived because the opposition accepted it too.

Actually, the conservative order at the turn of the century blended liberal centralism of Buenos Aires with provincial hierarchical traditionalism. Roca was the consummate compromiser and shrewd bargainer who combined these skills with his military prestige to unite provincial political organizations. Technological advances such as the railway and telegraph also contributed to Roca's extension of federal power. Moreover, the expansion of trade enlarged federal coffers to such a degree that Roca had more largesse for traditional forms of patronage. His friends and supporters benefited from the land rush that followed his Conquest of the Desert. The expansion of the railways and burgeoning agricultural exports provided a rise in land values and opened up new opportunities for political insiders. Locally based elite families continued their dominance of provincial politics and competed for state control. The national government at Buenos Aires could resort to federal intervention, that constitutional centralizing instrument, to introduce adjustments between conflicting local rivalries. It did not, however, effect fundamental change in the principles of political participation at the local level.

While the landowners retained political authority in the provinces, national power had a more complex constituency in the liberal age. Not all the politicians came from the "best families." Many, in fact, represented recently acquired wealth, near-wealth, or a mixture of provincial status and new connections. The PAN may have ruled in the interests of the wealthy oligarchy, but the politicians remained a distinct class of operatives and influence-mongers. The state in Argentina was not the passive instrument of the economic elite but rather had developed aspirations and powers separate from and increasingly antagonistic to those of the oligarchy itself. This separation of state and oligarchy would become apparent in due time. In general, the unprecedented era of political peace was underwritten by a vibrant and expanding economy.

## Technological Change and Economic Growth

The Argentine economy of the liberal age absorbed new technologies in its most dynamic sectors. In terms of foreign investment, railway building, trade with the industrialized nations, and peopling of the prairies, this period appeared to fulfill the dreams of Juan Bautista Alberdi, the Argentine economist and jurist who died in 1884. Agricultural exports boomed, and old industries in the interior provinces, such as wine in Mendoza and sugar in Tucumán, experienced significant expansion. The country did not industrialize during this time of economic transformation, yet manufacturing did expand.

Some Argentines have seen the lack of industrialization in the period before 1930 as having created a long-term problem for Argentina. While it did grow, they argue, the country nevertheless remained "underdeveloped" because the Generation of Eighty failed to generate the "self-sustained" economic growth that industrialization would have provided. Critics have developed a variety of explanations that emphasize the discrepancies and pathologies in export growth: control of capital and commercial assets by a landowning elite little interested in manufacturing, foreign investment only in the export and food-processing industries, government indifference toward industrial develop-

| Indicators of Economic Growth in Argentina, 1880–1914 (Expressed as annual rates of growth) | |
| --- | --- |
| Population | 3.5% |
| Urbanization | 5.4% |
| Railroad trackage | 10.6% |
| Value of exports | 15.2% |
| Value of imports | 6.8% |
| Manufacturing | 9.3% |
| Gross Domestic Product | 5.0% |

Sources: Comisión Nacional de Censos (1916–19, I:119; VIII:16; X:406–7); *Censo industrial and comercio* (1913, 9); Comisión Directiva del Censo (1898, III: 271); Díaz Alejandro (1970, 3)

ment, lack of political influence among immigrant manufacturers, and competition from the import of foreign consumer goods. These characteristics are accurate, yet Argentine industry did make impressive gains, as the yearly growth rate of 9.3 percent attested.

Argentina participated in the prevailing trends of the world economy and profited greatly from its changing structure. Falling prices, especially for foodstuffs, characterized the European economy from 1873 to 1898, an era of peace and low interest rates, which facilitated, in particular, British investment in technological innovations such as railway construction and steam-powered and steel-hulled shipping. At the same time, the British population increased, and per capita food consumption also surged. Here was a market for cheap Argentine foodstuffs.

The Argentine state responded to the international market by vigorously promoting the construction of a national railway system and designed its economic policies in order to attract foreign capital in building and operating the railways. In 1862, the government of President Mitre had granted land and stations to foreign entrepreneurs, offered incorporated status in Argentina to foreign companies, and insured them against governmental expropriation. He also guaranteed investors an annual profit rate of 7 percent. Before too long, however, these guaranteed payments came to be a leading budgetary item and even led to scandalous abuses in the late 1880s. Corrupt friends of the liberal politicians often constructed duplicate railroad lines and laid poorly planned track just to collect the guaranteed profits from the government. Of the 28 separate railway companies registered by 1892, most were barely solvent.

Government promotion of rail construction was effective, nonetheless. By 1880, almost 61 million gold pesos (the equivalent of approximately $61 million, or £12.5 million) had been invested in some 1,360 miles of track in Argentina. Railway investments increased by 150 percent from 1900 to 1914, while trackage rose to 21,390 miles. Freight tonnage and the number of passengers carried by Argentine railroads increased impressively (see table). Cultivation of cereal crops on the Pampas, a negligible commercial activity in the 1870s, developed relative to the extension of rail lines. Rail freight also included greater amounts of livestock, manufactured goods, and construction materials. Argentina had become the leading railway country in Latin America.

Railway construction was not the only sector in which foreign—and domestic—investors placed their capital. Resources flowed into merchant companies, land and mortgage corporations, urban utilities,

| Cargo and Passengers Carried on Argentine Railways, 1880–1914 (In millions) | | |
|---|---|---|
| Year | No. of Passengers | Tons of Cargo |
| 1880 | 2.8 | 0.8 |
| 1885 | 5.6 | 3.1 |
| 1890 | 10.1 | 5.4 |
| 1895 | 14.6 | 9.7 |
| 1900 | 18.3 | 12.7 |
| 1905 | 26.6 | 22.4 |
| 1910 | 59.7 | 33.6 |
| 1914 | 75.1 | 33.5 |
| Sources: Comisión Nacional de Censos (1898, III: 462); Tornquist (1919, 188) | | |

banks, meatpacking plants, and construction companies. Total foreign investments in Argentina, including French, German, and American capital, occasionally amounted to more than 3 million gold pesos ($3 million, or £500,000) per year.

Banking and credit institutions flourished in this intoxicating milieu of liquidity. By 1913, 143 banks were operating in Argentina with capital assets of more than $552 million gold pesos. Their financial policies tended to promote trade and commerce, especially between Argentina and Europe. The Banco de la Nación Argentina, established in 1891 at the instigation of a group of Argentine "industrialists," loaned an overwhelming proportion of its capital to agricultural and commercial enterprises. Many politicians used their influence to draw on the national bank's assets, too. President Roca himself took out loans amounting to more than 1 million gold pesos.

## The Export Sector

Argentina constructed its national prosperity around the export of pastoral and agricultural products. In this, policy makers and landowners showed themselves to be amazingly receptive to new economic opportunity. They capitalized repeatedly on the changing structure of world markets and ably absorbed necessary technologies.

| Major Argentine Grain Exports, 1880–1915 (In thousands of tons) | | | | |
|---|---|---|---|---|
| Year | Wheat | Linseed | Maize | Oats |
| 1880 | 1 | 1 | 15 | |
| 1885 | 79 | 69 | 198 | |
| 1890 | 328 | 31 | 707 | |
| 1895 | 1,010 | 276 | 772 | 18 |
| 1900 | 1,010 | 223 | 713 | 8 |
| 1905 | 1,930 | 665 | 2,222 | 17 |
| 1910 | 1,884 | 605 | 2,660 | 371 |
| 1915 | 2,512 | 981 | 4,331 | 593 |

Source: Ernesto Tornquist (1919, 30)

The dynamism of the era did not depend on one or two products but on the vigorous expansion of new staple exports as old ones stagnated. For instance, raw wool earned the bulk of the foreign exchange for Argentina in the late 19th century, while wheat and grain expanded rapidly to become the leading export items in 1910, when Argentina challenged the United States as the world's leading exporter of wheat. Frozen mutton and beef then became popular after the turn of the century to challenge the export leadership of wheat. Argentina even enjoyed diversified markets despite close commercial ties to England. Three-quarters of Argentine exports from 1909 to 1913 went to countries other than Great Britain.

Sheep raisers represent a fine example of how Argentine landowners improved their production to take advantage of new technological possibilities. Raw wool surpassed hides as the leading export sometime after 1850 and continued to dominate exports until 1900. The perfection of the mechanical wool comber in British mills had stimulated Argentine wool exports, and sheep men, who were now breeding fine merino stock, were able to export 216 million pounds of raw wool in 1880 and 310 million a decade later. At the turn of the century, Argentine sheep breeders readily switched to the fuller-bodied Lincoln sheep as the era of refrigerated meatpacking came to Buenos Aires in 1900. Argentina then supplied Great Britain with 30 percent of its fresh mutton and 45 percent of its imports of live sheep and lambs.

## CHANGING PRODUCTION ON THE SANTA ISABEL *ESTANCIA* NEAR ROSARIO, SANTA FE

Some years after my visit in 1888 the flood of Italian colonists, spreading outward from Buenos Aires, had reached Santa Isabel [an estate of 60 square miles]; and it had been through them that the changes had been brought about.

The land was let out to them, ten square miles at a time, and what they found as rough camp [countryside], they left as alfalfa pasture. Better stock was introduced, the camp was subdivided by fences, more care was taken in breeding; and so, in a very short time, the profits of the estate rose by leaps and bounds. I will give some figures.

| 1888 | | 1908 |
|------|------|------|
| 5,650 native longhorn. | **Cattle** | 9,000 head of cattle of good breed, chiefly Durham. |
| 1,200 "native" sheep. | **Sheep** | 10,000 head of sheep of Merino breed. |
| 425 horses, mostly "native." | **Horses** | 630 horses of the Cleveland breed. |
| Practically none. | **Crops** | The *estancia* drew from the colonists on 20 square miles, without any expense, one-quarter of all the produce as rent. When the colonists, after holding the land for four years, were about to move on, the *estancia* at its own cost sowed alfalfa with the colonists' last crop; that was all. The colonists had ploughed and prepared the land. |

■

*(Larden 1911, 51–53)*

Cattle raisers turned to grain farming with equal agility. Three factors made the cultivation of wheat profitable in this era: the extension of railroads across the prairies, the arrival of immigrants to work as agrarian laborers, and the increasing reliance of Europe on foreign grains. Argentines imported foreign farming technologies—machinery, barbed wire, and windmills—and thus transformed rural production. A British visitor returned to Argentina in 1900 after a 20-year absence to notice "an entirely new feature; the sentinel-like forms of the windmills now used all over Argentina for pumping water into the reservoirs that supply the houses or feed the drinking-trough; tapering columns of open ironwork some 30 feet [high], surmounted by the untiring vanes" (Larden 1911, 35).

In the 1860s and 1870s, agricultural colonies of European settlers first began the cultivation of grains in the provinces of Santa Fe and Entre Ríos. Thereafter, wheat cultivation shifted to the more fertile terrain of Buenos Aires province, where landowners altered their operations in response to market pressures. Tenant workers plowed up the cattle ranges and sowed wheat crops for several years. They then planted alfalfa and returned the land to cattlemen in the form of improved pastures. By 1910, Buenos Aires had become the leading province in wheat production, cultivating more than one-third of the 15 million acres in the entire nation.

The development of grain carried with it the necessity of improving the commercial system and of using new technologies in farming and food processing. Imports of wire fencing increased as cultivation spread to the cattle areas of Buenos Aires province. In the years before World War I, more than 89,000 tons of fence wire passed through Argentine customs each year, and the country also began importing large numbers of reapers and threshers. Grain elevators improved storage and port facilities, and the quantity of wheat transported in burlap bags, which produced handling problems that backed up valuable railway cars during the harvests, was rapidly reduced. Soon flour mills sprang up in the port cities of Buenos Aires, Bahía Blanca, and Rosario. By 1912, Argentina milled all its domestically consumed flour and still exported 145,500 tons, principally to other Latin American nations.

The story of Argentine meat exports is also one of technological change that allowed the country to capture large world markets. Salted and dried beef had been an important agricultural export since 1820 but was not popular among European consumers. Finally, in 1876, a successful experiment with ammonia cooling and compressed air refrigeration signaled a major technological breakthrough. It took 20 years to perfect the processing and marketing of chilled and frozen meats, during which Argentine *estancieros* were replacing their native longhorns with English shorthorn stock. The old *saladeros* were closed down, and several *frigoríficos* (refrigerated packing plants) near Buenos Aires began processing chilled and frozen meat. On the eve of World

War I, the *frigoríficos* were processing nearly 440,800 tons of chilled beef and 66,100 tons of mutton yearly for export.

These striking developments in the rural sectors and in the processing industries aided Argentina in a limited process of import substitution. That is, the country began to produce domestically what it used to import. While food, drink, and tobacco items had totaled 40 percent of all imports in 1880, these same items were reduced to 13 percent in 1913. Much of Argentina's construction materials, industrial and agricultural machinery, and transport equipment still came from abroad. Capital goods totaled one-third of all imports prior to World War I. Also imports of all types of manufactured consumer goods remained high—37 percent of total imports. Clearly, the export of staple products accounted for the expansion of the entire Argentine economy and set the pace for its social and industrial development.

## Immigration and Urbanization

The social dimensions of Argentina's growth prior to World War I were as impressive as the export of staple products. Urban centers grew, a national market developed, rural enterprises found cheap sources of labor, and foreign-born entrepreneurs initiated an array of manufacturing ventures. In large measure, social development in Argentina was the result of massive immigration, which Liberal politicians and the landed elite always considered essential to economic growth. Nearly 2.9 million immigrants settled permanently in Argentina between 1880 and 1916, when at least 30 percent of the nation's population was foreign-born. Another million immigrants arrived in the 1920s. At the outbreak of the European war, the Argentine population had grown to approximately 8 million. It surpassed 10 million in 1930.

Wages increased throughout the 19th century in both the countryside and the city, particularly in the more dynamic export economy of Buenos Aires and the littoral provinces. The scarcity of rural workers in a time of intense frontier settlement drove up wages. The prices of foodstuffs and other commodities may also have offset somewhat these wage movements, but urban wages rose well above the cost of living in the last quarter of the 19th century. As late as 1907, one senator still worried about Argentina's chronic problem of labor scarcity, fearing that the high wages paid by the railroads would lure all the male agricultural workers away from the harvest.

Workers emigrated from Europe to Argentina in order to improve their lives, or *"hacer la América"* (to make America). This rise in real

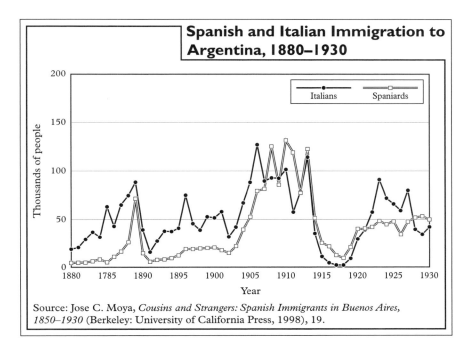

**Spanish and Italian Immigration to Argentina, 1880–1930**

Source: Jose C. Moya, *Cousins and Strangers: Spanish Immigrants in Buenos Aires, 1850–1930* (Berkeley: University of California Press, 1998), 19.

wages provided the pull factor attracting thousands of European immigrants to Argentina. Except for the depression years of 1891 and 1895, when many Europeans returned home, Argentine wages consistently exceeded Italian and Spanish wages. This trend favored those workers who came to the city. "Life here in Buenos Aires is always the same," wrote one immigrant to his parents in Italy. "There is a tremendous amount of construction work. The workers took advantage of it and have managed to get an eight-hour day at a pay that varies according to the trade. The average is four pesos, but no one works for less except the unskilled laborers" (Baily and Ramella 1988, 66). By 1895, more than 80 percent of both skilled and manual laborers in Buenos Aires were foreign-born.

Argentina received its largest portion of newcomers from the Mediterranean countries. Italians comprised almost 49 percent of all immigrants between 1857 and 1914. In contrast to the United States's experience of massive immigration from southern Italy, Argentina attracted most of its Italian immigrants from the agricultural regions of the north. Spaniards comprised the second largest number of immigrants to Argentina, while the French, Germans, and Russians (especially Russian Jews) contributed smaller numbers.

| Nationality of Foreigners Residing in Argentina, 1914 | | |
|---|---|---|
| Nationality | Total Number | Percent of Total Immigration |
| Italian | 929,863 | 39.4 |
| Spanish | 829,701 | 35.2 |
| South American | 203,129 | 11.6 |
| Russian/Austro-Hungarian* | 131,757 | 5.7 |
| French | 79,491 | 3.4 |
| Ottoman (Arab/Middle Eastern) | 64,369 | 2.7 |
| British | 27,692 | 1.2 |
| German | 26,995 | 1.1 |
| Swiss | 14,345 | 0.6 |
| Other | 50,610 | 2.1 |
| Total | 2,357,052 | 100.0 |

\* Mostly Russian Jews
Source: Carl Solberg (1970, 38)

Argentina's growing economy tended to absorb numbers of immigrants in the newer, expanding sectors. Many immigrants went into agricultural occupations (nearly 12 percent) and into commercial trades (9 percent), but a greater number worked in manufacturing and crafts (17 percent). Foreigners who crowded into Buenos Aires and other cities found opportunities as proprietors, managers, and workers. While foreigners shunned traditional native enterprises, still 40.9 percent of all landowners in 1914 were foreign-born. More than three-quarters of manufacturers and shopkeepers were alien, and 62 percent of wine producers were immigrants. Furthermore, the immigrant found jobs, better wages, and possibilities of advancement as an urban worker. Real wages averaged about 25 percent more than those earned by workers in Paris. Suburban home ownership became a reality for thrifty skilled workers, as an expert mechanic in Buenos Aires was able to buy a lot and build a house after saving regularly for a decade.

The population of the city of Buenos Aires increased more than eightfold between 1869 and 1914, from nearly 178,000 to more than 1.5 million. Another million more people lived in Buenos Aires when

*Between 1880 and 1916, nearly 3 million immigrants came to Argentina, principally from Europe. Many immigrants lived in squalid circumstances as shown in this view of tenant housing in Buenos Aires around 1910.* (Patricia Harris Postcard Collection, Benson Latin American Collection, University of Texas at Austin)

census takers counted residents in 1936. Immigration increased the overall ratio of men in the city, as foreign males outnumbered foreign females. The capital of Argentina experienced its most radical transformation and growth during this period when both working-class and middle-class suburbs blossomed and proliferated. Buenos Aires was the most populous urban center in Latin America and among the 10 most

| Population of the City of Buenos Aires, 1914–1936 | | | | |
|---|---|---|---|---|
| | 1914 | | 1936 | |
| Argentine males | 394,463 | 35% | 726,524 | 30% |
| Argentine females | 403,506 | 35% | 816,583 | 34% |
| Foreign males | 455,507 | 19% | 476,522 | 20% |
| Foreign females | 323,338 | 11% | 394,200 | 16% |
| Total | 1,576,814 | | 2,413,829 | |
| Source: Richard J. Walter, in Stanley R. Ross and Thomas F. McGann (1982, 69, 71). | | | | |

# AN ITALIAN IMMIGRANT DESCRIBES HIS WORK OPPORTUNITIES

Buenos Aires, 3 May 1903

Dearest parents, brother, and sister,

As you will see from the heading, I am once again in Buenos Aires.... I am fine here, in excellent health; business is also good. As I had written you from Santa Teresa [Entre Ríos], it is just that I had to keep on the move. I left there toward the end of February and went straight to Santa Fe, where I had to take a job with a French railway firm. I worked a few days, but then, since Frenchmen and Italians don't get along with each other, I went on my way. The next day I left for San Cristobal. I stayed there for only three days since they are still all negroes,* and I headed straight for Tucumán, where I had an excellent job. But since there is malaria in that area ... and at that time there was also smallpox, and it seemed to be spreading, I got scared and took off again. I would have liked to go to Bolivia, but since I was rather far away from the big cities, it was not convenient for me. So I headed for the capital. Almost two days and three nights on the train. I assure you that I am tired and have had my fill of traveling.

For about a month I have been here and have been employed in the work on the Congreso Nacional, which is under construction; the work will last at least a half dozen years. I am doing very well here, and if I did not have to do my military service [in Italy], I would stay on to the end.+ That would be of great advantage to me....

Oreste [Sola]

* The writer probably was referring to the native-born workers.
+ He never did return to Italy.

■

*(Baily and Ramella 1988, 52–53)*

populous cities in the world. Nearly one-third of all Argentines lived in Buenos Aires.

Immigrants also settled in the interior, but the second-largest Argentine city—Rosario in Santa Fe province—had a population of only 223,000, or just one-sixth the size of Buenos Aires. Still, 47 other Argentine cities had residents numbering more than 10,000 people each; in fact, half of Argentina's people had been urbanized by World War I. Together with the railways, the rising urban population had created a national market that stimulated the domestic wine and sugar industries of the interior. Between 1895 and 1914, annual wine production in the Andean foothills increased by 940 percent. The sugar industry, centered in Tucumán, more than doubled its output. Imports of foreign wine and sugar, therefore, began to dwindle after the turn of the century.

With its rapidly increasing population, Argentina's capital city received the services and utilities that accompanied modern urban living. British financiers and technicians constructed a modern port complex with docks, grain elevators, and hydraulic equipment within view of the presidential palace. The British-owned gas company in 1888 began installing gas lighting in the city. At the turn of the century, electrification and a tramway system permitted the city to spread into suburban neighborhoods. Horsedrawn and electric trams ran on more than 1,860 miles of tracks throughout the city and carried nearly 400 million urban passengers in 1914. Telegraph and telephone lines arched through the city and out to provincial centers. Coastal and river shipping, whose traffic expanded ninefold between 1880 and 1910, linked the littoral provinces to the commercial and communications hub of Buenos Aires.

Furthermore, the export economy of the era induced significant investment in schools so that Argentina became the educational leader of Latin America. The literacy rate reached 62 percent of the total population, driven more by the fact that most immigrants were already literate on arrival than by Argentine educational success. More immigrants were able to read and write than native-born Argentines. By 1909, some 59 percent of eligible school-age children in the nation attended primary school. For the city of Buenos Aires, the number was far greater: 83 percent. One of the weaknesses of the system (so far as the nation's economic development was concerned) lay in the continued dominance of classical education. Few secondary students received any technical training at all. In addition, most education stopped at the primary level.

Even though general standards of living may have improved for all workers, European immigrants participated in the economic improvements to a greater extent than did Creole (native-born) laborers. Elite prejudice against the working class had been a constant theme throughout the 19th century. Moreover, sons of the gauchos still preferred to work in the familiar ambience of cattle production, leaving farming, sheep raising, and urban jobs to the immigrants.

# ORIGIN OF THE ARGENTINE TERM *CHE*

**C**he has become one of the hallmarks of colloquial Argentine Spanish, as in *"¿Como estás, che?"* ("How are you, man?"). Everyone calls one another *"che."* The tango singer Carlos Gardel liked to speak in the café slang and sprinkled his conversations with comments such as *"Macanudo, che, macanudo,"* a very characteristically Argentine expression for "Good, man, very good." Later, the young revolutionary Ernesto Guevara used the word so frequently in conversation during his travels through Latin America that by 1955, when he first met Fidel Castro and other Cuban insurrectionaries, he was already nicknamed Che Guevara. Later he would come to be known simply as "el Che."

The term *che* may have derived from the indigenous language of Araucanian, which had become the lingua franca among the Indian

While Argentine urban society denigrated natives of color, it also produced social conformity in the children of immigrants. The dress, language, and culture of European immigrants became objects of derision at all levels of *porteño* society. Sons of immigrants at the turn of the century began to reject their parents' heritage and embrace *"lo argentino"* (that which is Argentine). A leading proponent of a return to Hispanic values in Argentina was Emilio Becher, grandson of a Dutch immigrant. José Razzano and Carlos Gardel, sons of immigrants, in 1917 became the leading innovators in the revival of traditional "Creole," or gauchesque, music. This singing duet was managed by another immigrant's child, Max Glucksman.

Because conformity preserved the social hierarchy, it became a powerful mechanism to blend the immigrant into Argentine society. The drama *Juan Moreira* about a gaucho had many successful runs between 1886 and 1920. No longer did genteel Argentines consider the gaucho as uncouth, ignorant, arrogant, violent, and lazy—characteristics Domingo F. Sarmiento had ascribed to them more than a half century prior. Now the gaucho was the source of the basic traits of Argentina's national character: compassion, elegance, honor, loyalty, and generosity. In reaction to the massive immigration of the period, Argentines suddenly embraced the gauchesque literature of the late 19th century,

bands inhabiting the southern Pampas and the Patagonia in the 18th and 19th centuries. Following is the explanation of Lucío Mansilla, who spent much time along the frontier in 1870:

> The night was mild and clear, an inviting one for conversation, and we needed only the starlight and the moonlight to read. I seized the opportunity to take a lesson in Araucan. Finally I came to understand certain words whose meaning I had sought for some time, such as the Picunche, the Puelche, and the Pehuenche Indians. *Che* is the word that, depending on its context, can mean "I," "man," or "inhabitant." Thus, Picunche means "inhabitant of the east."

■

(1977, 224–225)

especially *Martín Fierro*. This 1872 epic poem by José Hernández depicted the country folk as noble and honorable; in turn, the businessmen and politicians from the city appeared duplicitous and corrupt. As Hernández wrote, "A gaucho'd live in his home country / as safe as anything, / but now—it's a crime! / things have got to be so twisted / that a poor man wears out his life / running from the authorities" (1967, 21). Urban Argentines even became accustomed to a most popular form of address originating among the Pampas Indians and brought to the city by the gaucho: Friends and relatives began to call one another *"che."*

## The Beginnings of Modern Manufacturing

The story of industry before World War I was one of remarkable expansion but not of self-sustaining growth. In the 1890s, censuses show that tanneries, blacksmith shops, carpentry and metalworking plants, cigarette and match factories, burlap bag works, and shoe and shirt manufacturing had developed to meet the needs of a wider domestic market. Immigration obviously proved a boon in terms of labor and entrepreneurship. Most owners of domestic industries were immigrants and foreigners. In 1910, only 21 percent of all owners were Argentine-born. While social conventions may not have conferred prestige upon those natives who chose careers in industry, immigrant entrepreneurship certainly redressed the imbalance.

Argentina's food processors appear to have gained overwhelming predominance among the primary manufacturers. Flour milling, meatpacking, wine pressing, and sugar refining had become the dynamic industries of the era. While native and immigrant entrepreneurs dominated the flour and wine businesses, much of the sugar refining and the meatpacking industries remained under the control of foreign managers. These foreigners had little interest in spreading their technologies to other domestic industries.

Argentina's secondary industries grew impressively as the national economy became integrated. Yet these, too, confronted obstacles. Argentina's electrical generators, steam engines, and railroad locomotives ran on imported coal and coke. Lacking both coal and iron ore deposits, Argentina had to import much of the raw materials for secondary industry. In fact, the iron and steel manufacturers depended on foreign sources for nearly 80 percent of their raw materials.

World War I provided both a stimulus and an obstacle for Argentina's economic boom. Most of its trade partners went to war in Europe and ceased buying Argentine products. Similarly, Great Britain and France converted their industries to wartime production, making few items that Argentine consumers customarily purchased. Consumer prices shot up. The middle class and workers faced the stress of rising unemployment at a moment of rising cost of living, and 1917 saw sharp labor strikes and class conflict. Nonetheless, domestic manufacturers of consumer items expanded production of various items traditionally imported. Argentines bought more locally-produced textiles and leather goods. Small mechanical shops began to turn out the machinery and glasswares that previously had come from foreign sources.

## The Landed and the Landless

Argentine elite families had been able to preserve their socioeconomic status through three generations. The Spanish merchant elite of the viceregal era had provided the capital for their sons and daughters to expand into the ranching business after independence from Spain. By the 1880s, the grandchildren of colonial merchants were diversifying their *estancia*-based portfolios with investments in urban real estate, railway and bank stocks, and joint stock companies. These first families had consistently intermarried during the entire previous century in order to remain culturally and racially European.

The Argentine elite was open to an extent to infusions of non-Spanish Europeans: The economic expansion of the 19th century allowed the bluebloods to admit a limited number of very successful immigrants and sons of immigrants into their inner circles as well as people whose fortunes were made in politics or through politically connected businesses. Many wealthy British and other foreign merchants had married into Creole elite families throughout the century. Names like Bunge, Santamarina, Cambaceres, Gowland, Tornquist, and Armstrong connoted considerable status. The second generation of these wealthy families aspired to join the country's elite in their most prestigious social and economic organizations. The big landowners were members of the Rural Society (Sociedad Rural), which lobbied for their interests in public forums. Socially, the elite families gathered at the very exclusive Jockey Club, located in the stylish Barrio Norte of Buenos Aires. The Rural Society and the Jockey Club served as two powerful symbols of the country's influential oligarchy. Newly wealthy families could only expect membership in these organizations in the second generation, for only inherited wealth distinguished a family; the nouveau riche were held to be undeserving.

While the export expansion had made them wealthy, the landowning elite turned out to be poor entrepreneurs. They preferred to invest their money in certain ventures—land and cattle, joint stock companies—that preserved, rather than generated, wealth. Few Argentines invested in railway building. They left this risky business to foreigners, especially the British, and to the government. However, the Argentine elites did aspire to trade their family prestige and political influence for seats on the boards of foreign companies operating locally. One could do this without risking the family's fortune in modernization projects.

In 19th-century Argentina, there were other prerequisites for elite status besides mere wealth. Coming from the correct family, maintaining an effete bearing, and being educated and cosmopolitan counted more than ability in gaining status in society. Anyone who was non-white, illegitimate, or from dubious family origin could not hope to penetrate elite circles. These principles of exclusivity even extended to the rising middle class. Members of immigrant families on the rise tended to marry within their French, Spanish, or Italian social circles and seldom into Creole working-class families. Respectable families, whether elite or bourgeois, guarded their racial status closely over several generations.

The dominant elite utilized its sociopolitical status to capture the largest increments of the wealth created by economic progress. At the beginning of the 19th century, the elite families had lived in the center of Buenos Aires cheek-to-jowl with the working poor. As in the colonial tradition, the wealthy families resided in fortresslike one- and two-story homes near the main square (the Plaza de Mayo), the president's palace, and the cathedral. In Buenos Aires, trade had also centered on the Plaza de Mayo, which lay within two blocks of the riverbank over which passed the nation's cargoes. The 1871 epidemic of yellow fever thus plagued the elite as well as the poor in the unhealthful and crowded downtown area.

By the dawn of the 20th century, however, the elite had moved out of the city center into the Barrio Norte. Laborers may have come to work in this exclusive neighborhood of Parisian-style town houses, but only the household servants resided there. On the *estancias*, the landowners erected sumptuous chateaus and abandoned the traditional huts with thatched roofs. As a contemporary British writer observed, "Increasing wealth no doubt has set a bar betwixt the classes, making the poor man feel his poverty, and the rich know that isolation is the best weapon in the fight that he must wage" (Walker 1978, 150).

One interpretation holds that the expansion of cattle raising concentrated land ownership among the elite, coerced free gauchos into working on the *estancias,* and prevented the spread of farming on the Pampas. This is an exaggeration. Recent studies of frontier settlement have uncovered more variety in landownership and rural production. Prior to 1880, a process of subdivision was already working to reduce the size of the first great cattle estates. General Julio A. Roca's Conquest of the Desert temporarily reversed that trend, as speculators and political insiders rushed to gobble up frontier land by the hundreds of square miles. Soon, however, railways and cereal production began to push the cattle herds farther out into the Pampas. Then herds of sheep left the Pampas and migrated to Patagonia. The Pampas was now available to dirt farmers. This agrarian transformation set in motion new forms of production and caused the older cattle *estancias* to be subdivided.

The rural district of Baradero is a convincing example of this trend. Properties smaller than 1,000 hectares (about 2,500 acres) occupied only 14 percent of Baradero in 1895; huge *estancias* accounted for the rest. Within 15 years, however, those "modest" units had multiplied at the expense of the big estates to cover nearly 85 percent of the Baradero's total land. These indications suggest that export growth fostered the subdivision of older landholdings as well as the settlement of new land. Likewise, the growth of pastoral and agricultural exports resulted in a diffusion of occupations. While big landowners were becoming wealthy, a group of rural middlemen arose, composed of shopkeepers, small growers, warehousemen, buyers, and sellers.

*This rural woman posed with a large stone montero, which was used to manually grind wheat.* (Casa Figueroa, 1900)

Nonetheless, it is certain that immigrants did not benefit initially from the diffusion of landownership, at least not on the Pampas, where cattlemen and speculators relegated the immigrants to public lands far from markets and rail traffic. Rather, newly arrived immigrants settled on unused public lands in isolated sections of Santa Fe, Córdoba, Entre Ríos, and Corrientes. One area of the interior of Entre Ríos, whose farms were settled under the financial sponsorship of the German Jewish philanthropist Baron Maurice de Hirsch, became famous for its "Jewish gauchos."

Most foreigners on the Pampas, nonetheless, were sharecroppers and farm tenants. Entire immigrant families signed tenancy contracts with *estancieros* to fence off a section of cattle pastures, plow the land for the first time, and cultivate wheat. The tenants then shared with the owner in the proceeds from the sale of wheat. In other words, Argentine cattlemen on the Pampas were getting into the export of wheat without becoming farmers. One agricultural journal of the time described the common tenant's contract: "The land is first divided into fenced grazing pastures of four to five thousand acres and then subdivided into surveyed numbered lots of five hundred acres each without any intervening wire. These lots are rented on a three-year contract . . . to Italian farmers who bring their own equipment and supplies and agree at the end of the period to leave the land sown with alfalfa, the seed being supplied by the owners" (Scobie 1971, 118).

Needless to say, farm immigrants led a precarious existence dependent on the benevolence of landowners and good grain prices. Their relations with the *estanciero* could become strained in falling markets for agricultural produce, at which time the tenant farmers resorted to rebellion and demanded that their contracts be liberalized. One such occasion was the Farm Tenants' Strike in Entre Ríos in 1912. A few succeeded by working hard, living thriftily, and saving money to rent or purchase their own farmsteads. The big *estancieros* of the Pampas also sold portions of their estates to the nouveau riche and political insiders from the city.

---

# A CONTEMPORARY VIEW OF THE CAUSES OF THE FARM TENANTS' STRIKE OF 1912

The colonists [tenants] are paying the proprietor 33 per cent of the crop with selected grain, threshed, placed in bags and delivered at the railway stations; they are only allowed to thresh their crops with machines provided by the landlord, buy their bags from him, and unless with his consent cannot sell their crops to third parties but must sell it to him; they are only allowed 10 per cent of the camp rentage for pasturage purposes and they have to pay for this $30 [30 pesos] per square per year, and if they require more pasturage land they have to pay double the price. All their provisions have to be obtained from the store indicated by the owner. Of the four pigs which they are allowed to have, one has to be given to the owner; he making his own selection and with the guarantee that it shall not weigh less than 120 kilos [265 pounds]. The colonists now demand that the rent be reduced to 25 per cent of the crops, and that they shall only deliver same at the foot of the thresher, ready bagged and of export type; that they may be allowed to sell their crop to whom they please giving preference to the owner under similar conditions, and that he has to receive same eight days after threshing. Liberty to buy bags where they please, and also all their store goods, and that they be given 6 per cent of the camp without charge for pasturage purposes.

∎

*Review of the River Plate July 5, 1912 (Scobie 1964, 154–55)*

---

Land purchase may have been easier in the interior provinces, where the arrival of railways commercialized several regional economies. In Córdoba, urban immigrants bought up suburban plots and farms, which they then leased to migrants and landless natives. The number of small holdings also increased in Tucumán, although this province had fewer immigrant settlers. In Mendoza, Italians gained access to subdivided land through contracts to cultivate grapes. The immigrant role in establishing *bodegas* (grape-pressing plants) and developing vineyards enabled the wealthiest foreigners to join the local oligarchy. Immigrants moved in as *contratistas,* who took charge of employing and supervising the unskilled workers in the various tasks of making wine. The local Mendoza oligarchy utilized these immigrant middlemen to discipline "indolent" migrant workers. Land was being subdivided in interior areas undergoing capitalist expansion, and after the local gentry, foreigners appear to have benefited.

Nowhere is the evidence more conclusive than in Santa Fe, where the railway stimulated intensive agricultural growth. In the north of that province, foreigners began to acquire land in 1872 and established family-based production of corn, flax, and peanuts. In the central wheat-growing colonies of the province, there were indications of social mobility among small- and middle-sized producers. The incidence of landownership by producers themselves was greater in the oldest agricultural colonies, while the newer ones were dominated by renters and sharecroppers. Thus, the expanding wheat exports of the late 19th century enabled renters to buy the land they worked. In 1895, about 48 percent of farm families in Santa Fe owned their own land, the national average being approximately 30 percent. This rural middle class was composed of immigrant Italians, Germans, and Swiss. The Argentines remained peons on the cattle ranches of the elite.

But the story does not end with the differential sharing of wealth. Social distinctions and ethnic discrimination engendered resentments and rivalries that Argentine elites were able to utilize to maintain a semblance of the old order in the face of economic change.

## Gringos and Criollos

Massive immigration in this traditional postcolonial society deepened the distinction between natives and Europeans. Immigrants came to be known as *gringos,* a term that meant "foreigner," "newcomer," or "greenhorn." While the elite grew wealthy and distant, massive immigration spawned the development of a skilled working class and a white

*The term* criollo *came to refer to a specific class of mixed-race native-born workers. Shown here is a group of rural criollos in the 20th century.* (Patricia Harris Postcard Collection, Benson Latin American Collection, University of Texas at Austin)

middle class that further marginalized the native-born workers. In fact, the meaning of the term *criollo* had already begun to change. In the colonial period, a Creole was an Argentine-born Spaniard. At the end of the 19th century, *criollo* came to denote the Argentine-born working class of mixed racial background.

Creoles were swarthy in skin color due to their indigenous, African, and European heritage, while immigrants were white. In addition to racial differences, culture and language often divided gringos and criollos. So criollos and gringos continued to be separate and unequal—and mutually hostile. Politicians exploited this animosity to maintain social control, alternately balancing the interests of immigrants and natives so that both groups remained dependent and nonthreatening. Argentina in the liberal age was *not* a melting pot.

Though both groups may have worked with their hands, criollos and gringos lived separate existences, and only one of them—the gringos— had opportunities for upward social mobility. It is true that the workforce in Argentina expanded in proportion to the economy, but Creoles suffered systematic exclusion from advancement. Gringos were more literate than the Argentine criollos. Skilled immigrant artisans hired only other immigrants as journeymen and apprentices, thus relegating Creoles to the less skilled positions in the building trades. Part of the reason for immigrant hegemony in the artisan trades was the appetite among the elites for European-style goods, whether homemade or imported. Immigrants thus retained control of Argentine shopkeeping and manufacturing establishments. In 1910, 80 percent of all manufacturing shops had foreign-born owners. While urban occupations offered more jobs for women, immigrant domination of small manufacturing meant that immigrant women enjoyed more opportunities in employment than did the native-born.

Family life among the Creole working class scarcely measured up to traditional Hispanic values. Widespread adultery, illegitimacy, and abuse of women had existed among Argentina's working poor since the colonial period. Large numbers of abandoned children inhabited many working-class barrios of Buenos Aires. In the countryside, less than one-third of the native-born were married. Family life was difficult because men and women of the Creole working class lived such extraordinarily separate lives. In urban Córdoba in 1895, for example, the number of female Creoles exceeded that of male Creoles by 6,000. But criollo men vastly outnumbered females in the countryside. Creole workers lacked a cohesive family structure that could have provided security and advancement in society.

Those immigrants who went to the countryside distanced themselves from Creoles. As rural shopkeepers and farm renters, the gringos often became the employers of Creole peons. The Italian farmers of Entre Ríos, moreover, came to resent the criollos for their uncouth behavior and violent temperaments. They called them "Negroes" and seldom intermarried. On the Pampas of Buenos Aires, foreigners found work as petty merchants, tradesmen, and sharecroppers, competing effectively with Creoles for these positions. Meanwhile, the gaucho class that had once roamed freely across the countryside found that it had to settle down as pliant peons. The new barbed-wire fences prevented the unfettered vagabond roaming of an earlier age.

Some were not troubled by the disappearance of the gaucho. It was good for the country, lectured the prominent intellectual Leopoldo Lugones in 1913, because the gaucho possessed "part-Indian blood, an inferior component" (Méndez 1980, 85). Nonetheless, the general marginalization of the criollo did not prevent the glorification of the mythical gaucho as the repository of traditional Argentine national character.

Yet the Generation of Eighty like Rosas, saw the advantages of pandering to the dispossessed. To counter the demands of the immigrants, the government recruited members of the Creole working class for the military and the police. Gringos were exempt from conscription; therefore, native-born men of the countryside filled the ranks of the army, criollos who made the army a career were noncommissioned officers. According to an army publication, "most of our soldiers are recruited from the social stratum of field workers, men without much money, poorly dressed and fed even worse, without house or home, who since infancy have acquired unfortunate habits and predilections, no doubt to counteract their organic poverty or as an unavoidable consequence of their idle or errant life, until pressing need makes them enlist for a pittance, or impulse leads them to commit a crime and (a judge) settles the account by assigning them to an army unit as punishment" (Ramírez 1987, 123). These men were led by an officer corps drawn overwhelmingly from the provincial and rural gentry. The officers suffered two glaring deficiencies: their excess numbers and poor training. In 1891, there were 1,360 officers for nearly 6,000 soldiers.

The Generation of Eighty believed it could count on the police and the army against immigrant workers and farmers. In 1893, immigrant grain producers of Santa Fe rebelled against a new production tax intended to support the provincial government controlled by the PAN. To crush this gringo resistance, the politicians marshaled Creole cattle workers, who were only too willing to attack foreigners. Throat cutting temporarily reappeared as an expression of political preferences. The politicians counterbalanced the two working classes elsewhere, too. Indians and mestizos from the northern provinces formed the elite cavalry units of the Buenos Aires police forces. They particularly relished breaking up immigrant labor disturbances and union rallies.

Army officers, however, proved to be less loyal to the oligarchy in the long run. They were recruited principally from the class of marginal elites of the poorest provinces. Sons of the landholding oligarchs eschewed the dull life of a bourgeois officer rising up through the ranks; therefore, the army officers as a group tended to support their own middle-class interests. They resented the elite for its ability to travel abroad and its fascination with all things European; they remained suspicious of first-generation immigrants who "mangled" Argentine Spanish and formed trade unions; and they became a reservoir of resentments against the power of foreign capital—particularly that of British railroad tycoons and American oilmen. Although current officers were not a threat to the government of the elite (there were no military coups between 1880 and 1930), a trend was developing in which officers in the future would identify with public order and nationalism but not with continued rule by the oligarchs.

If a young Argentine had left the country in 1870 and returned 35 years later, he or she would have been amazed by how radically national life had changed. The indigenous peoples had been eliminated from the frontier regions, and gringo farmers harvested wheat where once only cattle had roamed. More than 1 million people lived in the capital, and one out of every three *porteños* was foreign-born. The skyline and modern port facilities revealed few traces of the colonial origins of Buenos Aires. The tree-lined paved avenues looked like Paris. Even the cattle estates of the Pampas had changed; Herefords and English shorthorns grazed on alfalfa pastures behind barbed wire fences.

And yet things below the surface were much the same. Social discrimination prevented native-born people of color from getting ahead, and educated whites and the foreign-born monopolized the middle-sector occupations that provided opportunities for social mobility. The landed oligarchy still remained aloof; in fact, the first families of Argentina had become wealthier and even more remote. While the phenomenal export-led development between 1880 and 1916 had expanded the nation's wealth, it had done nothing to equalize the distribution of income. The rural and urban working classes contributed to exports but did not share enough of the nation's income to eliminate poverty. Moreover, the returning Argentine would recognize in his nation's politics the corruption and the rigged elections of a previous age.

Argentina, nonetheless, was not the same country, and national politics had taken on new constituencies. An emerging middle class was demanding participation in public affairs, and so was a boisterous urban working class. These new contestants for power did succeed in gaining entry to political life before the end of the liberal age, even though in the long run their enfranchisement did not sustain the political stability guaranteed by the Generation of Eighty.

# 7

# THE DECLINE OF
# LIBERALISM, 1916–1930

After more than three decades in power, the conservatives of the National Autonomist Party (PAN) began to lose their political edge. General Julio A. Roca finished a second term as president in 1904 and died shortly thereafter. Factionalism began to erode the will and direction of the PAN. The Generation of Eighty and their political descendants faced a serious challenge from the opposition Radicals. Formed by dissident oligarchs, the Radical Party had gained support from farmers and rural tenants in the provinces of Santa Fe and Entre Ríos. The sons of immigrants (women could not vote) supported the Radicals as a viable alternative to the corrupt conservatives of the PAN, who seemingly kept themselves in power only through electoral fraud. Three minor rebellions within the military in 1890, 1893, and 1905 showed that many officers also favored the Radicals.

Finally, one faction of the PAN proposed a novel approach to save the party. President Roque Sáenz Peña sought to outflank the opposition Radicals with a series of electoral reforms. Under the Sáenz Peña laws, the responsibility of overseeing elections fell to the army, a supposedly neutral observer. Voting became compulsory (as a way of "forcing" voters to be good citizens) for all male citizens over 18 years of age. Balloting became secret. The Sáenz Peña laws of 1912 enfranchised the native-born working and middle classes because their leaders considered them controllable; aspiring foreigners, on the other hand, were not to be trusted with such rights. Altogether the electoral reforms added much needed transparency to the electoral process and expanded the electorate, but they did not accomplish what the conservatives had hoped.

## Political Transition

The first presidential elections following these reforms proved monumental. Not only did the Radicals win the presidency and control of the Congress in 1916, but the Socialist Party gained power in the city of Buenos Aires, where voters would consistently elect Socialist congressmen into the 1950s. Suddenly the battered remnants of the PAN became an anemic party of opposition. The day belonged to the Radicals, and jubilant party loyalists at the inaugural parade unhitched the horses from the presidential carriage and pulled their leader, Hipólito Yrigoyen, through the streets. The elections of 1916 marked the first time that one national party transferred political power to another through a peaceful process. Argentines had reason to believe that the era of criollo politics and military coups were behind them.

The oligarchy in the provinces did not fare any better in the 1916 elections. Public life in Mendoza had been transformed during the period of rapid economic growth, symbolized by the arrival of the railway at the end of the 19th century. The local landowners, in order to protect their sociopolitical hegemony, welcomed the railway and economic change almost in self-defense. They did not wish to be overrun by powerful national economic forces. But if they had intended to retain their social and economic monopoly, they were mistaken. Modernization brought in its wake new local social groups, especially an immigrant bourgeoisie that increasingly captured a share of land and financial resources. Immigrants developed the province's modern wine industry. While Mendoza's oligarchy still controlled access to land, water, and finances, it found itself weakened by older family divisions and by the need to permit participation of new social groups. True, the old *mendocino* elite had become wealthy, but in the end, the oligarchy lost the hegemony it had hoped modernization would preserve. In 1916, three decades after the arrival of the first railway, the local Conservative Party fell from provincial power in Mendoza.

President Yrigoyen was the longtime leader of the national Radical Party. He rose to power through the support of the farmers, the farm tenants, the urban middle classes, and, unexpectedly, the working class. Yrigoyen was a man of property and his inner circle of Radical leaders, also, belonged to the landed oligarchy. The families of many Radicals had been members in good standing of the Generation of Eighty, so the economic policies of the Radical government did not depart significantly from those of the conservatives. However, the other constituencies

*An early-20th-century view of downtown Buenos Aires* (Patricia Harris Postcard Collection, Benson Latin American Collection, the University of Texas at Austin)

of the Radical Party added new and potentially contradictory tendencies (social reformism and nationalism) to Argentine politics.

The emerging urban middle class made up part of the Radical electorate for seemingly conflicting reasons. On the one hand, the middle class hated the landed oligarchy for monopolizing politics and economic opportunities. And despite its immigrant origins, the middle class was becoming quite nationalistic in its politics in the early 20th century. It castigated the oligarchy for its cozy relationship with British interests and supported the expansion of the state bureaucracy as a way of regaining control over the foreign-dominated economy. On the other hand, the middle class accepted many elite values. One was a respect for university education as a mark of prestige, and the other, a fear and loathing of the uncouth working classes.

Yrigoyen could deal with the educational aspirations of the middle class more easily than with their antilabor sentiments. The university strikes of 1918 and 1919 gave him the opportunity to address the former. When Yrigoyen came to power, Argentina had three institutions of higher learning: the University of Córdoba, which had colonial origins; the University of Buenos Aires, founded just following independence; and the University of La Plata, established in 1890 in the capital of Buenos Aires province. Government budgets supported the universities, and although enrollments in the universities had risen to 14,000 in 1918, the schools remained bastions of the elite. Their administrations were conservative, and instruction favored law and the classics over the sciences. If the government was becoming more democratic, why not the universities, too? The growing body of middle-class university students boycotted classes beginning in 1918 in an effort to democratize the administration.

The Radical government seized this opportunity to reform the universities. Each received a new charter giving the students a voice in administration. Budgetary controls were tightened, and the student bodies were expanded to include more middle-class entrants. The state also founded two new universities, one in Santa Fe and the other in Tucumán. University education expanded in a manner that subsidized the middle class and extended additional opportunities to people in the interior.

## Controlling the Popular Classes

The Radicals had found it convenient to cater to another political constituency: the urban workers. They had learned from the 1916 elections that the middle class, still quite small on a national scale, did not suffice by itself to overturn conservative rule. Yrigoyen purposely appealed to urban laborers, but not to rural peons, who remained under the thumb of the landed oligarchy. The courtship made political sense: The city of Buenos Aires contained about one-fourth of the nation's voters, most of whom belonged to the working class, who in turn were casting a majority of their votes at the time for the Socialist Party.

Politicians who appealed to the labor vote trod a very fine line. As the urban working class grew along with economy, the workers became increasingly aware of their second-class citizenship. Even immigrant workers did not accept this status. Many of them had brought with them syndicalist traditions from the old country, advocating labor organizing to defend workers' interest. As early as the 1890s, skilled laborers introduced labor unions and strikes. Anarchist labor leaders, who threatened working-class violence if necessary, many of them foreign-born, mounted the first general strike in 1902 and succeeded in shutting down the city. Also in 1902, a radical attempted to assassinate President Roca. The government responded by passing the Residency Law by which foreign-born "troublemakers" could be summarily expelled from the country.

Working-class violence was frightening to both the oligarchy and the emerging middle class. Their nightmares seemed to come alive in 1909 when an anarchist succeeded in assassinating the *porteño* chief of police. Moreover, rapid urbanization and growth of the urban working class gave new visibility to women laborers. Their presence in the streets and newfound economic independence provoked men to equate poor working women with prostitutes and, thus, threats to public health and the traditional Catholic family. Nervous elites had another issue to debate: social control through the regulation of legalized prostitution. Despite the fearsome ideology of international anarchism, however, Argentine labor leaders actually preferred collaborating with government officials rather than "smashing the state" and challenging capitalism. Many voted for Yrigoyen in 1916. The Radicals in power, therefore, chose to negotiate with organized labor.

The economic crisis of World War I put the state-labor alliance to the test. Suffering from layoffs, falling wages, and rising prices, workers in the larger industries staged numerous strikes in 1917 and 1918. They demanded job security and wage increases to compensate for the price inflation. For the most part, the Radical government intervened in these strikes. The politicians coerced foreign employers in the port works and railways to give in to labor demands and ordered the police to protect the picket lines rather than repress them as the PAN governments had previously done.

# GENDER AND SOCIAL CONTROL OF THE MASSES

Public authorities sought to deal with the perceived dangers of rapid social change by uniting men of all classes behind the control of women. Male workers resented women taking jobs from them, and men of the middle and upper classes did not want their wives and daughters to pursue independent careers. The very idea of women's freedom to work threatened family patriarchy and social order. Although few women worked as prostitutes, public authorities sought to identify poor women with the sex industry, thereby justifying their regulation through legal restrictions. Here was an issue that united men of all classes, a rare commodity in public life.

The Argentine congress first legalized prostitution in 1875. Thereafter, the country changed rapidly as the wealth created by agricultural exports stimulated immigration, urbanization, and the development of an urban working class. Women too found new opportunities in the urban environment. By 1914, more than 13,000 found employment as schoolteachers in Buenos Aires, 80,000 as domestic servants, and 68,000 as industrial workers. In textile factories, women held more than half the jobs.

Public officials in the early 20th century attempted a number of different measures to control women. They outlawed the white slave trade through which European prostitutes supposedly entered Buenos Aires. They inspected and regulated the bordellos. The police rounded up streetwalkers and jailed poor women for disturbing the peace. They used immigrant prostitutes as scapegoats and blamed them for the spread of venereal disease, even though most women in the sex trade after 1920 were native-born. Public health officials even sought to force prostitutes to submit to periodic physical examinations in order to protect their customers.

It did not occur to the authorities to regulate the well-to-do men who frequented the bordellos, to inoculate men against syphilis, or to prosecute men for abandonment and for lack of child support. The fact remained that a few women engaged in prostitution out of economic need. Having failed to succeed in controlling women through the legal regulation of prostitution, the public authorities once again outlawed prostitution in 1936.

Many of the foreign interests whose striking workers received government support protested to no avail. One editor responded in 1917, saying that "[the British railway managers] accuse [Yrigoyen] of carrying out a pro-labor policy hostile to capital; they do not see that . . . this is the wisest course in view of the phenomena which are now transforming the social and political structure of the world" (Wright 1974, 123). Workers reacted to government overtures by voting for the Radicals over the Socialists in the 1918 congressional elections.

However, the middle class shared some of the oligarchy's misgivings about the new influence of labor. So did the army. The January 1919 workers' strike led to a breach in the Radical-labor coalition during a week of violence in Buenos Aires remembered as the Semana Trágica, or "Tragic Week." The police had moved in to quell a metal workers' strike, and a three-day melee resulted in the deaths of one police officer and five workers. Gangs of secondary-school youths then descended on the city from the middle-class suburbs. The mobs looted and burned the Jewish quarter of Plaza Once, blaming local shopkeepers and tailors for labor agitation. The police simply stood by. Hundreds of working-class residents, particularly those who "looked like" immigrants, died in the right-wing violence. The U.S. embassy reported that 1,500 people had been killed and 4,000 wounded,"mostly Russians and generally Jews." Many women had been raped.

Radical government policies toward labor changed overnight. Yrigoyen gave in to the newly energized right wing of the middle classes, which organized the Argentine Patriotic League. This new organization expressed some of the antilabor and anti-immigrant sentiments of the emerging middle class, notwithstanding its immigrant and artisan antecedents. The Patriotic League also found members and support among army officers. Yrigoyen now turned to listen to his military and middle-class constituents. When the port workers and the shepherds of Patagonia launched a series of strikes in 1921 and 1922, Yrigoyen handed over the problem to the army. Troop commanders crushed "rebellious Patagonia" and executed countless workers and labor leaders. They said that the strike had posed a threat to national sovereignty, inasmuch as many of the workers in Patagonia were Chilean migrants.

The Radical government turned decidedly conservative in the 1920s, heralded by the 1922 election of Yrigoyen's handpicked successor, the landowner Marcelo T. de Alvear. Yet there was no turning back to the unabashedly liberal policies of the 1880s. The disparate Radical constituencies, after all, were able to overcome their internal contradictions when dealing with the foreign interests.

# AN EYEWITNESS ACCOUNT OF THE SEMANA TRÁGICA, JANUARY 1919

[Juan E. Carulla] heard that they were burning the Jewish quarter, and there I directed my steps.... Only when I reached Viamonte [Street], opposite the School of Medicine, was I able to witness what could be called the first pogrom in Argentina. Piles of books and old furniture were burning in the middle of the street. One could recognize among them chairs, tables, and other domestic chattels. The flames sadly illuminated the night, making prominent with reddish glare the faces of a gesticulating and shaking multitude. I made my way through the crowd and saw fighting in and around buildings nearby. I was told that a Jewish merchant was accused of making communist propaganda. I thought, nevertheless, that other Hebrew homes were suffering from this cruel punishment. There was noise of furniture and cases violently thrown into the street mixed with voices screaming "death to the Jews, death to the maximalists [anarchists]." Every now and then long bearded old men and disheveled women passed by me. I shall never forget the livid face and supplicant look of one of them who was being dragged by a couple of youngsters; or that of a crying child who held fast to the old black coat, already torn, of another of those poor devils. Not without repugnance, I could not but see similar pictures wherever I set my eyes, because the disturbances provoked by the attacks to the Hebrew stores and homes had spread to various blocks around us.

■

*Juan E. Carulla, Al filo del medio siglo (Mirelman 1990, 63)*

## The Beginnings of Economic Nationalism

Following setbacks during World War I, the Argentine economy resumed its vigorous export development in the 1920s. Foreign capital inflows, railway building, immigration, and expansion of the domestic capital market continued their prewar trends. Little new territory was opened up to agricultural exploitation after the war, but rising capital investment in agricultural machinery and a developing regional specialization in breeding and fattening cattle for the *frigoríficos* improved rural productivity. Meatpacking continued to expand in the 1920s with a new influx of investment from the United States. The arrival of the automobile industry added to the vigor of Argentina's light industries, as evidenced by the growth of the shoe and textile Alpargatas plant of the Fraser family, a third-generation Scots-Argentine clan, and the expansion of the S.I.A.M. company owned by Torcuato Di Tella, an immigrant.

By 1930, Argentina had made progress toward alleviating its dependency on foreign sources of energy. The creation of the state-owned oil enterprise Yacimientos Petrolíferos Fiscales (Federal Petroleum Deposits), or YPF, helped the country cut its per capita use of foreign coal by supplying more than half of its petroleum requirement. Argentina's economic growth in the 1920s even outstripped that of many "industrial nations": Its annual growth rate for gross domestic product was 6.7 percent. At the end of the 1920s, Argentines compared themselves favorably to France in terms of material progress.

Economic nationalism meant exercising the political will to absorb and internalize the benefits of economic growth by restricting the influence of foreign interests. In Argentina, it specifically meant the state's steady accretion of power to regulate foreign-owned economic assets such as railways, meatpacking plants, and petroleum companies. All of the foreign enterprises gaining entrée to Argentina would eventually suffer state interference. Economic nationalism also served as the foundation for the state-run industries for which Juan Perón's presidency became known in the 1940s. In Argentina, economic nationalism originated among the landed oligarchy; the Generation of Eighty that had given foreign investors great liberties, after World War I, began to restrict their activities.

The railways serve as a good example. Back in the 1880s and 1890s the landed oligarchy had wanted to build railways to increase the value of their rural properties. This same oligarchy had even supported subsidizing British railroad companies through government borrowing. As soon as the companies were established, however, landowners began to resent paying high freight rates and pressured their friends in government to prevent the British managers from raising prices. Lower railway profits inhibited the companies from investing in sufficient capacity. During harvest time, when the *estancieros* needed to deliver their perishable crops to the port, the railways never had enough rail cars. Bags of wheat would be stacked up along the rail lines, slowly rotting in the sun.

To make matters worse, in the eyes of the landowners, the foreign companies never were able to control their workers. Laborers in the British-owned railways formed the vanguard of the Argentine labor

*A train station along the Western Argentine Railway. There was a boom of railroad building in Argentina between 1880 and 1910.* (Patricia Harris Postcard Collection, Benson Latin American Collection, University of Texas at Austin)

movement. British railway construction in Argentina ended in the mid-1910s, during a critical political period in which the first democratically elected government replaced the conservative regime that had strongly supported the railway companies. While the popular Radical Party was in power, from 1916 to 1930, the workers initiated their most important struggles for the enforcement of work rules. These rules governed work conditions and procedures on the shop floor, protected the workers, and restrained the companies from wielding arbitrary power at the grassroots level. Two unions led the resistance. Founded in 1887, the Locomotive Fraternity (La Fraternidad) constituted the craft union of the engineers and firemen. The nonlocomotive workers did not have their own organization until 1922, when they successfully formed the highly centralized Railway Union (Unión Ferroviaria) after numerous failures over a long period of time. Only the unskilled and itinerant roadbed laborers, most of them criollos, were not organized. The Radical Party governments proved more responsive to workers' demands than their conservative predecessors had been.

The railway unionists seemed to find grievances over which to halt operations in protest, and most vexing to the landed oligarchs, often right at harvest time! For these reasons, the governments of both the Conservative and Radical Parties paid a great deal of attention to how the Britons operated the rail system that they had built and maintained. Politicians who were tough with the foreign companies gained support among the elite. As one deputy said in 1913, "I would not fear the trust if I did not know that the railways, like all industrial trusts and monopolies, exercise a depressive influence, especially upon the morale of a country" (Wright 1974, 107).

There were instances of labor unrest in the Argentine oil fields as well. Oil field workers, most of whom were foreign-born, protested the rising cost of living and the poor housing conditions in Comodoro Rivadavia. Private companies such as Shell and the British railways provided electricity and clean barracks for their workers, but the government did not. In 1917, workers struck the government oil fields for a period of 51 days. Navy personnel operated the oil fields while the government negotiated, but as soon as the workers returned to the job, the police arrested and deported their leaders. In the 1920s, the government continued its tradition of dealing harshly with strikes in the government oil fields. Argentine military administrators did not look kindly upon "unpatriotic" labor organization by Spanish, German, and Romanian workers. The army ended the brief strikes of 1924 and 1927. What explains the government's leniency toward railway workers and its intransigent attitude toward oil workers? The railway workers worked for foreigners.

The same may be said for the British-owned meatpacking plants, the *frigoríficos*. Landowners had transformed their cattle-raising enterprises to satisfy the new demand of the meatpacking industry for fat livestock of good quality. They had rid themselves of the skinny, lanky longhorns of Rosas's time. They put up fences, improved the pastures, built barns and sheds, and hired more peons to tend to the shorthorn stock they imported—at great expense—from England. Moreover, the nation's cattlemen had reorganized the system for the new beef markets. The *estancieros* in the dryer grasslands of Mendoza and Córdoba specialized in breeding the cattle. They shipped the cattle as yearlings—by British rail, no less—to landowners of the humid Pampas of Buenos Aires province, where cattle fattened for market on the dense alfalfa pastures. British meatpackers supported this whole productive industry when they paid good prices for the *estancieros*' cattle. But they did not always pay well.

The British companies, after all, were businesses that served world markets. International prices determined their own profits and what

# A RAILWAY UNION LEADER PROTESTS ACTIONS OF A BRITISH-OWNED RAILWAY, 1929

**T**he Assembly in Mendoza Was Large and Enthusiastic

[Union leader Becerra stated,] "The Directing Commission [of the Mendoza Railway Union] demonstrated that during this year the company had earned three million pesos more than in the previous year despite the fact that the profits of 1928, as this same company has established, were considerable, which is the reason why we cannot comply with the economics that the company desires.

"The company has acquired in Europe a half million square feet of finished wood, pursuing without doubt the aim of favouring the interests of foreign governments while damaging those of our Nation.

"The national government" said Becerra in his talk, "obliges our industrialists to utilize Argentine wood, very excellent and cheaper than the foreign product, with the objective of developing our wealth and benefiting the working class. The company violated these dispositions and has conspired to undermine the stability of our workers.

"We will struggle to defend the interests of the laborers who work in our nation and who, with their intelligence and effort, contribute to the greater prosperity of the country.

"The money that the company obtains in our nation should be invested, at the least, in works that translate into advantages for the Argentine people.

"We will defend nothing less than a just cause," Becerra affirmed in closing. "We do not ask for a raise in salaries without respect and work for the laborers who contribute to the progress of the country, and this is legitimate.

"The times in which we live demand intense action to prevent this company, imitating the other enterprises, from triumphing in its aims against our union, and forcing workers to lose all of their successful conquests.

"Happily, our union has deep roots. ... The capitalist reaction will not be able to bring it down."

■

*(El Obrero Ferroviario [Buenos Aires] March 16, 1929)*

they could afford to pay to the Argentine oligarchs. Any downturn in international demand, as in 1885, 1892, 1902, 1908, and 1914, undermined the capacity of British meatpackers to pay top prices for beef steers. *Estancieros* blamed the foreigners for monopolistic pricing and for remitting "excessive" profits abroad. They demanded government action. The Radical government responded in the 1920s with police confiscations of company account books and with congressional investigations of British meatpacking operations. When some British interests sold out to such American meatpackers as Swift and Armour, Radical politicians doubled their oversight. Many Argentines believed they could deal with the British firms. But the Americans had the reputation of being especially aggressive and monopolistic in their operations. "[W]hen North American capital arrives," the conservative newspaper *La Prensa* editorialized in 1928, "it is said . . . that the country is being invaded" (Wright 1974, 132).

There was a limit to elite pressure on the foreign companies, however, for the latter remained indispensable links to foreign markets for Argentine exports. As a spokesman for the Rural Society said, "We are not even thinking of the possibility that the State, by construction, purchase, or nationalization of freezing establishments should become directly involved in the economic management of the firms, convinced [as we are] of the superiority of individual initiative which, in the case, has shown itself in the admirable development of the meatpacking industry in this country. It could well be . . . that the destruction of wealth brought by official management would exceed the harm which the monopolistic combinations could cause to us rural producers" (Smith 1969; 123). But not all modern production was exported. This is the reason that the nationalists in the liberal age had made more progress in regulating and owning the Argentine petroleum industry.

## Petroleum Nationalism

Argentina was the first country of Latin America to establish a state oil company to compete against foreign capital. It represented the initial phase of the nation's many subsequent forays into state-run enterprise.

Argentina's extraordinary economic growth had made it the leading consumer of petroleum fuels, all of them imported. The British-Dutch Shell company and the Standard Oil Company of New Jersey (later renamed Exxon) established offices in Buenos Aires to import oil products. Petroleum began to compete with imported British coal in fueling the nation's railways and electricity plants, meatpacking factories, and military installations. Then, in 1907, government drillers discovered petroleum deposits in federal lands in the Comodoro Rivadavia region of the Patagonia.

The government prevented the foreign companies from entering the Patagonian oil lands while a political debate ensued about the proper relationship between the Argentine state and the private foreign companies in developing this modern source of fuel. On one side, the older conservatives favored open markets and relatively unrestricted foreign investment. On the other side, the rising nationalist movement made common cause with the Argentina military. In a telling incident, one of the first Argentine military aviators, Colonel Enrique Mosconi, recounted how a Standard Oil clerk had refused to refuel Mosconi's army plane until he was paid in cash.

It seemed to Mosconi and other Argentine officers that foreign interests were controlling the defense of the nation. Radical politicians agreed. The existence of a government oil field at Comodoro Rivadavia, accounting for nearly 80 percent of Argentine production by the end of World War I, meant that the foreign oil companies of the 1920s did not enjoy the monopoly that the British rail operators had enjoyed in the 1890s. The government already had extensive experience with foreign entrepreneurs under its belt and soon adopted a nationalistic stance with new foreign oil interests. For example, one British group attempted to negotiate a joint enterprise with the Argentine government to operate the 12,350-acre national oil reserve at Comodoro Rivadavia. Under the proposal, the state would have received 65 percent of the net profits; however, not only did President Yrigoyen reject the proposal, reported a British agent, but he "also refused to acknowledge receipt of the memorandum or give a reply to it, desiring to avoid leaving any record of our negotiations for political reasons" (Brown 1989, 16). Clearly, politicians were wary of granting territorial concessions of any sort to foreigners. The nationalists reserved special animus for Standard Oil.

The government of President Marcelo T. de Alvear formed the government oil fields into the first Latin American state oil company, known as YPF. Its first director, army aviator Mosconi, now a general, felt a moral and nationalistic obligation to break the sales monopoly of the foreign companies. He built YPF refineries and sales outlets, cut the prices of petroleum products, and used political pressure to prevent the private companies from expanding their production. Mosconi's nationalistic views applied to all foreign companies. But he particularly harbored suspicions of two of the biggest petroleum corporations in the world—Royal Dutch Shell and Standard Oil of New Jersey.

# GENERAL ENRIQUE MOSCONI'S VIEW OF THE FOREIGN OIL COMPANIES, 1928

I have been asked which of the two trusts, the Royal Dutch Shell or the North American Standard Oil, was preferable because of its technical capacity, method of work, and procedures. I replied that both of them responded, as is logical, to the characteristics that distinguish European culture from the North American.

The North American group is less scientific, more audacious and impetuous, disposes of unlimited financial resources, and for that reason develops splendid energy in its enterprises. The company belongs to a people who have enriched themselves extraordinarily in a brief lapse of time [and] has impetuousness, assets, and freedom from bias, if not contempt, for outside sentiments and models of behavior, characteristics that distinguish "the newly rich." [These characteristics] do not acknowledge limitations in the pursuit of [the group's] objectives, and from there are derived the reactions that provoke [the company's] rugged procedures, which begin with personal demonstrations and are extended to nonrecognition and attacks on the sovereignty of other peoples.

The European group is more scientific, has greater respect for tradition than the North American group, and is more enlightened by the world's technical and scientific bibliographies; as it is less wealthy [the Royal Dutch] is more prudent, more methodical in its plans, and more gentle in its labor systems, to the extreme that in certain moments it passes unnoticed. Not the less for this, it succeeds in obtaining with skill and with all possible respect for the means and the environment in which it operates, the goals that it pursues.

When all is said and done, the two groups are equivalent, and the North American firm would compare to a hemp rope, and the European, to a silk one; so that, in response to the question that was made to me, I replied that between the two cords, coarse the one and smooth the other, both would serve to hang us...

■

*(Mosconi 1957, 230–31)*

These British and American companies suffered from the government restrictions of the 1920s. Prompted by Mosconi, President Alvear, in a 1924 decree, converted the Patagonia into a federal oil reserve.

That act restricted all oil companies but YPF from expanding their holdings in the proven fields of the Patagonia. The decree struck Shell harder than Standard Oil, as the latter was actively exploring oil reserves elsewhere, in the province of Salta. There the state government supported the activities of the foreign companies as independent sources of revenues for the local oligarchy. Mosconi engineered a second assault on the international oil companies in 1929. After having expanded the retailing and refining apparatus of YPF, he decreed a national petroleum price cut of 17 percent and established a uniform price throughout the nation. The private companies were forced to follow suit.

Argentina's burgeoning appetite for petroleum, the result of economic expansion and the proliferation of automobiles and trucks, saved the foreign companies from a complete nationalist onslaught. Mosconi's YPF simply could not handle all the demand. Also, the Alvear government favored British oil investments over Standard Oil, a legacy of both of the elite's pro-British sentiments and Standard Oil's notoriety. By 1927, 13 private oil companies were still operating in Argentina. The Royal Dutch Shell company was the country's largest, but Standard Oil was moving up fast.

Shell and Standard Oil dominated the lucrative Buenos Aires market, but the national price equalization established by Mosconi in 1929 rendered marketing in the interior cities unprofitable. Shell and Standard Oil left that market to YPF, which weakened the national company in its struggle with the international firms over the market in the capital. Shell, however, had been shut out of much of Argentina's growing markets for gasoline because it lacked a refinery. In 1927, it finally obtained permission from the Alvear government to build a refinery in Buenos Aires to compete with both YPF and Standard Oil. But the following year, President Yrigoyen returned as president for a second term and rescinded the permit. Instead, he pushed a bill before Congress to nationalize the oil industry completely. Nationalization would have eliminated all private firms from Argentina's production and sales; however, the nationalization bill proved too controversial, and Yrigoyen backed away. Ultimately, Shell received permission to built the refinery in exchange for providing on-the-job training for students of the new Petroleum Institute of the University of Buenos Aires.

President Yrigoyen and the nationalists did not yet possess the capacity for nationalizing the Argentine oil industry. The nation needed the foreign oil companies because YPF could not produce, refine, and market sufficient domestic petroleum to supply the market, and the

| | | | YPF Production as % of Total Consumption |
| Year | Total Argentine Consumption | Imports as % of Consumption | Total Argentine Production | |
|---|---|---|---|---|
| **Argentine Petroleum Consumption, Production, and Imports, 1922–1930 (In thousands of cubic meters)** | | | | |
| 1922 | 1,495 | 70 | 455 | 23 |
| 1923 | 1,720 | 69 | 530 | 24 |
| 1924 | 2,031 | 64 | 741 | 27 |
| 1925 | 1,802 | 47 | 952 | 35 |
| 1926 | 2,348 | 47 | 1,248 | 32 |
| 1927 | 2,772 | 51 | 1,372 | 30 |
| 1928 | 3,142 | 54 | 1,442 | 27 |
| 1929 | 3,393 | 56 | 1,493 | 26 |
| 1930 | 3,431 | 58 | 1,431 | 24 |

Source: Carl E. Solberg in John D. Wirth (1985, 66)

nationalists could not keep out the foreign oil companies while maintaining development of the national economy. A more propitious moment would come later for the nationalist movement.

When that moment arrived, neither Yrigoyen nor the Radicals were around to usher the country into the age of national industrialization and populism. Instead, the Great Depression came first and exposed all the shortcomings of the age of liberalism.

## The Depression and a Military Coup

The depression affected Argentina deeply. The industrial nations suffered a severe fall in investment and production beginning in 1929. They sent less capital abroad and purchased fewer imports from South America. Export prices collapsed in Argentina, and the foreign businesses responded by laying off thousands of workers. The oligarchy had to curb its conspicuous consumption. Even the middle class was sullen and discontented when it became increasingly difficult to pay home mortgages in the suburbs and support sons at university. Those who worked for the government bureaucracy were no better off. Yrigoyen could not sign their pay vouchers for lack of customs revenues.

Everyone blamed the Radicals for the depression. A man who once was perceived as mystical and powerful, Hipólito Yrigoyen suddenly seemed old and remote. His Radical sycophants in power were now seen as corrupt and subservient to the foreign interests, just as the conservatives had been. What was to be done? Yrigoyen had four more years to go in his presidential term, and his popularity and ability to rule had plummeted to impossibly low levels. In moments such as these in the 19th century, invariably a military caudillo had stepped forward to capture the popular imagination and "save the nation." But the army had not been involved in a political transition since the 1880s when it helped launch the liberal age under General Roca and the Generation of Eighty. Now, in 1930, the national army would be involved in undoing liberal rule. Some of the conspiring army officers said they were saving the constitution.

The conspiracy to oust Yrigoyen from power had its origins in 1929 but required a year and a half to collect sufficient support inside and outside the military. General José F. Uriburu represented the hard-liners within the military who resented Yrigoyen's interference in military promotions and his use of the army to intervene in provincial politics to the benefit of Radical Party interests. General Agustín Justo led the more moderate and larger faction of officers, whose penchant for caution dissolved as Yrigoyen grew increasingly senile, autocratic, and obscurantist. This moderate faction of the military proposed "to take by arms the road of the Constitution and from this base to return as soon as possible to normalcy" (Potash 1969, I:44). The deepening depression did not help the president to hold onto his office.

The conspiracy was no secret. Prominent civilians sobered by the economic crisis also questioned Yrigoyen's abilities and called for drastic action against him; the political opposition hoped to profit from the Radical's demise and stood by. Even Yrigoyen's vice president did nothing, as he may have expected to be promoted to the presidency by the military conspirators.

On September 6, 1930, the resolute Uriburu faction took the initiative. Six hundred cadets from the military academy and 900 troops from the Campo de Mayo army base marched down Buenos Aires's Avenida San Martín toward the presidential palace, the Casa Rosada. Yrigoyen fled to La Plata, as large crowds turned out to cheer on the military procession. Ultimately no one in the military or from the civilian sectors

*Large crowds turned out in Buenos Aires in September 1930 to support the coup d'état led by General José Uriburu that ousted President Hipólito Yrigoyen.* (Archivo General de la Nación)

# MILITARY MANIFESTO OF THE COUP OF SEPTEMBER 6, 1930

Responding to the clamor of the people and with the patriotic assistance of the army and navy, we have assumed control of the government of the Nation.

Exponents of order and educated in the respect for the laws and for institutions, we have witnessed in astonishment the process of disorder that the country has suffered in the last few years.

We have waited serenely in the hope of a redeeming reaction, but faced with the anguishing reality that places the country at the brink of chaos and of ruin, we assume, before it, the responsibility of avoiding its definitive collapse.

*Demonstrators cheered the arrival of troops at the National Congress during the coup d'état of September 1930.* (Archivo General de la Nación)

The administrative inertia and corruption, the absence of justice, the anarchy in the universities, the improvisation and mismanagement in economic and financial matters, the decadent favoritism as a bureaucratic system, the politicking as the principal task of government, the destructive and denigrating interference in the army and navy, the international discredit brought about by arrogance in the contempt for law and by the revealing attitudes and expressions of an aggressive uncouthness, the exaltation of the subordinate, the abuse, the outrage, the fraud, the systematic robbery, and the crime are scarcely a pallid reflection of that which the country has had to support.

On appealing to the power to liberate the Nation of this ominous regime, we have been inspired by one high and generous ideal. The facts will demonstrate that we are guided by no other aim than the good of the Nation.

■

*(Sarobe, 1957, 250–51)*

openly opposed the coup, and Yrigoyen was imprisoned briefly before being allowed to return quietly to his home in the capital. Public opinion supported this breach of constitutional rule, and singer Carlos Gardel recorded a congratulatory tango:

> An airplane cut through the gray mist,
> it was the triumphant dawn of the revolution.
> And as of old, in the immortal year 1810,
> the people, radiant with pride, filled the streets.
> Long live our nation! And the glory of being free ...
> Proud to be Argentines
> as we trace our new destiny.

■

(Collier 1986, 116)

Once in power, however, the military government took on a program of its own. The generals announced that they had saved the nation.

Uriburu's audacity and success permitted him to rule the country according to his hard-line philosophy for the following two years. No one perceived it at the time, but this coup marked the end of the liberal age and the tentative beginning of another in which the state would become more interventionist. Politics also were to become less stable, and for the remainder of the 20th century, more generals (14) than civilians (11) would serve as head of state.

# 8

# THE RISE OF POPULISM, 1930–1955

The year 1930 was a turning point. Liberal age leaders cannot be faulted for having produced too little economic growth and expansion. The Generation of Eighty had succeeded in taking advantage of favorable developments in international markets, making good use of foreign talent and capital and liberating the economic potential of the population. At no other time had Argentina experienced such an economic boom. Technological transformations in transportation, food processing, and port facilities had paved the way for phenomenal growth. Agricultural exports had diversified to raise productivity in the countryside, and interior provinces such as Mendoza and Tucumán had become more integrated into the national economy. Even domestic manufacturing had received a boost in productivity. The nation, nonetheless, was unable to overcome other shortcomings in order to carry the economic dynamism beyond the Great Depression.

Neither the Generation of Eighty nor the Radicals had been able to solve the country's social and political problems. On the one hand, the liberals did not address social discrimination, growing caste and class antagonisms, and the increasingly skewed division of income. Nor, on the other hand, did they change the criollo politics they had inherited. Corruption, insider deals, manipulation of the political process, and administrative fiat thrived during the entire liberal age. Also, the *porteño* powerbrokers collected taxes throughout the country but spent most of it in Buenos Aires, a pattern little changed from viceregal times. These shortcomings ultimately diluted the country's economic dynamism, and conditions implied that economic growth had unjustly favored the few over the many. It increased the rancor between the haves and the have-nots.

Just as the entire national fabric became more intricately interwoven and society became urbanized and industrialized, the Argentines could no longer sustain the old dynamism. Fifty years of export-led development came to an end in the depression of world trade. The dynamic agricultural sector stagnated. Politicians blamed the wealthy oligarchs and the foreigners for the nation's problems and turned to national industrialization as the panacea. After 1930, the state bureaucracy grew in order to satisfy the demand of the middle class for jobs worthy of its educational achievement. Workers eager for participation in public affairs exchanged their political loyalties for the security of unionized jobs in state industries. Hoping to satisfy the workers as a method of controlling them, politicians obliged by nationalizing the foreign interests. Thus did the age of populism rise out of the rubble of liberalism.

## The Infamous Decade

The substitution of populism for liberalism took time, for the bankruptcy of liberalism did not manifest itself immediately. General Uriburu turned out to be too rigid and right wing for the tastes of many Argentines. He appointed members of his own hard-line faction as cabinet ministers and ignored the moderates among his fellow officers. The Uriburu administration purged the bureaucracy of Radical officeholders as a method of cutting public expenditures. His government banned the Radicals from participating in politics and annulled provincial elections in which his own handpicked gubernatorial candidates were losing. Uriburu, as acting president, supported paramilitary nationalist groups that spread antiforeign sentiments and attacked labor strikers with clubs. Some of the same middle-class youth who had marched in protest against Yrigoyen just 12 months before returned to the streets to protest the repressive policies of the military government. Thereupon, the moderate faction of the military persuaded Uriburu to hold elections in order to have General Agustín Justo elected.

In 1932, Justo won the presidency, after some voting irregularities, with the support of the anti-Yrigoyen Radicals, the old PAN conservatives, and the Socialists of the city of Buenos Aires. General Justo remained in office for a full six-year presidential term but kept his supporters in the provincial statehouses and the federal congress only through wholesale electoral fraud. It seemed as if the politicians of the 1930s were returning to the days before the 1912 electoral reforms. Not without reason, critics have called this the "infamous decade." Partisans of the Yrigoyen faction of the Radical Party were excluded, although they still represented the largest single political group in the country, and the Radicals could not nominate candidates for about 10 years. They had one great occasion for protest, however: Yrigoyen died in 1933, and multitudes of mourners filled the streets of Buenos Aires to mark his passing. Their public homage to Yrigoyen indicated yet another quick turn in public opinion and a reproach to manipulative politics.

The public demonstration of affection for the former president at his death would be equaled only by two other demonstrations in the 15-year period following the 1930 military intervention. One, which will be discussed later in this chapter, had political significance: the demonstration on October 17, 1945, that saved Juan Perón's political career. The other great public display came in 1936, at the burial of tango singer Carlos Gardel.

In 1938, another election marked by irregularities and fraud brought to power the first civilian president since Yrigoyen. The presidency of the Conservative Party's Roberto M. Ortiz succumbed to rising nationalism, unstable political alliances, and the president's health problems. In addition, the outbreak of World War II in Europe cut off Argentina's agricultural exports to the Continent. As an alternative, the administration sought to reestablish cozy diplomatic and trade relations with Great Britain, but nationalist groups whipped up public opinion against concessions to British meatpackers and railways. When Great Britain imported Argentine meat and cereals but postponed the payment for these items with British gold reserves for the duration of World War II, the South American producers became ever more indignant. They could not even exchange their produce for manufactured goods, as British industry had been converted to producing the machinery of war. Thus, a large Argentine gold reserve was building up in Britain.

A pro-U.S. policy also contained little satisfaction for the nationalists. As the Argentine government equivocated while all other Latin American nations declared war on the Axis in 1942, the United States began criticizing Argentina as being pro-Nazi. Indeed, German doctrine had been a part of every officer's training from the military academy through the general staff college. The generals who served as heads of state in the 1930s proudly stood for photographs in the army dress uniforms that featured the spiked helmets and Prussian capes similar to

# PUBLIC MOURNING IN BUENOS AIRES, 1936

**C**arlos Gardel was born in Toulouse, France, and came as an infant with his mother to Buenos Aires. At a young age, he gained a reputation for a strong voice, flawless interpretation, and a charming personality. After an early flirtation with gauchesque songs, Gardel participated in the tango craze of the 1920s that made Argentina famous in the world of music. Gardel and his guitar accompanists toured Madrid, Barcelona, Paris, and New York between 1928 and 1930. His many recordings and several movies spread his reputation to the rest of the Spanish-speaking world.

This immigrant tango singer was beloved in his adopted city of Buenos Aires for a number of reasons. Though of humble origins, he dressed impeccably and flourished in the café scene and nightlife of the capital. He was *simpático* (charming) and took a lively interest in the Creole culture of Argentina. Moreover, Gardel sang his tangos with the plaintive and ironic cadence that expressed the inner yearnings of a majority of Argentines. One of his famous tangos is "Volver" ("Return"):

> And although I did not wish to return,
> one always returns to one's first love . . .
> To return, with withered brow,
> the snows of time silvering my temples,
> to feel that life is but a puff of wind,
> that twenty years is nothing.

> ■

> (Collier 1986, 239)

Gardel died in a plane crash in June 1935, while on tour in Colombia. The day of his funeral in Buenos Aires, in February 1936, the city came to a halt and *porteños* filled the streets. His tango recordings of longing, nostalgia, and unrequited love continue to appeal to Argentines today. No artist has since replaced Gardel in the hearts of Argentines.

those worn by the kaiser's officers in World War I. But the United States had never been a good trading partner to Argentina. U.S. farm lobbies had always pressured Congress to keep Argentine wheat and meat off the domestic market.

Faced with the sharp decline in exports in the early 1940s, the civilian administration found it difficult to carry out any coherent policies in the polarized political atmosphere. The transition of power was bound to be troublesome as the 1943 presidential elections approached. President Ortiz's health declined, and he resigned in 1940. His vice presidential successor, Ramón S. Castillo, represented the pro-Allies Conservative Party oligarchs of the interior. As president, Castillo was planning for the 1943 election of another interior oligarch—presumably through voter fraud—which appealed neither to the nationalists nor to the Radicals. A profound sense of pessimism afflicted the political climate in 1943, preparing the public for another military intervention.

*The tango singer and actor Carlos Gardel, shown with actress Anita Campbell, was Argentina's most popular cultural figure of the 20th century.* (Archivo General de la Nación)

The June 1943 coup d'état had no particular plan except that its army leaders had decided not to share power after the coup with civilian politicians. Civilians were nevertheless involved. Politicians from both branches of the Radical lineage and even some Conservatives who abhorred their own candidate had held talks with military personnel about a possible ouster. Officers of all political persuasions—some pro-Allies, some pro-Axis, and others nationalist—were mildly supportive. Even the president had heard rumors of military conspiracies but could do little to fend them off. The so-called Grupo de Oficiales Unidos (United Officers' Group), or GOU, a secret lodge of field-grade and company-grade officers, none of them ranking higher than colonel, planned the whole affair. Colonel Juan Domingo Perón, then an anti-communist nationalist with fascist leanings attributable to his work as military attaché in Italy, was among the leaders of the GOU. No single policy issue united this secret clique. Instead they felt contempt for venal civilian politicians, resentment of political interference in military affairs, and fear that political unrest would lead to communist rebellion on the part of the working class.

More than 10,000 troops took part in the Revolution of 1943, a far grander movement in scale than the anti-Yrigoyen affair 13 years before. Cavalry and infantry troops spilled out of their suburban encampments in three great processions that met at the Casa Rosada. No great public celebration attended this coup, nor did any overt opposition. Perón apparently helped pen a manifesto that justified in florid language the coup, denouncing the Castillo government for "venality, fraud, peculation, and corruption"—the usual crimes. It also called for "national sovereignty" in international affairs. "We support our institutions and our laws," the manifesto stated, "persuaded that it is not they [at fault] but men who have been delinquent in their application" (Potash 1969, I:197). Over the first several days of military governance, the GOU eliminated two generals who had claimed the interim presidency and settled on its favorite, General Edelmiro Ferrell.

At the time, few took note of the announcement that President Ferrell had appointed Colonel Perón as head of the Labor Department. Soon Perón would take advantage of Argentina's transition to an industrial society.

## Industrialization and the State

The 1930s witnessed a continuance of the fundamental changes in the economic infrastructure and social makeup peculiar to urban Argentina. The Great Depression proved a second stimulus for the nation's industrialization, the first having been World War I. Once again, consumers could not purchase imported items either because they were not available due to the industrial downturn in Europe or because they lacked sufficient income to purchase foreign "luxuries." The alternative was to buy domestically manufactured goods. In fact, the long-term industrialization of the country permitted industrial production to eclipse gradually agriculture and livestock raising.

National industrialization received a great deal of help from governmental promotion, despite a desperate and successful attempt in 1934 not to lose the British market for agricultural exports. Great Britain had responded to the depression by giving preference to trade within the British Commonwealth of Nations and importing wheat and meat from Canada, New Zealand, and Australia even though the Argentine alternatives were lower priced and of higher quality. The British policy greatly affected Argentina's exports, so President Justo promptly dispatched Julio Roca, Jr., son of the late president, to draw up a new agreement with Great Britain. The Roca-Runciman Treaty preserved British markets for Argentine exports in exchange for Argentina's promise to give preference to British manufactured imports and to pro-

| Growth of Manufacturing within the Argentine Gross Domestic Product (GDP), 1900–1955 (Based on 1935–1939 price weights) | | |
| --- | --- | --- |
| Year | GDP in millions of pesos | Manufacturing |
| 1900 | 2,226 | 244.9 |
| 1905 | 3,248 | 367.0 |
| 1910 | 4,196 | 549.7 |
| 1915 | 4,668 | 485.5 |
| 1920 | 5,424 | 634.6 |
| 1925 | 6,938 | 992.1 |
| 1930 | 8,206 | 1,198.0 |
| 1935 | 8,976 | 1,319.5 |
| 1940 | 10,257 | 1,620.6 |
| 1945 | 11,642 | 2,037.4 |
| 1950 | 14,709 | 2,662.3 |
| 1955 | 16,532 | 2,942.7 |

Source: Laura Randall (1978, 2–3)

tect British companies in the railway and meatpacking industries. In the final analysis, Great Britain was declining in importance to Argentine economic health, and the treaty turned out to be more rhetorical than effective, but it did serve to help the eventual recovery of Argentina's economy from the shock of the Great Depression. Exports soon returned to and then grew beyond levels of the late 1920s.

Government policy in the 1930s, however, tended to favor the development of domestic industry, for such a policy had wide appeal. It swelled the pride of middle-class nationalists and satisfied the working class seeking job opportunities in the modern sector. The government therefore continued with tariff protections and tax rebates for infant industries. The economics ministry went so far as to intervene in foreign exchange transactions in order to facilitate the import of industrial machinery and raw materials, and the government favored industry with credit and financial resources through its control of the banking system. Customs duties on foreign trade still provided the government with 70 percent of its revenues (in the absence of an effective income tax) so that agricultural exports had a tendency to underwrite industrial expansion.

The military also approved of industrialization because it provided the resources for national defense. In fact, the state purposely involved the army and navy in the development process. In the same vein that General Enrique Mosconi had been instrumental in developing the production and refining capacity of the Argentine oil industry, in 1941 the government created Fabricaciones Militares to produce war supplies and develop related industries. Army administrators ran the pig iron factory, the arms industry, and an airplane manufacturing plant. The navy became involved in the shipbuilding industry and explosives. The only problem was that state enterprises such as these never resulted in high productivity levels. From the beginning, they were overstaffed with administrative personnel and political appointees.

Economic nationalism continued its upward trajectory in the 1930s, and the international oil firms remained targets because the nationalists suspected that Standard Oil and Shell meddled in domestic politics and fomented war. Many Radicals, for example, claimed that the oil companies bribed the Argentine military to overthrow President Yrigoyen in 1930. Other nationalists charged the oil companies with promoting the Chaco War of 1932–35 between Bolivia and Paraguay as a method of competing for oil resources. Standard Oil supposedly supported Bolivia while Shell backed Paraguay. (Over time, the Chaco region has not proved productive, however, and no one has been able to prove the conspiracy of the oil companies.) Argentine foreign minister Carlos Saavedra Lamas helped negotiate the peace treaty ending the Chaco War and consequently won the Nobel Peace Prize.

| Growth of the Argentine Oil Industry, 1922–1940 | | | |
|---|---|---|---|
| Year | Total Production | YPF | Private Companies |
| 1922 | 0.5 million cubic meters | 89% | 21% |
| 1925 | 1.0 | 66 | 34 |
| 1930 | 1.4 | 58 | 42 |
| 1935 | 2.3 | 42 | 58 |
| 1940 | 3.3 | 61 | 39 |
| Sources: Solberg (1982, 389) and (1979, 174–75) | | | |

The state-run oil company YPF's production expanded enough during the 1930s to reduce dependency on oil imports. In 1930, Argentina had imported more than 58 percent of its petroleum. Within 10 years, that number had dropped to 37 percent. The combined production of Shell and Standard doubled during the 1930s, but YPF's growth as producer was more spectacular. In 1934, problems arose between YPF and the private companies. Just as YPF attempted to expand its marketing in Buenos Aires, the companies lowered retail prices. There was a nationalist outcry, and critics accused the international trusts of "dumping" in Argentina in order to destroy YPF.

The government in 1936 decreed that YPF henceforward would control all oil imports and distribute them as it saw fit. But President Justo did not wish to antagonize the British, whose market for imported wheat and beef partially supported Argentina's economic recovery. In 1937, the government rescinded its oil import controls. Instead, it reached a market-sharing agreement between YPF, Shell, and Standard Oil that lasted for a decade. The companies conceded half the Buenos Aires market to YPF. The expansion of the oil industry, in the meantime, was stimulating industrial modernization in the country.

As the oil industry expanded, the railways reached a period of stagnation and outright decline in services and profits. Freight transportation in the 1930s fell by one-quarter, and railway profits, by nearly one-half. Burgeoning road construction and growing motor transport diverted cargo and forced the British-owned railways to reduce their own rates. Perhaps the companies could have remained competitive by modernizing operating equipment and adopting new technology, but the British managers completely suspended capital investment in tracks and rolling stock. By 1940, half of their locomotives were more than 50 years old. A British diplomat observed, "The railway authorities are themselves to blame . . . for the state of affairs that has been allowed to arise" (Brown 1997, 138–39).

Rather than improving railway services themselves, the British railway companies resorted to petitioning the Argentine government. They requested protection against the growing motorcar competition, sought tax exemptions, and requested permission to raise freight rates and passenger fares. The government did not always see fit to comply. The British ambassador himself attempted to explain the government's ambivalence: "It must be borne in mind," he said, "that most of the landowners who constitute the real governing classes here, are bound to have small personal grievances [poor services and high freight charges] against the particular railways which they may use" (Brown

# ARGENTINA'S GREATEST INDUSTRIALIST: TORCUATO DI TELLA

**A**rgentina's economic growth unleashed a remarkable spirit of entrepreneurial opportunism among several generations of landowners and manufacturers. Italian-born Torcuato Di Tella (1892–1948) immigrated to Argentina with his parents in 1895. At 18 years of age, Di Tella seized upon a new market opened up by a health ordinance banning the hand-kneading of bread dough. He began the manufacture of a dough mixing machine to be used in bakeries throughout Buenos Aires. Next, Di Tella capitalized on the expanding petroleum industry by manufacturing gasoline pumps and storage tanks, signing contracts with YPF as well as with the Shell company. Financial backing for his metallurgical company came from several banks, especially from German financiers.

In the 1930s, Di Tella's company, S.I.A.M., constructed a new factory in the Buenos Aires industrial suburb of Avellaneda, employing hundreds of skilled Italian workers. They began producing refrigerators, washing machines, and electrical appliances. By 1940, he had manufacturing and sales subsidiaries in Brazil, Uruguay, and Chile. Though not overtly involved in politics, Di Tella allowed his antifascist sentiments to show when he commented on the arrest of Colonel Juan Perón in October 1945: "The democratic struggle of our people has begun and will continue until the last vestige of fascism has been eliminated" (Cochran and Reina 1962, 165). The military government came to an end, but Perón never forgave Di Tella for his precipitous remarks. Later, during Perón's presidency, S.I.A.M. encountered difficulty in getting import licenses and government contracts.

Following Di Tella's death, his metallurgical and engineering company expanded into electric fans, power station generators, and automobiles. The first Di Tella 1500 sedan came off the assembly line in 1960. It was to be the only Argentine automobile competing against domestically assembled foreign models. Taxi drivers particularly favored their spacious interiors and drove many customers along the broad boulevards, invariably playing tango music on the radio.

1997, 141). The government, therefore, resisted the requests of the railway interests—except on labor issues.

The growth of the state's power to regulate the foreign interests, of course, opened up new forms of corruption. The remaining British meatpackers profited due to government favoritism after the Roca-Runciman Treaty was signed in 1934. They benefited from government tax rebates and enjoyed favorable exchange rates that other foreign enterprises did not. The relationship did not result in high profits for landowners, who were averaging less than 4 percent on their meat sales in the 1930s. And a congressional investigation revealed that the British-owned *frigoríficos* also falsified their account books in order to escape additional taxes while the government looked the other way. Why? Because the minister of agriculture, himself an *estanciero*, had nurtured a special relationship with the British owners. They bought all the steers coming from the minister's *estancias* at a price 10 times higher than that paid to other cattlemen. The situation illustrated once again the economic prerogatives of those with political power.

## The Social Question

What was possible politically and socially in the era of Juan Perón was due to Argentina's transformation from a primarily agricultural society to an industrial one. The industrial workforce had expanded from roughly 430,000 in 1935 to more than 1 million in 1946 in a nation of 16 million people. The population of Greater Buenos Aires, home to more than 70 percent of these workers, had grown from 3.4 million to 4.7 million between 1935 and 1947. Migrants from the nation's rural interior settled in the industrial enclaves of Argentina's cities, supplementing southern and eastern European immigrants as a source of cheap, unskilled labor. The newcomers worked in textile and metallurgic factories. Others labored in the booming construction trades or in the immense meatpacking plants that supplied Europe with Argentine beef.

Although the economy had expanded, the workers lived in crowded neighborhoods strained by housing shortages and shrinking real wages. Most industrial laborers suffered arbitrary treatment by employers while the government stood by, unwilling to enforce existing labor codes. Meanwhile, electoral fraud and corruption among civilian politicians denied the working class an effective voice in the political arena.

The depression had terminated the era of massive immigration in Argentina, though some Europeans and Asians found niches in the urban and rural landscape thereafter. The new workers of the 1930s and 1940s were native-born migrants. The first wave of rural migrants consisted of sons and daughters of European immigrants, gringos, who chose to move to the city, particularly Buenos Aires, after a generation of working as tenants on the land. This trend had begun early and continued into the 1930s. Increasingly, however, mixed-race criollos of the interior arrived looking for job opportunities in provincial cities and in the national capital. Di Tella's manufacturing plant experienced a wholesale turnover of its 4,000 laborers from skilled Italians to semi-skilled and unskilled Argentines.

The new influx of Creole workers added to the cultural and racial antagonisms within urban society. As the sons and daughters of gringos moved into the middle class, their factory jobs were taken over by darker-skinned migrants. These newly arrived workers crowded into the unhealthy shantytowns known as *villas miserias* (miserable little towns). On the streets, they were disparagingly called *cabecitas negras* (black-headed ones), for their Indian and African features. The middle class in particular found new reason to worry about the problems of crime and social control in a rapidly changing urban society. They believed the migrants to be undisciplined and given over to deceitful and tricky behavior known as *viveza criolla* (native's deceit).

Tensions also rose in the workplace between foreign and middle-class supervisors and the multicultural workers. The railways were employing nearly 2,000 British citizens at the outbreak of World War II, and the company's policy of placing British subjects in the highest positions necessarily affected the majority of the workers. Of the other railway employees, 49,516 were Argentine, 19,515 were Italian, and 12,062 were Spanish. The tension between British and non-British employees was not the only ongoing ethnic conflict. Animosity also existed between Argentine citizens and immigrants and between the unskilled migrants and the skilled workers.

The directors tried to increase worker productivity in order to compensate for the railways' technological stagnation and increasing decay. To do so, they needed the Conservative's support to annul the work rules sanctioned by the previous Radical governments. One of the military government's first measures in 1930 was to repeal the eight-hour workday that had been legislated just before the coup. A subsequent decree by President Justo allowed the companies to cut wages and violate seniority rules. Bereft of political protection, workers looked to their unions as the principal means of advancing their interests.

By the early 1940s, 20 percent of Argentine workers held union cards, a high level of unionism compared to most Latin American countries. The railroad workers still had the nation's most powerful union, as they made up more than one-third of the union members affiliated with the Confederación General del Trabajo (General Labor

Confederation) or CGT. Communist labor activists had been aggressively organizing the less-skilled workers in labor-intensive industries like meatpacking and construction. They also carried their union drive to the rural sector, particularly to the criollo laborers in the sugar industry of Tucumán province. Communist-led unions accounted for more than 90 percent of new members. Their unions thus received the unfavorable attention of the police, who harassed labor activists, prohibited union meetings, and arrested striking workers. Communist inroads in the labor movement concerned the new military junta.

## The Seventeenth of October

The 1943 military coup initially may have been responding to the growing inflexibility and lack of consensus within the ruling classes, but it ended up profoundly transforming labor's relationship with the state. The military's intervention generated working-class expectations for social reform as well as general anxieties over the neofascist leanings of some of its leaders. Colonel Juan Domingo Perón as labor minister encapsulated both qualities.

During hundreds of meetings with union delegations, visits to factories, and tours of working-class neighborhoods, Colonel Perón addressed the issues confronted by workers on a daily basis. That he often did so in a language particular to Argentina's lower classes enhanced his popular appeal. Recognizing the potential political strength of the working class, Perón used his official position to mediate a growing number of labor conflicts. The Labor Department enforced existing labor legislation and negotiated collective agreements that raised wage scales and improved working conditions. To soften the effects of wartime inflation, the state lowered fares on public transport, froze rents, and set controls on food prices. These reforms quickly garnered the allegiance of most rank-and-file laborers, but many union leaders were suspicious of Perón's larger designs.

The motive behind Perón's concessions to worker demands was to undermine labor's capacity to act autonomously. Colonel Perón as labor minister sought to organize workers into state-controlled unions and to eliminate antimilitarist dissent from the labor movement. The military government escalated the repression of Communist Party members and other labor leaders who refused to collaborate with Colonel Perón. New unions emerged, and established ones were reorganized under the leadership of Peronist sympathizers. Most important, however, Perón's

# LABOR MINISTER JUAN PERÓN ON THE DANGERS OF COMMUNISM, 1944

There are agitators among the masses who provoke disorder, and besides cooperating actively with these there are political instigators who add their purpose to that of the Communists. All these contribute to the real causes of disturbance common among masses. These are the real post-war enemies whom we shall have to face and fight with systems that will have to be as effective and radical as circumstances require. If the struggle is free from disturbance it will be fought quietly; if the struggle is a violent one the means to suppress it will likewise be violent. . . .

The Communist party, hypothetic beneficiary of the campaign against the government, has adopted a more skillful and well known procedure; viz, infiltration among the workers. It acts like a wolf in sheep's clothing. They pretend to support many acts of the government but on the other hand they try to spoil social work. They promote strikes to claim the success of the solutions for themselves and shout, Hail Perón! when they consider it the right moment. In spite of which they try to mix with the masses to cause anarchy among them and see if they can deviate them from their route. They claim to have broken relations with the Democratic Union, yet like the latter they fight against the social justice of the government and against the economic independence of the country. They try to bring about a decrease in the production on land and in factories; to promote increases in the salaries, to encourage petitions declaring unhealthy work conditions; all these in the hope that a moment will come at which the government will have to put an end to these excesses and face the workers. It is evident that they obey foreign orders in an organized sabotage. . . .

We wish to get rid of the extremists from trade union organizations as they have, in our opinion, no matter what extremes they represent, alien ideologies such as we Argentines have never felt an inclination for and because they, with their sentiments of ancestral hatred bring us their problems which neither interest nor concern us.

■

*(Perón 1948, 326–28)*

ability to identify himself with working-class aspirations earned him the loyalty of the blue-collar workers.

As soon as Colonel Perón assumed leadership of the Labor Department, he chose the railway unions as the main beneficiaries of his political projects and granted them major concessions. A new decree resurrected the eight-hour workday and other rules won by labor prior to the depression. The owners gave up their efforts to rationalize the operations of the railways solely by requiring the workers to bear the costs. The Argentine railway workers, with Perón's assistance, had successfully resisted these plans. "Decrees are being issued forcing the railways to grant concessions which we have stood out against in the past," remarked one British manager. "We are in for a spell of strict totalitarian government in this country" (Brown 1997, 146).

Subsequent to becoming labor minister, Perón was appointed vice president of the junta and emerged as the most visible figure in the military government. He also became the target of a growing middle-class opposition movement. By 1945, middle-class demands for replacing the junta with an elected government and supporting the Allied forces in World War II increasingly divided Argentine society. The military junta was notoriously sympathetic to Germany during the war.

As the opposition movement gained momentum, its street demonstrations and rallies implicitly carried an increasingly antilabor content. In September 1945, more than 200,000 Argentines marched from the wealthy Barrio Norte district to central Buenos Aires, demanding a return to constitutional government. Many carried banners denouncing the *chusma*, a pejorative term referring to the working-class "mob." Early in October, a coalition of military officers forced the junta to arrest and imprison Perón, seemingly ending his mercurial rise to prominence.

Argentine workers feared that Perón's arrest would annul the social reforms and reverse the material gains they had just won. Sensing the inevitability of a large-scale popular mobilization, the CGT called a general strike for October 18, but Argentine workers took to the streets a day early in Avellaneda, an industrial suburb just south of Buenos Aires. At the same time, sugar workers were converging on downtown Tucumán; likewise, protesters emerged from suburban industrial zones and congregated in Córdoba, Rosario, and La Plata. They demanded Perón's release and attacked sites symbolic of elite culture: the Jockey Club, university buildings (and students), banks, and newspaper offices.

In Buenos Aires, hundreds of thousands of working-class men, women, and children converged on the Plaza de Mayo, the political hub

*These are among hundreds of thousands of workers who turned out to demonstrate for their hero, Juan Perón, on October 17, 1945.* (Archivo General de la Nación)

of the nation. The military junta debated its options, ultimately deciding to release Perón from custody. The 300,000 workers at the Casa Rosada greeted the news with victorious chants of "Pay-ROHN, Pay-ROHN!" It was nearly midnight when Perón himself climbed to the balcony of the Casa Rosada to address his supporters. The workers' mobilization of October 17, 1945, shook the social and political foundations of the country.

## The Populist Project

Given this opportunity to forge the illusive "national unity," Perón formally gathered together the strands of the political program known as populism under his own term, *justicialismo*. It was to be neither capitalist à la the United States nor communist à la Eastern Europe. *Justicialismo* represented the "third way." Perón himself may have been guided by the fascist and corporatist policies he had encountered as military attaché in Mussolini's Italy, but populism had sturdy roots at home in Argentina and needed little cross-pollination from foreign plants. Indeed, some have viewed Perón's brand of nationalism, developmentalism, militarism, and appeal to the masses as having antecedents in the policies of Juan Manuel de Rosas.

Basically, populism was a multiclass political alliance formed by middle-class and military leadership that incorporated the growing working classes into national affairs. In Argentina, the new populist coalition finally eclipsed the last vestiges of oligarchic power. Perón also combined political strategies that had been developing since War World I. They included economic nationalism, national industrialization, a civil-military alliance, and state negotiation with labor as a method of controlling the masses. Perón received the support of many of his fellow military officers. He pledged that the military would receive an enlarged role in industrialization and that a future Perón presidency would modernize the military and fortify national security. A grateful army promoted Perón to the rank of general just before he resigned his commission in order to run for the presidency.

Perón's project also appealed to the middle class. His support of national industrialization catered to the educated youths who anticipated the managerial and political appointments that would accompany the expansion of the state into economic affairs. His nationalism always hinted strongly of antiforeign sentiment. The antioligarchic rantings of the Peronists may have caused some middle-class misgivings but not much, since historically the elite landowners had always conspired to keep the urban bourgeoisie from power.

Moreover, the oligarchy had traditionally kept the Catholic Church from intervening in political affairs. President Roca had presided over a series of anticlerical laws that removed religious instruction from public schools as early as 1884. Many urbanites of the middle class had rallied to the new Catholic Action organization that had grown in the 1930s as a counterweight to the Conservatives' return to political prominence. When Perón, in 1943, endorsed the military government's reinstatement of Catholic religious instruction in public schools, he gained support among members of Catholic Action. Indeed, Catholic priests attended all Peronist labor rallies up to 1950.

Perón ultimately ran for the presidency as a candidate of the Labor Party. This party had been formed and led by union bosses who came to support Perón during his tenure as labor minister. Workers also viewed Perón as the man who recognized their valuable contributions to industrialization. He praised rather than demeaned their physical labor. Perón had removed the pejorative connotations from the term *los descamisados* (the shirtless ones). Whereas the word was once used dismissively by the well-attired elite and middle class in reference to workers, it now became a symbol of honor and citizenship. As Perón would say as he removed his suitcoat, "Now we are all *descamisados!*"

But it was the United States that added the last brick to the populist edifice Perón was constructing during his first presidential campaign. The new U.S. ambassador to Argentina, Spruille Braden, was disturbed by the military government's tardy and lackadaisical entry into World War II on the side of the Allies. He drew up a "Blue Book" detailing the pro-Nazi activities and sympathies of members of the military government, of which Perón had been the most prominent. The Blue Book hit kiosks around the country just before the February 1946 election. It was intended to undermine the popularity of Perón, but it had the opposite effect. His opponents appeared to be beholden to the foreign interests, while Perón mobilized nationalist sentiment by stating that the 1946 election amounted to a choice between "Perón or Braden." Perón won a five-year presidential term in the most transparent national election since the 1920s. He received 54 percent of the vote.

## Perón in Power

The populist coalition, however, proved to be quite fragile as Perón—and his successors—tried to balance social justice with national industrialization. Perón believed that harmonious class relations would encourage industrial growth. Peronist authorities thus sought to centralize the labor movement in order to limit union autonomy, thereby, they believed, disciplining the rank and file and preventing costly labor disputes. Yet even Perón recognized that "no one can preserve or impose discipline until he has first instituted justice" (Brown 1997, 165).

During the next four years, the Perón regime broadened its control over the structure and leadership of the nation's principal labor federation. The government intervened in the internal affairs of established unions, replacing dissident leaders with Peronist sympathizers. The General Labor Confederation evolved into a virtual appendage of the Peronist government. State-sponsored organizational drives incorporated the nonunionized industrial workforce, and membership of the CGT multiplied. Between 1945 and 1950, the number of unionized wage earners in Argentina jumped from roughly a half million to more than 2 million. Even household servants and bootblacks organized unions within the CGT.

The post–World War II expansion of industrial output provided workers with the bargaining power necessary to realize their aspira-

*A Peronist rally in 1947 marking the two-year anniversary of the October 17, 1945, demonstrations that brought Juan Perón to power.* (Archivo General de la Nación)

tions. European and North American factories had not yet converted to peacetime production, protecting Argentine industry briefly from foreign competition. The Peronists inherited an economy growing at an annual rate of nearly 6 percent between 1945 and 1949. Industrial production rose 25 percent, and employment levels increased 13 percent over the same period. Workers seized on these favorable economic conditions and struck in record numbers from 1946 to 1948. They anticipated Perón's tolerance. The state's gradual elimination of non-Peronist union leaders did not end blue-collar militancy, and the CGT's lack of success in stifling labor strikes in the meatpacking and the metal trades suggested that these militants still could sustain a degree of union autonomy.

The rank and file emerged victorious during these early years of the Perón government. Between 1945 and 1948, real wages for skilled and unskilled workers rose 22 and 30 percent, respectively. More important, the portion of national income earned by workers grew from 40 to 50 percent. The majority of industrial laborers enjoyed medical compensation, maternity leave, paid vacations, and protection from arbitrary dismissal. Their attachment to Perón cannot be measured completely in material benefits, however; working-class loyalty also reflected the workers' gratitude for "the dignity ... that the oligarchy always denied us," as one labor leader observed (Brown 1997, 172).

The railway nationalization has to be considered the high point of the Perón regime because it satisfied nearly everyone in the populist alliance—workers, nationalists, military officers, and the middle class. The new president was not one to pass up a symbolic act, so in 1948, he exchanged 2.5 billion gold pesos worth of Argentine beef and gold reserves for 16,000 miles of British-owned railways. Whether people knew the railways were run down, the public responded enthusiastically to Perón's nationalistic act. However, once the British-owned railways became Argentine property, problems arose. The workers criticized the new railway administration, which was filled with middle-class appointees with no expertise in industrial management, and they particularly resented the imposition of new union leaders "qualified only by their influence in a certain political sector [and] completely ignorant of matters related to the railroad industry" (Brown 1997, 176). The politicians sought to streamline railway operations at labor's expense. To cut operating costs, the government kept most of its newly hired political appointees but laid off some 17,000 workers. In late 1950, dissident leaders organized hundreds of wildcat strikes and paralyzed the industry. Ultimately, Perón gave in to the strikers, giving them a pay raise and abandoning efforts to reduce the number of personnel.

Despite these problems, the populists could still mobilize popular support at election time. The creation of a network of Peronist political clubs in working-class neighborhoods helped, as did the government's 1947 decision to grant women the right to vote. Perhaps due to the prominent political role of Perón's wife, Eva Duarte de Perón (popularly called Evita), women proved to be more ardent supporters of Perón than men. In late 1951, they helped elect Perón for a second presidential term, this time giving him 64 percent of the vote. Within a year, a full-blown recession would threaten the cohesion of the populist alliance.

Part of the economic problem could be traced to rising state deficits, for the Peronists were discovering that inflation had become the Achilles' heel of populism. To satisfy and balance his middle-class and labor constituencies, Perón's government engaged in deficit spending. Management overstaffing and production inefficiencies increased expenditures in the outmoded railway system as well as other state companies in petroleum, electricity, telephones, and meatpacking. With bureaucratic sleight of hand, therefore, government accountants carried each year's growing deficits over into next year's ledgers.

The Peronists further contributed to their own deficits by democratizing corruption, heretofore the prerogative of the privileged few. Perón's election marked the first time that labor leaders and party hacks of working-class background received invitations to the political banquet. Perón's public housing initiatives serve as a case in point. He launched a much-needed program to construct modest homes that workers could purchase on easy terms. But Peronist stalwarts, obedient labor bosses, and bureaucratic insiders scrambled to get their hands on as many public housing units as possible.

Moreover, the usual insider deals and corrupt practices continued, though the benefactors changed and the opportunities multiplied geometrically as the state took over industry after industry. Many people cite Eva Perón's charity foundation as the prime example of Peronist corruption. True, Evita and her staff practically extorted millions of pesos from businesses and labor unions and whimsically distributed largess to the needy with no accounting whatsoever, but these were not public monies. More pernicious were the increasing numbers of political appointees to the bloated bureaucracy and the state industries who supplemented their embarrassingly low public salaries with shady deals. One car dealer used his political contacts to obtain licenses to import new automobiles duty-free. He then sold half of his yearly stock of 22,000 cars at cost to politicians, each of whom could resell the autos at high market prices. The Peróns even bought cars from him. The government, however, lost tariff revenues with which to pay down the rising deficit.

Meanwhile, the Peronists were presiding over the unraveling of the populist alliance. Foodstuff production declined as the government held down the prices to urban workers and the middle class. Shortages of basic commodities soon became evident, and Perón's government had to ban sales of beef on certain "meatless days"—this in Argentina! Prices on unregulated commodities rose, industry turned out shoddy and expensive consumer items, and the middle class and workers began to feel the loss of their real wages. This was the inflationary cost of populism. Welfare and job security for union workers and government jobs for the expanding middle class could not be sustained despite the transfer of unearned wealth from the countryside to the city.

The decline in traditional agricultural exports after the close of World War II accounted for much of the 1952 recession as well.

Increased internal consumption and severe droughts in 1951 and 1952 caused agricultural exports to fall drastically. The depletion of foreign exchange undermined Argentina's capacity to import the capital goods and raw materials it needed for manufacturing. Inflation rose from 4 percent to 40 percent in just five years and was eroding workers' earnings. In 1952, average real wages for unskilled workers in Buenos Aires stood 21 percent below the 1949 average.

The Perón regime responded to the crisis with an austerity program: It froze workers' wages. In the long run, the austerity program proved effective, because inflation in 1954 returned to the single digits. Yet the economic crisis dealt a harsh blow to labor. An estimated 40,000 textile workers and 25,000 meat workers were laid off in 1952 The state also abandoned its commitment to mediating strikes to the benefit of labor. Perón declared that workers should raise their own standards of living through increased productivity. "Today, as always," he said, "our slogan is Produce! Produce! Produce!"

*Striking railway workers in 1953. A faltering economy brought hardship to many working-class Argentineans, who often responded with strikes and demonstrations.* (Archivo General de la Nación)

# THE PERONIST SAINT: EVA DUARTE DE PERÓN

**E**vita Duarte's meteoric rise in the Peronist movement has resulted in much controversy and myth about her role in Argentine history. She was born in a small Pampean town in the 1920s, the product of a relationship between her single mother and a married man of "the respectable classes." She got ahead in the only way available for a beautiful young woman of her social circumstances. Arriving with a male consort in Buenos Aires in 1935, she launched a career in acting. Apparently she found advancement in the radio industry by exploiting her relationships with powerful men. By 1944, Evita had her own radio talk show and became courtesan to officers in the new military government. Several film appearances yielded little critical acclaim. Then Evita met Colonel Juan Domingo Perón at a fund-raising benefit, and they married shortly before his presidential inauguration.

Due to her "common origins," the respectable middle class shunned the new first lady. The elite loathed and ridiculed her, even as she began to dress like them in expensive designer gowns and fur coats. But the energetic Evita embraced the mission to which her husband had assigned her: to serve as a bridge between President Perón and his working-class followers. Evita immediately became a patroness of the *descamisados* and *cabecitas negras,* creating a charity foundation to provide orphanages, medical clinics, and nursing homes for the poor. In her speeches, she extolled the virtues of Juan Perón and subordinated herself to his guidance. Evita championed the new Peronist law providing women's suffrage in 1947 and formed the feminist wing of the Justicialista Party. More women served in Congress during the second presidential term of Perón than at any time since then.

Evita's health deteriorated in the early 1950s, and she died from cancer shortly after Perón's second presidential inauguration. The public mourning and funeral cortège surpassed even those of President Hipólito Yrigoyen and Carlos Gardel. In death as in life, Evita remained controversial. The pope rebuffed an effort to have her declared a saint in recognition of her work for the poor.

Eva Perón's death in 1952 had also cast a shadow over the Peronist movement. Evita symbolized the Perón regime's commitment to championing the rights of laborers and the poor. Although myth has obscured her historical role, individual workers perceived Evita as the official most sympathetic toward the working class. Her passing coincided with the government's harsh response to popular protest.

The recession exposed the Perón government's long-term inability to sustain manufacturing growth while promoting working-class interests. Late 1954 witnessed a resurgence of civil unrest. University students and the church emerged as the focal points of middle-class opposition to the Peronist regime. In October, a university strike spread nationwide and hundreds of students faced arrest. It was also a time of rising tensions between the church and the state.

The Catholic clergy had initially supported Perón in 1946 when he reestablished religious instruction in the public schools; however, the church hierarchy withdrew its backing in the early 1950s. When Catholic Action started proselytizing within the working-class barrios, Perón accused the church of attempting to undermine Peronist labor unions. The government ended subsidies to Catholic schools, and the state-controlled press became vehemently anticlerical. Then authorities began arresting priests and closing churches, as large numbers of middle-class Catholics joined the students in opposition.

Events began to happen in quick succession. In May 1955, the government proposed a constitutional amendment legally separating the church and the state. In June, 100,000 middle-class protesters marched through the streets of downtown Buenos Aires. Several days later, thousands of Peronist workers gathered for a counterdemonstration in the Plaza de Mayo, the city's main square. Rebel officers mutinied against Perón and sent warplanes to bomb and strafe Peronist workers in the open plaza, killing 156 people and injuring hundreds more. Loyal officers ultimately thwarted the coup. In the aftermath, however, crowds of Peronists sacked several churches near the plaza.

Within several weeks, General Eduardo Lonardi launched the Revolución Libertadora, a military coup intended to conclude the Peronist regime's "destruction of the culture and economy [of Argentina]" (Verbitsky 1987, 61). In September, Perón resigned and fled to Paraguay.

Once again, the military had intervened in a national political and social crisis. Perhaps a strict constitutionalist might not fault the officer corps in 1943 for replacing one corrupt and unrepresentative government with an equally unrepresentative military one. Twice now in the 20th century, however, the military had ousted heads of state (Yrigoyen and Perón) who had been popularly elected in transparent and free electoral contests—all in the name of "saving the nation." In the military's view, civilian politicians had once again endangered the nation by provoking a rebellion among the middle class.

*Demonstrators in the Plaza de Mayo supporting the seizure of power by General Lonardi in what they called the "Liberating Revolution"* (Archivo General de la Nación)

His opponents had branded Perón as fascist and autocratic. It is true that he revised the constitution to permit his reelection and jailed people without charges, one of whom was Victoria Ocampo, one of Latin Americas' greatest women of letters. Perón also attempted to manipulate public opinion, expropriated anti-Peronist news media, indulged in demagogic rhetoric, passed a woman's suffrage law in an effort to double his electoral majority, and used the police to repress strikes and control middle-class protests. But Perón's brand of populism did not confiscate the property of the oligarchs. He did not defraud the electorate. He did not socialize the means of production, and he did not murder sizable numbers of his opponents.

It is ironic that the dominant modernization theory of the time equated industrialization and growth of the educated middle class with the development of democracy. If the theory had been accurate, Argentina would have enjoyed the most democratic government in South America. Instead, massive civil disobedience on the part of the middle classes had preceded military coups d'etat, and the middle class

215

# PROCLAMATION OF GENERAL EDUARDO LONARDI'S REVOLUCIÓN LIBERTADORA, 1955

To the Argentine people and the soldiers of the fatherland:

In my role as chief of the revolution, I turn to the people and especially to my comrades in all the armed forces, in order to request your collaboration in our movement.

The navy, the air force, and the army of the fatherland are abandoning its bases and barracks once again in order to intervene in the civic life of the nation. We do it impelled by the imperative of love of liberty and of the honor of a subjugated people, who wish to live in accord with their traditions and who are not resigned to indefinitely serve the caprice of a dictator who abuses the power of the government to humiliate his fellow citizens.

Under the pretext of underwriting the postulates of social justice that nobody disputes, because in the present hour it is the common desire of all Argentines, he has annihilated the rights and guarantees of the constitution and has substituted the juridical order with his subjugating and despotic will. This ignoble oppression only has served to bring out the apogee of corruption and the destruction of culture and the economy, of all that which is fearful symbol, the burning of the churches and of the sacrosanct archives of the Fatherland, the enslavement of the justices, the reduction of the university to dishonest bureaucracy, and the tragic crucifixion that compromises the future of the republic with the handing over of its sources of wealth.

. . . We say it simply, with full and reflective deliberation. The sword that we have unsheathed in order to defend the standard of the nation will not fulfill its duty without honor. Life without honor does not interest us, and we pledge our actions to the future of our children and to the dignity of our families.

■

*"Primer mensaje del general Eduardo Lonardi," September 17, 1955*
*(Verbitsky 1987, 60–62)*

# VICTORIA OCAMPO IN A PERONIST JAIL, 1953

Though she remained apolitical throughout her long career, Victoria Ocampo still ended up in a Peronist jail. Ocampo was born to a distinguished family of the old oligarchy, grew up in a sumptuous home on the banks of the Río de la Plata north of the capital, and spent summer months at her family's *estancias* and vacation homes. She and her parents frequently traveled abroad. Young Victoria always maintained literary aspirations and wrote poetry and essays. She avidly read European and Latin American literature. An unhappy marriage to a domineering husband—hardly a rarity in the male-dominated milieu of the day—ended in legal separation.

Personally wealthy, Ocampo indulged herself in an independent lifestyle beyond the means of the vast majority of Argentine women. She founded the literary review *Sur* in 1922 and associated with Albert Camus, Aldous Huxley, Jorge Luis Borges, and other literary figures of her time. Ocampo also advocated the rights of women. When Juan and Evita Perón succeeded in passage of the law granting women the right to vote, however, Ocampo declined to support them. She equated Peronism with fascism and told her friends that she could not condone the kind of Argentine feminism that Peronistas had in mind. Her private contempt of the Peróns landed Ocampo in jail shortly after an attempted assassination of the president in 1953. She remained imprisoned for 26 days until a personal plea by the Chilean poetess and Nobel laureate Gabriela Mistral motivated Perón to release Ocampo.

The experience of imprisonment did not dampen Ocampo's zeal for feminist causes. "Friday, I am going to talk on television about my jail experience and about the changes that I believe should be made in the women's prison," she confided to Mistral following Perón's ouster. "All these things concern me and keep me busy, as you can imagine" (Meyer 1990, 167). Ocampo died in 1979.

had joined the oligarchy in denouncing elections if they portended working-class victories. Nonetheless, Peronism would remain—at the grass-roots level—a firm source of social identity and the basis of a working-class culture of resistance well after Perón's fall in 1955. The new military government would discover that soon enough.

# 9

# THE FAILURE OF
# DE-PERONIZATION,
# 1955–1983

The generals and admirals who overthrew Juan Perón in September 1955 presided over a period of political instability and indecision. Not having to deal with opposition in Congress or with a powerful judiciary (Argentine courts were traditionally weak), the general officers should have been able to formulate a unified policy, but this was not the case. They disagreed among themselves over whether Peronism should be repressed, how to deal with labor, and how much power to share with civilian politicians who collaborated with them. The first head of the military government, General Eduardo Lonardi, for example, welcomed the leaders of the Radical Party and the Socialist Party to the Casa Rosada in a grand display of post-Perón political unity. He then tried to come to an accommodation with labor union leaders in order to win their support for the new regime. Some labor leaders welcomed the attention, but the rank and file still resorted to strikes in order to recapture wages lost in the economic decline. The continued labor agitation goaded the hard-liners among the officer corps. They mounted a movement within the military to displace Lonardi in favor of General Pedro E. Aramburu.

## Military Government and De-Peronization

General Aramburu became president in November 1955, and under his leadership, the government cracked down on the Peronists. He purged the government of party supporters, intervened in the unions, and jailed recalcitrant union bosses and striking workers. The new hard-line military government then tried to impose industrial rationalization on the shop floor and dismissed thousands of Peronist activists from the confederated CGT unions. Hundreds of military officers, who were deemed to have been too compliant during Perón's presidency, received early retirement. In an effort to discredit the exiled Perón, the government displayed the luxuries that Juan and Evita had collected during their time in power—designer wardrobes, fur coats, expensive automobiles and motor scooters, and Evita's jewelry collection. They spread rumors that the Peróns had diverted millions of dollars into Swiss bank accounts.

Aramburu's zeal to de-Peronize Argentina extended to the dead as well. He ordered a military subordinate to remove the embalmed body of Evita Perón from its resting place at CGT headquarters and make it disappear. For the next 17 years, no one knew what had happened to Evita's corpse. The general intended to deny the Peronist faithful their potent symbol c f resistance, but little did he know that this gesture was to make him a target of a future generation of Peronists.

The generals under Aramburu's leadership did not plan to control government indefinitely, merely to manage the return of power to "acceptable" civilian politicians. The strategies paralleled those of the 1930s when the Radicals (then the largest party in the country) were persecuted; now, in the late 1950s, the military excluded the Peronists from the political arena. In the elections of 1958, no Peronists could present themselves for office. This exclusion should have benefited the Radical Party presidential candidate; however, the second-largest political group in the country had just split into two groups. One of these factions, led by candidate Arturo Frondizi, had made a secret pact with the exiled Juan Perón, living in Venezuela at the time, to increase its chances of winning. Frondizi bargained for Peronist votes in the presidential election in exchange for permitting Peronist candidates to run in subsequent congressional and gubernatorial contests. Frondizi defeated the candidate of the rival faction of the Radical Party and assumed the presidency under a cloud of uncertainty.

Frondizi ruled for three and one-half years of his five-year term. The military generals stood behind him suspiciously, watching his every decision for betrayal of the "secret" deal about which they had heard rumors. Frondizi made a triumphant state visit to meet President John F. Kennedy in Washington, D.C., and returned with promises of economic assistance under the new Alliance for Progress program; however, the generals became alarmed when Frondizi met with the expatriate revolutionary Ernesto "Che" Guevara. The Radical president went ahead, in compliance with his agreement with Perón, and allowed Peronist candidates to participate in the gubernatorial elections of

# CHE GUEVARA RETURNS TO ARGENTINA, 1961

**E**rnesto Guevara grew up in a well-to-do if slightly decadent family in Córdoba province. His playmates later told of a childhood filled with defiant nonconformism that only privilege could support but also one plagued by debilitating asthma. Young Guevara took little direct interest in politics, except that he approved of Juan Perón's nationalistic stance against the foreign interests. He passed his medical exams in 1953 and took off on a motorcycle trip through Latin America with a friend. Guevara's travel experiences stimulated his political views, as he witnessed the CIA-assisted military counterrevolution of 1954 in Guatemala.

He next traveled to Mexico City, where he met the Cuban lawyer and political dissident Fidel Castro. When Perón fell from power in September 1955, Guevara was training with the Cuban revolutionaries and answering to "Che," the nickname his Cuban comrades used with him. Landing in the mountains of Cuba, Guevara gained legendary status as a guerrilla fighter. When Castro came to power, Guevara proved to be an effective spokesman for the revolution.

Under the circumstances, Argentine president Arturo Frondizi could not pass up the opportunity to interview Guevara, who had just arrived in Uruguay to attend an inter-American diplomatic conference. Guevara secretly entered Argentina on August 19, 1961, drove to the Casa Rosada in the presidential limousine, dined with the president, rode secretly through the streets of Buenos Aires to visit an ailing aunt, and departed before nightfall. Guevara never again set foot in his native country.

That evening, a bomb blew out the front door of the apartment house in which one of Guevara's uncles lived. The man told the press that unfortunately, he had not seen his famous nephew. "I'm going out to dinner now with some friends," he added, "if a bomb hasn't been placed under the hood of my car" (Anderson 1997, 521).

1961. Peronist victories in 10 of 14 provincial elections proved too much for the military. The generals annulled the elections, arrested Frondizi, and replaced him with a civilian caretaker.

At this point, factionalism within the military came to a head. At issue was the military's attitude toward the popular forces underlying

Peronism. One faction of the military, called the Azules (blues), recommended a return to the conciliatory approach. They proposed to negotiate the reentry of the "moderate" labor union leaders into the public arena as allies of the military, a kind of Peronism without Perón. The Colorados, or "crimson" faction, adamantly opposed this strategy and suggested that the military assume formal control of the government, if necessary, to crush the Peronists and their labor movement once and for all.

The weak interim president could only stand by helplessly as the two military factions began to fight. The Azules and Colorados skirmished in La Plata and at several army and navy installations around the nation's capital. The tank forces of the Azules prevailed. They purged the officer corps once again by retiring the hard-liners, but not without causing rancor among the surviving officers. The policy of the Azules failed anyway, as workers refused any collaboration without Perón himself, as we will see below.

A new election in 1963 offered little escape from the cycle of instability. The military prevented Frondizi, Perón, or a Peronist stand-in from running, and the winning candidate, Arturo Illia, became president on the basis of having received just one-quarter of the vote. Illia came from the opposite Radical Party faction from Frondizi, which did not prepare him for dealing with the unstable political atmosphere. Controlling government deficits and inflation demanded strong political will, but Illia's decision to devaluate the peso had the immediate effect of further reducing the earnings of wageworkers. The unions reacted with massive strikes in late 1964. Then many Peronist congressional candidates avoided the military proscriptions in the 1965 elections, won seats in the Congress, and attacked all the legislative proposals of President Illia.

Despite their earlier reluctance, the Azules decided to take complete control of government. The Azules' military leader—the mustached, polo-playing tank commander General Juan Carlos Onganía—sent a group of officers to "invite" President Illia to vacate the office of the presidency so as to avoid acts of violence. "What violence are you talking about?" Illia is reported to have replied, "Violence has been unleashed by you in the Republic. . . . You have nothing in common with the Army of San Martín and Belgrano; you have caused great harm to our country and will continue to do so by such behavior" (Potash 1996, III: 192). The officers' answer was apparently persuasive, and Illia walked out of the Casa Rosada to return to his life as a country doctor in Córdoba. The generals had come to the conclusion that only a military government without resorting to the constitutional pretense of civilian rule could complete the de-Peronization of Argentina. But General Onganía confronted several difficult national problems. The inflation that had begun under Perón's rule was now endemic, and the worsening political and economic situation was stirring up serious resistance in the working class.

## An Economy of Dynamic Stagnation

Two contradictory phenomena had been occurring since the 1930s, the combination of which ultimately undermined the continued industrialism of the 1960s. On the one hand, the state sector of the economy was burgeoning, as successive governments had taken strong measures to stimulate national industry, even to the point of taking over much of the economic infrastructure, such as petroleum, railways, electricity, telephones, and eventually meatpacking. But as the size and importance of the state-run economy increased, the political environment grew steadily more unstable. Between 1930 and 1983, only three heads of state actually completed their terms of office. Each president averaged just two years in power. The typical tenure of the economics minister was even briefer: Each president replaced his minister for economic affairs on average every year.

All the political upheaval naturally resulted in the opposite of General Roca's old dictum of rule: Roca's prescription in 1880 had been "peace and administration," but the chaos only produced much politics and little administration. With so slender a hold on power, each regime tended to dispense as much patronage as possible to its partisans so that the expansion of the federal bureaucracy often exceeded that of the gross domestic product. Politicians overstaffed the state-owned companies with white-collar workers and pencil pushers, few of whom had any expertise in or training for the industry they were to manage. Favored labor leaders also added redundant workers to secure, high-paying jobs. These public entities began to bubble with inefficiency, cost overruns, and equipment failures. Instead of producing profits to invest in new equipment and technology, the state industries fell into deficit spending just to maintain services. Customers waited up to two years for the state telephone company to install a new line, and calls were occasionally misrouted. The lack of oversight permitted corruption to flourish in these industries as well.

The result was inflation. Argentina's peso had begun to lose value even before Perón's first administration. The 1948 and 1952 economic

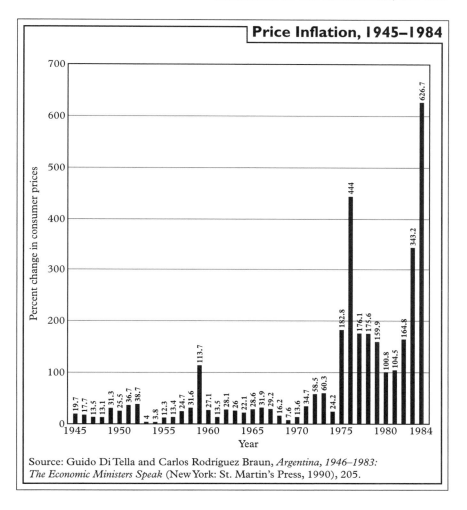

## Price Inflation, 1945–1984

Source: Guido Di Tella and Carlos Rodríguez Braun, *Argentina, 1946–1983: The Economic Ministers Speak* (New York: St. Martin's Press, 1990), 205.

slumps further eroded the value of the peso, and workers and the salaried middle class had to pay more for consumer items. As a populist, Perón froze prices of basic items of popular consumption, such as bread and beef, which won him the gratitude of urban workers but discouraged the landowners from planting more wheat and raising more livestock. Inflation became endemic as economic ministers floundered in search of the least objectionable policy to correct the problem. To hold the value of the peso meant that urban consumers could still buy imported goods and domestic products at reasonable prices, but Argentine exports eventually became overpriced, and foreign consumers switched over to Australian wheat and American beef. If the

223

economics minister had the temerity to devalue the peso, agricultural exports again became competitive, but urbanites suffered from sharply rising prices for consumer items. The rate of inflation brought intense pressure on the peso's value every two years or so, forcing the government to make another unpopular no-win economic decision. The two-year cycle also coincided with the life expectancy of an Argentine presidency.

The military and civilian governments that followed the revolution of 1955 essentially carried on with Perón's populist economic policies. Army and navy officers spent part of their careers in the state industries, some of which were traditionally run by a general or an admiral. All of them deemed industrialization to be a matter of high national security. Neither military nor civilian presidents ever seriously considered cutting back the public sector, for their tenuous holds on power could not withstand the outcry of bureaucrats and workers who would lose their jobs. Even in the private sector, the industrialists depended on political favoritism to protect market monopolies and obtain licenses to import technology and exchange currencies. When a government appeared weak, the domestic investors sought safety by cutting back on investments and sending the money out of the country. When the occupant of the Casa Rosada appeared powerful, the private entrepreneurs repatriated their savings and invested in domestic expansion.

Foreign investment, however, flourished in this unstable milieu, at the expense of domestic private industrialists. Multinational corporations had the advantage of sources of capital independent of government favoritism. They generated their own technologies in their home economies and benefited from their prior experience in efficiently manufacturing the latest consumer products. International Business Machines (IBM), Palmolive, DuPont, and Monsanto all expanded in Argentina in the 1950s and 1960s, while Argentine companies sold out to the multinationals. Overseas investors bought nearly 40 local businesses in banking, cigarette manufacturing, and chemicals between 1962 and 1968.

As in the days of British investment, the new companies brought in their own non-Argentine top managers. This time, however, middle management, supervisors, and manual workers were mostly Argentines, and the presence of foreigners in the new industries was not so prevalent as in the liberal age. It was simply recognized as good business for the multinational companies to train managers and workers from the ample pool of educated Argentines, because it saved on the high wages that foreigners demanded. Eventually, the head manager at companies such as IBM would be Argentine, although he was subject to the frequent visits of executive consultants from company headquarters abroad.

American investments in Argentina grew appreciably. By 1969, U.S. capitalists contributed nearly $790 million to industrial ventures, up from $230 million at the time of Perón's fall. American companies controlled nearly half of all foreign capital coming into the country. In 1972, U.S. investments totaled $1.8 billion.

The automobile industry expanded in Argentina during this time, but it was 23 foreign car companies rather than domestic car manufacturers (with the exception of S.I.A.M.) that set up new assembly lines. (Nine of the 23 went out of business in the next 10 years, and S.I.A.M. sold its auto plant in 1964.) In an effort to develop the interior provinces, government policy chose Córdoba as the site of the new automobile plants. Fiat and Kaiser (later acquired by Renault) established factories in the province. In the 1960s, several other U.S. and European car companies set up assembly plants in Buenos Aires. Ford, Chrysler, General Motors, Citroën, and Mercedes-Benz all contributed to putting Argentines on the road to urban traffic jams and air pollution. (Some wags began calling the capital "Malos Aires"[Bad Airs].)

Petroleum was the one exception to the success story of foreign investment in Argentina. Politicians had been wary of the multinational oil companies since the days of General Mosconi. The state-owned YPF expanded with government support, but the rapid growth of the numbers of trucks, buses, and cars in the country taxed the capacity of YPF to keep up with the demand for gasoline. Argentine petroleum production fell below demand and acted as a drag on the economy. To stimulate economic recovery, Perón in 1954 and Frondizi again in 1962 proposed to bring in Standard Oil under contract with YPF to develop new oil fields in Patagonia. Many nationalists in the country were struck dumb by the news. Had not both Perón and Frondizi been critical of the foreign interests? Perón himself had nationalized the British railways; Frondizi had honed his political reputation on criticism of Perón's 1954 flirtation with the big oil companies. Both presidents had to back off their petroleum proposals because public opinion vehemently disapproved of any new production concession to the foreign oil companies. Standard Oil remained in Argentina but mainly as an importer and refiner.

The economy exhibited stop-and-go patterns. It was unable to sustain growth for more than two or three years at a time, as investors tended to follow the shifting political winds that determined marked

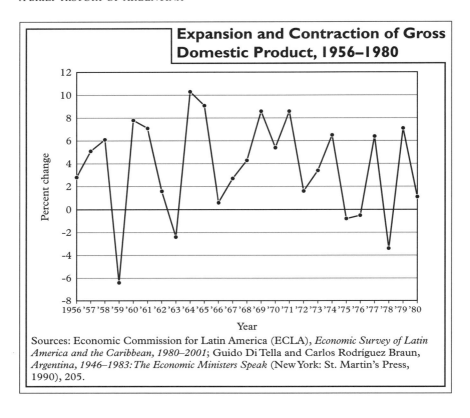

## Expansion and Contraction of Gross Domestic Product, 1956–1980

Sources: Economic Commission for Latin America (ECLA), *Economic Survey of Latin America and the Caribbean, 1980–2001*; Guido Di Tella and Carlos Rodríguez Braun, *Argentina, 1946–1983: The Economic Ministers Speak* (New York: St. Martin's Press, 1990), 205.

opportunities. In one year, the gross domestic product would expand by as much as 4 or 5 percent, and the very next year the economy would contract. Economic downturns and regime changes were synonymous, and it became difficult for analysts to measure whether governments fell because of economic failure or the economy fell because of the government's failure. But this was the sort of perverse scenario Argentine pundits liked. One of them called this "the economy of dynamic stagnation," and this term, in all its simplicity, spoke volumes about what Argentina had become in the 1960s.

## Resistance of the Peronist Workers

The majority of workers in the country had become orphans, so to speak, when the military coup forced Perón into exile in 1955. True, they declined to take up arms for "the old man" or even to take to the streets as in 1945, but they remained *peronistas* in their hearts. The loyalties of the old workers would not have sufficed to bring back Perón, for the older workers were being replaced on the shop floors by newcomers. The rural-urban migration patterns continued in the 1950s and 1960s. Another million or so migrants came to Buenos Aires seeking industrial jobs.

Immigration, once again, played an important role in the making of the urban working class of Argentina. This time, in a new wrinkle that held through the rest of the century, the immigrants came not from Europe but from neighboring Latin American countries. Paraguay and Bolivia had always provided seasonal labor for the sugar industries of Tucumán and Salta, and the Mapuche of southern Chile crossed the Andes to harvest grapes in Mendoza and shear the sheep of Patagonia. Now these neighbors were settling down permanently in Argentina, the young *marochas* (dark-skinned women) taking up positions as maids in middle-class households and the men in factories. It was as if the criollos were reclaiming Argentina.

These new immigrants and migrants from rural Argentina, who settled in the working-class neighborhoods south of Buenos Aires, in addition to the children of Peronist workers of the 1940s, were to burnish Perón's image. The military, too, inadvertently helped them. It soon became apparent to workers that the generals in power wished to carry out their development schemes on the backs of the working class. They repressed strikes, jailed militant union leaders, and permitted industrialists to reorganize production without consulting workers' delegations. Most of all, the generals promoted a kind of trickle-down agenda that encouraged the accumulation of profits among employers while holding down industrial wages. After 1955, Argentina's laborers lost all income gains they had made under Perón. Of course, the workers could object through the vote at election time, but the military rulers made sure that the names of the Peronist candidates for whom they would have voted did not appear on the ballots. The workers felt abandoned.

The younger generation of workers nonetheless resisted the new decrees from above and fought for recognition. In the factories and on the work sites, union members consistently cast their ballots for Peronist labor leaders. They used sabotage and work slowdowns on the shop floors. Their strikes became political statements protesting their subordination in the development process and their destitution from inflation and wage freezes. An unprecedented wave of strikes resulted in 7.5 million man-days lost in Buenos Aires in 1956, and 3.3 million, in 1957. It became evident that the older, conservative bosses had lost control of the unions, while younger, more militant leaders had gained the confidence of workers.

Certain countervailing legacies, present in the labor movements since the beginning of the century, however, produced conservative tendencies in union organization. Once in power, a young militant leader became more conservative in order to maintain his power. Labor unions in the 1960s remained powerful organizations. Employers still deducted union fees from workers' wages in order to sustain the union bureaucracy. Unions used these slush funds to run medical clinics, manage pension deposits, and maintain the union-owned vacation hotels in Mar del Plata and the Córdoba hills. Many a young militant became accustomed to dispensing discretionary funds and resorted to fraud and violence to remain the boss. Union politics gained a reputation for gangsterism. Sometime labor leaders collaborated with employers and military leaders. A labor boss's official recognition by the Labor Department helped solidify his control of the rank and file. As one worker in Córdoba later recalled, some labor leaders would "betray strikes and sell out to the bosses, and live in luxury like potentates, with a house in the mountains, fast cars, women" (James 1994,229).

More grass-roots militancy and strikes, especially after 1966, tended to undermine many comfortable labor bosses who seemed to have turned away from Perón. Because the repressive military was against Perón, the workers gained strength and resolve in identifying their interests with "the old man." In the union halls, they elected leaders they thought were closer to Perón's philosophy. The movement also had adherents among unorganized and poor Argentines. Many hovels in the *villas miserias,* where migrants first settled into urban life, featured corner altars complete with photos of Juan and Evita surrounded by burning candles.

First-generation workers in Córdoba also had been developing a strong Peronist identity. As many as 8,000 rural residents per year were moving from farms and rural villages to this expanding industrial city. Córdoba's population nearly doubled in just one generation. The unions that had formed in Perón's time had always resisted direction from the CGT in Buenos Aires and nurtured a strong regional and grass-roots identity. The young workers of the 1960s came around to Perón because they saw themselves as disenfranchised by the anti-Peronist military. The new generation of union leaders adopted the criticisms of the oligarchy and foreign interests that they subscribed to Perón himself.

228

In 1966, when General Juan Carlos Onganía took power in a coup d'etat, some workers were hopeful of a political alliance. Onganía had been leader of the moderate faction of the military, which sought a modus operandi with labor, thus some union bosses supported his coup, thought they would regret it later. But Onganía and his new economics minister decided on an antilabor policy of development, one that attempted to impose—with force, if necessary—increasing worker productivity while holding down wages. The new military government devalued the peso, which raised the cost of living, and laid off workers in the state industries to cut costs. Strikes were outlawed. In Córdoba, Renault cut wages and laid off dissident workers. Onganía's repressive policies provoked an explosive backlash among the autoworkers and others in Córdoba.

In May 1969, a group of metal workers held a rally to protest the mandatory lengthening of the workweek by four hours. Police intervention angered the workers, who marched into downtown Córdoba to protest. University students, who were undergoing a process of radicalization as well, joined the demonstrations. Several days of protests followed, and the police abandoned the downtown area to the protesters.

*Mounted police and demonstrators during the Cordobazo in May 1969* (Archivo Página 12)

229

Xerox and Citroën offices were set on fire, and rioters overturned cars and broke the windows of downtown businesses. Gradually, the workers withdrew, but the students carried on. Army forces arrived and in a bloody three-day period fought their way into student and working-class neighborhoods. In the end, up to 60 people lay dead, hundreds were wounded, and 1,000 arrested.

The violence of the Córdoba riot, which came to be called the Cordobazo, shook the nation. The strongman, General Onganía, was forced to resign within a year and a more conciliatory junta took control. The Cordobazo emboldened workers and students throughout the nation to stiffen their resistance and to demand that the military allow Perón to return to his homeland. Soon the military would contemplate elections again in order to placate the increasingly radical elements demanding Perón's return. During this process, university students had gone from being partisans of the right-wing Catholic Action that had helped bring down Perón's presidency in 1955 to left-wing guerrillas fighting to bring "the old man" back in the early 1970s. Argentina did not lack ironies.

## Rise of the Guerrilla Movement

The ongoing malaise gave rise to the radicalization of the country's middle-class youth, whose employment future looked very bleak. They were educated and proud of their heritage but ashamed of the political and economic ineptitude that clouded their future. The students at the University of Córdoba had struck a blow against the repressors. After the Cordobazo, a small cadre of around 200 active combatants in a dozen or so resistance organizations blossomed into a paramilitary army of 5,000 guerrilla fighters. The guerrillas announced themselves with a spectacular symbol of defiance. One group kidnapped General Aramburu, the retired head of the junta who had "disappeared" the body of Evita Perón. After interrogating him at a "people's prison" in a safe house, the guerrillas executed Aramburu and returned his body to his family. The military now confronted a wholly new set of Peronists, the middle-class youth.

The older guerrilla leaders had nurtured their militancy as members of Catholic Action, the anti-Peronist strike force of the early 1950s. Some began a leftward ideological transition while volunteering to work with socially active priests in the *villas miserias*. There they observed the reverence Argentina's poor felt for Juan and Evita Perón. Some concluded that only Perón could effect the radical change needed in the country and became converted *peronistas*. The guerrillas "are not drawn from the masses," two priests who knew them divulged to the public. "They were born and they grew up listening [to their elders] vomit abuse against Peronism. What drives them to react violently against the social milieu in which they grew up? . . . the conviction that only violence will sweep away social injustice. . . ." (Moyano 1995: 27)

Many students experienced the same kind of repression as the workers and emerged combative and radicalized from the experience. A decisive episode came in the 1966 police attack on a student protest at the University of Buenos Aires after Onganía ended university autonomy and purged administrators and professors. The military government repressed the student takeover with typically brutal violence. More than 200 students were jailed and 30 hospitalized. The incident was dubbed the Night of the Long Pencils (a euphemism for police batons).

In the wake of the Cuban Revolution—and fellow Argentine Che Guevara's role in it—the intelligentsia embraced a new critique of

# EYEWITNESS REPORT ON THE NIGHT OF THE LONG PENCILS, 1966

The police entered [the Department of Exact Sciences of the University of Buenos Aires] firing tear gas and ordered everyone to face the wall with our hands up. . . . As we stood blinded by the tear gas against the walls of the classrooms, the police . . . began hitting us. Then one by one we were taken out and forced to run between rows of police spaced about 10 feet apart. That is when I [Warren Ambrose] got seven or eight wallops and a broken finger. No one resisted. We were all terrified, what with the curses and the gas. Prof. Carlos Varsavsky, director of the new radio observatory in La Plata, received a fractured skull then. The eminent geologist Félix González Bonorino, who is about 70 [years old,] had his head bloodied. Those of us on our feet after running the gantlet were herded into trucks and taken to a police station . . . I was released at 3 A.M. but few of the others taken with me were freed at that time. At no time was any explanation given us for the police beatings, which is incomprehensible to me.

■

*Statement of Professor Warren Ambrose from Massachusetts Institute of Technology in the* New York Times, *August 1, 1955 (Moyano 1995, 19)*

national weakness that appealed powerfully to these youths. The doctrine was called the dependency theory. Argentina was trapped in the periphery of world capitalism dominated by the industrialized countries of Western Europe and especially by the United States. In Argentina's "dependent" society, the military and the elite collaborated with the foreign capitalists. Those powerful *vendepatrias*—"sellers of the fatherland," or "traitors"—extracted capital from the workers in the periphery and exported it to the industrialized nations. Dependent economic relations, therefore, resulted in underdevelopment in Argentina for the sake of development in the industrial metropolises.

According to the theory, only revolution would break these bonds of dependency and free the nation from the enslavement of foreign capital. Understandably, student radicals lionized Guevara and the Cuban Revolution, and Guevara's death while attempting to spread revolution to Bolivia vaulted him into martyrdom in 1967. But the guerrillas adopted Peronism as the expression of the Argentine revolution. If the elite and the military hated Perón so passionately, they reasoned, then he must truly represent it. Famous for her diatribes against the oligarchy, Evita became their patron saint. On walls throughout the city, they painted Evita's slogans such as "Peronism is revolution, or it is nothing!" without quibbling about her concept of revolution. Their admiration of Evita motivated them to strike out at the man who had made her body disappear. Thus, General Aramburu became the first victim of guerrilla justice in 1969.

But the guerrilla groups were as divided among themselves as any other class or political group, including the military. *Revolution* could mean anything from the Trotskyite sort favored by the Revolutionary Army of the People (ERP) to a vaguely nationalistic sort endorsed by the Montoneros. The latter group became the biggest of a score of guerrilla organizations, partly because they had pulled off the attack on Aramburu and also because their ideology was fuzzy enough to satisfy many followers. "The old man" in exile had blessed them all as the Soldiers of Perón. The Montoneros took their name from the pejorative term used by the 19th-century elite to discredit the mounted followers of the popular caudillos.

The fact that General Onganía finally relinquished power within the military to a moderate faction of officers did not deter the guerrilla groups; it emboldened them. They began a bombing campaign against the showrooms of the foreign car companies and the stores of the food chain Minimax (owned by American politician Nelson Rockefeller).

*Members of the Montoneros marched toward the Plaza de Mayo in May 1973.* (Archivo General de la Nación)

They assassinated labor leaders who were notorious collaborators and military officers known for their hard-line attitudes. They kidnapped foreign executives and exacted ransoms of millions of dollars for their release. Some groups attacked military bases, while others occupied small provincial towns as symbols of their audacity and the government's weakness. The numerous guerrilla factions mounted 114 armed operations in 1969, 434 in 1970, and 654 in 1971.

In concert with the resistance of the Peronist labor unions, the guerrillas made Argentina ungovernable. They left the military with only one option: call another election in 1973 and allow Peronist candidates to run. The junta also attempted to make peace with Perón by returning Evita's body. Living in exile in Spain, Perón located the body in a country cemetery in Italy, where Evita had been buried for 17 years under the fictitious identity of a deceased Italian-born widow. Despite these concessions, the junta manipulated the election to exclude Perón from the presidency by arbitrarily imposing a residency law for all candidates. However, years of military repression and guerrilla violence had left a bitter residue in the political environment. Extralegal action seemed more legitimized now than ever before in Argentina.

233

## The Troubled Return of Perón

As expected, the Peronists swept the elections of 1973 and the party candidate, Héctor Cámpora, took the oath of office amid jubilant hopes that the generals would never again return to power. Pedestrians spat on military officers on the streets. Of all the guerrilla fighters, Cámpora rewarded the Montoneros most of all. He set free all 371 political prisoners from the jails, most of whom were hard-core terrorists. Other Montoneros received government appointments along with Peronist union leaders and longtime party apparatchiks. The Montoneros celebrated with huge demonstrations, punctuated by jumping to the beat of *bombos,* big bass drums; youthful spectators at these celebrations filled up the stadiums of the professional soccer teams. But the Peronist right wing and many labor bosses resented having to share power with these presumptuous newcomers to the movement.

Perón sided with the right, especially after his triumphant return went sour. "The old man" and his young new wife, María Estela (Isabel) Martínez de Perón, arranged to arrive at Ezeiza International Airport on June 20. Nearly the entire city of Buenos Aires came to a standstill the day before as a million well-wishers headed to the airport, many having to walk when traffic became hopelessly snarled. The party and labor leaders took charge of setting up the stage where the Peróns were to greet the celebrants. When a column of Montoneros, accompanied by their *bombos* and banners, advanced in order to place themselves, as good Soldiers of Perón, in front of the stage, gunshots rang out, and a riot and firefight ensued between the Peronist right and left. A furious Perón had to divert his plane to an air force base. Everyone believed that the official statistics of 16 dead and 433 wounded vastly underreported the number of victims in this incident. Shortly thereafter, Perón forced Cámpora to resign and the interim president to call for a special election in which Perón won 61 percent of the vote in his third campaign for the presidency. His wife Isabel was elected vice president, an office that had eluded Evita.

Perón's new administration purged all the Montonero officeholders as he made conciliatory gestures to the opposition parties, industrialists, and the military. A state of euphoria gripped even members of the middle class, many of whom believed that only Perón could govern the country. Inflationary rates declined somewhat, and capital flowed back into the country. But Perón proved mortal, and in the middle of winter, on July 1, 1974, he died of heart failure. His state funeral surpassed even the massive outpouring of grief that had accompanied the burial of Yrigoyen, Gardel, and Evita. Thousands waiting to pass by his casket stood in a cold rain, setting a somber mood of grief mixed with uncertainty. Under these circumstances, Isabel Perón became the first female chief executive in the Americas.

Perón's widow, however, did not have sufficient training or character to handle the requirements of the job. Truth be told, perhaps no other living person did either, as the Montoneros immediately declared war on the government. The next two years showed a steady deterioration in public confidence; frightened people of wealth and foreign investors again sent their money to safe havens abroad. Inflation soared along with the nation's fatalism. Peronist workers again suffered losses of real wages that President Isabel Perón's decrees of pay increases could never make up, and they began to show up less frequently at Peronist loyalty rallies. Their chants of "Eez-sah-BELL, Eez-sah-BELL" never lasted as long as the old homages to "Pay-ROHN, Pay-ROHN, Pay-ROHN." Isabel turned to a shady, corrupt favorite of her late husband to help her run the nation. José López Rega, the minister of social welfare, consulted the stars before advising her and arranged to divert about a quarter of the federal budget to his ministry. Everyone knew that López Rega funded the notorious Argentine Anticommunist Alliance, the Triple A. Thugs within the Triple A undertook a positively Rosas-type reign of terror in the country, killing suspected guerrillas and leftist politicians, threatening left-of-center actors and folksingers, and leaving mutilated bodies indiscriminately along suburban roads and in burning cars near Ezeiza airport.

Guerrillas countered by taking up again their campaign of terror, bombings, kidnappings for ransom, and assassinations. In 1975, there were 723 incidents of guerrilla activity. "We are guided in this enterprise by the clean example of that great Argentine and great Latin American . . . commandant Che Guevara," stated one guerrilla communiqué. "[The regime's] puppet generals, its torturer policemen, have staged the comedy of finding our violence scandalous. . . . [T]hey are simply projecting on revolutionary combatants the image of their own methods, their own habits" (Moyano 1995, 61–62).

Neither side could easily get to the other, so they knocked off innocents in between. The guerrillas, unlike the Triple A, however, could never be faulted for lack of imagination. In 1974, they broke into General Aramburu's tomb and held his corpse hostage until Isabel and the military repatriated Evita's body from where it had been laid to rest in Spain. "If Evita were alive," they spray-painted on walls throughout the country, "she would be a Montonero." Seven hundred ninety people—soldiers, policemen, businessmen, politicians, and innocent bystanders—died at

# A REPORTER'S ACCOUNT OF A MONTONERO NEWS CONFERENCE, 1975

[**M**ario] Firmenich, descended from Yugoslav immigrants, was the supreme commander of the Montoneros. He had been among the founders, whose political apprenticeship has varied. Most of the twelve young men and women who (at the end of May 1969) had kidnapped and later murdered a former president of Argentina, had their origins in right-wing nationalism: their guidebooks not *Das Kapital* but the Scriptures. . . .

The guerrilla chief spoke with controlled excitement. The press conference had been called because it was Argentina's Flag Day and the second anniversary of Juan Perón's return to Argentina from exile in Spain. The "imprisonment" of the Born brothers [two wealthy businessmen] was proof that "we are now a force to be reckoned with, a political organization which cannot be ignored". . .

Firmenich lifted a hand and said that he wanted to tell us something special. . . . 'In a few minutes Mr Jorge Born will be brought here. We are presenting him to the press; he will be released today'. . .

'How much did you get for Born?' somebody asked. Firmenich smiled back and his smugness seemed to form a cloud around him, 'what we set out to get: 60 million dollars'. . .

Somebody called, 'There he comes!' Stepping carefully down a set of stone stairs with no hand rail, peering through dark glasses with some difficulty, Jorge Born arrived. It seemed simple; he looked quite ordinary; it was not clear to me what I [Andrew Graham-Yooll] expected to see. A man had to be different to the rest of his species after nine months of captivity. . . .

The journalists crowded around him, then stepped away as the German—or Swedish—television crew switched on the lights and focused their cameras. Born stared at the camera, stunned by the brightness of the lights, by the uncertainty of the situation and by the crowd of people—even though his guards had warned him to expect them. Finally the lights went out. It was exciting to be with him; he was worth 60 million dollars.

■

*(Graham-Yooll 1986, 43–45)*

the hands of guerrilla assassins. The Triple A murdered hundreds in retaliation.

By early 1976, public opinion clamored once again for a military coup d'etat. Newspaper editors, leaders of opposition parties, even workers desired respite from the mayhem of civil strife and triple-digit inflation. Those officers spat upon back in 1973 were deemed in 1976 to be the only saviors to whom most Argentines could turn. Yet, the generals waited. They wanted to build a real consensus for taking power again. They felt they had it in March 1976, when inflation was running at 600 percent. The military brought a swift end to Isabel Perón's constitutional presidency, which brought relief to the apprehensive public. Surely many must have suspected that the spasm of violence was far from finished.

## The Dirty War

The generals who seized power in 1976 instituted a far-reaching draconian program that they called the Process of National Reorganization, or el Proceso for short. They followed the Onganía example of 10 years before and filled the bureaucracy at the top with military officers.

*From left to right, Admiral Emilio Massera, President Jorge Videla, and General Orlando Agosti, members of the ruling junta that implemented el Proceso (Archivo General de al Nación)*

237

Purges followed. Peronists who had not already gone into hiding were dismissed from their government posts, and senators and deputies were locked out of their offices. While factionalism still existed among the top brass between the moderates and the hard-liners, the moderates consolidated control of the junta. General Jorge Videla, head of the army, assumed the presidency of a junta that consisted also of the heads of the navy and the air force. "The aim of the Process," Videla declared, "is the profound transformation of consciousness" (Feitlowitz 1998, 19). The new military government agreed on two policies that had broad support from the public. The junta promised to combat inflation, and it vowed to eliminate the guerrilla problem.

To remedy inflation, the junta assigned economic policy to José Martínez de Hoz, a Harvard-trained economist from an old landed family. He immediately inspired confidence in domestic and foreign investors, as he decreed economic policies that favored open markets and smaller public expenditures. Martínez de Hoz also welcomed foreign investment at a propitious moment. The Arab oil boycott of 1973 had succeeded in raising international petroleum prices fourfold, resulting in large profits for the world's oil exporters. Rising oil prices hurt the economy of Argentina, whose national oil company could not supply even the anemic economy with enough fossil fuels. However, international banks at the time had billions of petro-dollars on deposit and hired dozens of Spanish-speaking financial agents to scour Latin America for lending opportunities. Martínez de Hoz's decrees impressed the international lenders, who also exuded confidence in the military government's ability to "discipline" both the guerrillas and the workers. The new government eagerly seized the opportunity to achieve economic growth at a low rate of inflation through borrowing from abroad.

Under the onslaught of loans, the generals decided against downsizing the government, and every military governor and officer in charge of the state companies sought interviews with foreign lenders as a way to boost their personal power. They replaced the Peronist bureaucrats with an even greater number of their own friends and supporters. Argentina experienced a boom in its economy that made the military government very popular, but the generals succumbed to the age-old tendency of government officials entrusted with the nation's interests— their immunity corrupted them. The mayor of Buenos Aires, General Osvaldo Cacciatorre, was a fine example. In military politics, he represented the faction of hard-liners. His administration borrowed $1 billion to build a superhighway from Ezeiza airport straight into the heart

A villa miseria, *one of the urban slums in the Puerto Nuevo district of Buenos Aires* (Archivo General de la Nación)

of the capital. During construction, his minions bulldozed 32 shanty-towns (*villas miserias*) and displaced nearly 300,000 poor residents. The money ran out before the highway was completed. General Cacciatorre also conceived of constructing a great theme park, Interama, at the cost of $200 million. A few rides and exhibits were completed before the money disappeared. An accountant's report subsequently found "that the public funds for the park provided by the city and raised through bank loans, had gone mostly to deposit accounts in Switzerland and Luxembourg" (Simpson and Bennett 1985, 203). Under Cacciatore, the municipal government ran up debts of $2.5 billion, but the news media could not alert the public to these trends because the military government had outlawed all public criticism of its actions.

The external debt of Argentina climbed precipitously. Isabel Perón's government in 1975 had found it difficult to pay the interest on a total debt of $8 billion. Under the military government, the debt rose to $18 billion in 1979, then to $40 billion in 1982. The economic czar, Martínez de Hoz, was powerless to hold down external debt, as he had no control over generals and admirals pursuing other agendas. The availability of international funds kept the country's fictitious economic boom afloat for four of the seven years of military rule. Argentines remember it as a time of the "sweet money" (*plata dulce*), when even middle-class families could afford to travel abroad and purchase "six of everything." Though it mortgaged the future economic health of the nation, the prosperity of the moment enabled the junta to carry out its second objective: defeating the guerrilla movement.

The generals expressed their cause in medical terms: The nation had a "cancer" (left-wing terrorism) that they had to remove surgically. They believed that Argentina was the entryway through which communism chose to invade South America, and national security demanded harsh countermeasures.

General Videla and the military junta had very little control over the provincial commanders, troop leaders, and military bureaucrats, and the struggle against the guerrillas depended on the temperament of individual military leaders. This decentralized pattern of state repression thus took on a dynamic of its own and became a very blunt surgical instrument indeed. In order to wipe out the approximately 2,000 remaining hard-core left-wing guerrillas (the Triple A and other right-wing terrorists were exempted from the junta's repression of guerrilla groups), the military killed as many as 19,000 Argentines. The strategy was as follows: "First we will kill all the subversives," said General Ibérico Saint Jean, "then we will kill their collaborators; then their sympathizers, then . . . those who remain indifferent; and finally we will kill the timid" (Anderson 1993, 226). They also jailed, tortured, and raped many thousands more. An additional 2 million Argentines may have fled into exile.

The chief instruments of the counterinsurgency were the *patotas*, the arresting squads made up of six to 20 soldiers, sailors, or policemen. They struck at night, while victims slept, surrounding the house with their trademark government-issued green Ford Falcons. They took care to warn the neighborhood police ahead of time so that patrol cars would stay away. The *patotas* first secured the victims and their family members, then ransacked the home for evidence. They then led the victims away for interrogation. As their immunity grew, the *patotas* became common burglars. They raided middle-class homes that were under no particular suspicion for harboring terrorists merely to fill up trucks with furniture and personal effects to sell at flea markets. Some *patotas* hunted for pretty young girls to assault in broad daylight. These tactics vanquished the left-wing guerrillas fairly quickly, but the work of the *patotas* continued, not for national security reasons but for the sheer abuse of power.

# A MOTHER'S TESTIMONY

**M**y son was a student in La Plata but at the time of the coup, because of all the problems in the university, he was living here in Mendoza.... On the way home [one day] they drove into the middle of a police and army operation. He didn't have his identity card with him so they arrested him.... Effectively, he had disappeared....

A month after his kidnapping they returned to the house. At that moment our daughter Violeta, who was a student in La Plata, was staying with us and Ana María, the youngest who was at secondary school. It was 22 January 1977. They arrived at eleven or twelve at night in a number of cars, masked and with rifles. They invaded the house from the front and back, kicking in the doors. They didn't say who they were, but even though it was dark we could see that one of the cars was a police car. They were talking about drugs.

They ... threw us to the floor, threatening and insulting us, more than anything else about our jobs as teachers. They took away our two daughters aged sixteen and eighteen. They were both crying desperately. I suffered a nervous attack and, I don't know by what miracle, but they brought back the youngest.

... All this time the others were taking out everything from the house, anything they could carry. And they took Violeta ...

We heard our daughter weeping as they took her away ...

One night, a week later, my husband heard a noise and looked out of the window. He had a stick ready to defend himself against anyone who tried to get in. It was Violeta. She was naked, crawling on all fours, don't ask me in what condition—infections in her eyes, covered in bruises and with a terror on her face ... but she was there. She told us they had taken her to a place outside the city and kept her inside a car all the time, crouched up, with her hands tied, and blindfolded.... She could hear the screams of people being tortured. They tortured her too.

◼

*(Fisher 1989, 15–16)*

The *patotas* reported to commanders at houses of detention. In Buenos Aires, the military commands operated most of the detention centers, converting barracks and military classrooms to the task. For the most part, the police took a back seat to this activity, and the Triple A retired completely. The strategy of these operations changed somewhat, as the military tortured and killed in secret and disposed of the bodies discreetly, whereas the old Triple A had preferred, in Rosas fashion, to display them as warnings. The navy established one of the most notorious military detention centers at the Navy Mechanics School.

Each command maintained its own suspects' list, often enlarged by information obtained after torturing prisoners with electric shocks. The confusion of multiple lists meant that thousands of innocents ended up in detention for no reason. Loved ones never knew where those arrested were taken, complicating the process of following the already clandestine proceedings. Civil rights lawyers also disappeared, and few judges and journalists dared inquire into arbitrary arrests. One-third of the victims were labor leaders, testimony to the military's attempt once again to crush working-class resistance. Often physicians attended torture sessions in order to revive the victims long enough for the torturers to get more information. They buried the bodies of victims in isolated places without markers, thus giving rise to the term *desaparecidos,* or "disappeared ones." Military units with access to aircraft drugged their victims, flew them over a large body of water, slit open their bellies so they would sink, and dumped them overboard. In time, the torturers continued practicing their avocation—again with full immunity—merely for the feelings of power or sexual arousal it gave them.

A combination of fear and economic boom muted public reaction to the increasing evidence of disappearances. The government dealt harshly with attorneys, judges, and news reporters who inquired too closely about the missing. There was nothing at all in the newspapers about guerrilla activities, which had declined dramatically, or about state repression. Many did not want to know what was going on; however, a group of women—mainly mothers and wives of the disappeared—formed a protest group. The military officials rebuffed questions, telling mothers that their sons probably had run off with prostitutes and wives that their husbands had left to live with other women. Missing daughters were harder to explain away. In April 1977, a small group of these women gathered in silent vigil in the plaza fronting the Casa Rosada. Some passersby cursed them, and security officers threatened them. They marched in the Plaza de Mayo every Thursday thereafter, as they do to this day.

One of the leaders of the Mothers of the Plaza de Mayo, as the group came to be known, Hebe de Bonafini, believed that the international press and foreign diplomatic pressure was protecting these weekly protests, which grew with each passing month. The *New York Times* and the governments of Sweden, Spain, and France stood out in this regard.

*Mothers of the Plaza de Mayo during a rally in 1983* (Courtesy of Asociación Madres de Plaza de Mayo)

U.S. president Jimmy Carter in 1979 suspended loan negotiations with Argentina because of the military government's human rights abuses, Great Britain under Prime Minister Margaret Thatcher and the administration of Ronald Reagan in the United States, however, ignored or even applauded El Proceso. In fact, the Central Intelligence Agency under President Reagan invited Argentine army officers to train the first Nicaraguan counterrevolutionaries, the Contras, in 1981.

The military withstood the criticism of international human rights groups. General Videla presided triumphantly as Argentina hosted the international soccer championships in 1978, at which the home team won its first World Cup. Internally, though, he and the *moderados* had to put down a rebellion of hard-liners in Córdoba, led by General Luciano Menéndez, in order to pass along the presidency of the junta to another moderate. Despite the mounting evidence of gross violations of human rights, the military's grip on power did not relax until 1980, when the economy contracted severely and inflation again shot upward.

In addition to the Mothers of the Plaza de Mayo, industrial workers also initiated serious opposition to the military regime. Rank-and-file workers launched a series of wildcat strikes in 1976 and 1977, even as the *patotas* were decimating union leadership. A new generation of militant leaders called a general strike for April 1979. Subsequent strikes

243

of railway and auto workers resulted in wage increases rather than harsh repression from military authorities. Labor leaders were among the first to demand a return to democracy. "[O]nly by way of a government elected by the people," they announced, can the nation achieve "the anxiously awaited national unity" (Cox 1995, 82). The sharp contraction of the economy continued into 1981, provoking another shakeup in the junta and more questions about human rights abuses. In a second general strike, union leaders declared that "The Argentine people and the institutions that express the people's will have definitely lost their confidence in the process inaugurated in March of 1976" (Cox 1995, 95).

At this low ebb, General Leopoldo Galtieri took over as president of the junta and seized upon a dangerous opportunity to redeem the Argentine military. What ultimately dislodged the generals from power was neither their abuse of human rights, the labor agitation, nor the growing debt and rising inflation. It was the disastrous war with Great Britain over the Malvinas Islands.

## War in the Malvinas

In April 1982, General Galtieri ordered the navy and army to invade the Islas Malvinas, known in the English-speaking world as the Falkland Islands. The small British garrison on these windswept South Atlantic islands fell quickly. Thousands of Argentines filled the streets in reaction, not to protest the military government but to hail it. The sparsely inhabited Malvinas had been captured by the British navy as a coaling station in 1833 and held ever since. The advent of diesel-fueled warships rendered obsolete this imperial outpost, but 2,000 British citizens still lived in the Falklands. The United Nations had passed resolutions pressing for the return of the islands to Argentina, but negotiations between the two countries consistently broke down over the question of the rights of the British citizens who tended sheep there. The Malvinas nonetheless appeared on every schoolchild's map of Argentina, and patriotic pride was always just below the surface, even when politicians had solicited British investments during the liberal age, a century and a half before.

Although diplomatic right may have resided with the Argentines, General Galtieri miscalculated. On the evening he issued the order to invade, Galtieri had called his "good friend," President Reagan. The U.S. president was appalled that Galtieri expected him to uphold the Monroe Doctrine, the 19th-century canon that stated that an attack by

*Argentine troops were ill equipped and poorly trained when asked to defend the occupation of the Islas Malvinas against the British.* (Archivo Página 12)

any European power on any American republic would be considered an act of war toward the United States. It approved of Argentina's fight against "communism," but the Reagan administration wanted no disagreement with Britain, least of all over some South Atlantic islands of such minuscule importance. The American president and the British prime minister, Margaret Thatcher, had deep ideological affinities. Rather than supporting Galtieri, Reagan gave his moral support to Thatcher as she quickly outfitted a British task force to retake the islands.

Galtieri and his fellow junta members appointed General Mario Menéndez, a prominent member of the hard-line faction, as military governor of the "liberated" Malvinas and redeployed his defense forces, Argentina's crack combat units, to the Andean border with Chile. Although both military governments of the bordering countries cooperated in hunting down each other's fleeing leftists, Chile and Argentina still disputed certain regions in the Tierra del Fuego, particularly the Beagle Islands. Argentina worried about an invasion of General Augusto Pinochet's Chilean army, because he was the only head of state in South America to declare support for Great Britain. Consequently, the replacement forces sent to the Malvinas were all poorly trained and

# A CONSCRIPT DESCRIBES THE WAR IN THE MALVINAS, 1982

On the way there, when we were flying to the Malvinas, packed together, one of the boys sitting near me joked: "Stop grumbling lads, on the way back we'll be more comfortable." "Why?" someone asked him. "Well, there'll be fewer of us," he answered and there was a heavy silence. . . .

We finally got to our assigned place, but once there neither we nor the officers knew how to set up our position. At first we tried to sleep in tents and build fortifications to shoot from, foxholes, like the ones we dug in our training in Buenos Aires Province. But the soil on the islands was terrible; you dug a hole and within two days it was full of water. . . .

But the times our spirits were low, it was not because we were afraid of the English but because of the lack of food. If and when they arrived, the cold rations came in bags that had already been opened, with the odd tin and a couple of sweets. I [Daniel Kon] never saw the combat rations box. . . .

[O]n the final day of the English attack . . . they attacked us from all sides, from land and from four frigates. . . . At half past ten at night, the final shelling of our positions began. It was indescribable; about three rounds a second. We did what we could; all we could do was to protect ourselves and answer their fire every now and then. . . . They were boys from Córdoba who had just arrived from Comodoro Rivadavia. They were really terrified; they had never heard a bomb before and they'd been put there in the middle of hell. . . .

[We were held as prisoners of the English at the former Argentine headquarters.] And that was when we began to discover sheds and sheds, packed to the roof with food! When we'd gone down to steal, we'd found three or four warehouses, but it turned out there were more than forty. They couldn't get in, there was so much food. . . .

In the end we became quite friendly with some of the English soldiers. When I told them in one conversation that I'd only done five shooting tests and had fifty days' training, they banged their heads on the walls. They couldn't understand it. . . All the English soldiers had had at least three years' training. And however much patriotism you put in, you can't fight that.

■

*(Kon 1983, 12, 17, 26–27, 31, 38–39)*

equipped conscripts. Many were not issued sufficient clothing to withstand frostbite as they waited in wet foxholes for British troops. General Menéndez and his staff, meanwhile, hoarded supplies of meat and wine at their headquarters in Port Stanley, which was renamed Puerto Argentino.

The British forces met little effective resistance. Before landing at the islands, a British submarine sank the Argentine battleship *Belgrano*, and 800 sailors perished in the icy waters. An Argentine air force counterattack sank one British destroyer, taking 200 sailors with it. As the British fleet neared the Malvinas, however, most Argentine military hardware remained safe at the mainland bases. British marines faced minimal opposition, least of all from the Argentine officer class. Naval captain Alfredo Astiz, soon to be infamous for his human rights abuses at the Navy Mechanics School, surrendered the outlying Georgian Islands at the mere sight of British warships. British troops overran the main islands of the Malvinas, and General Menéndez quickly ran up the white flag of surrender over his comfortable headquarters. Back in Buenos Aires, General Galtieri announced the defeat the next day together with his resignation from the junta.

At first, patriotic Argentines were stunned by the news, then angered. They suddenly realized that the armed forces had been efficient in

*Argentine medics during the war in the Malvinas* (Archivo Página 12)

disappearing citizens, covering up their own corruption and human rights abuses, keeping the Peronists from power, intimidating the intelligentsia, taking the largest share of the national budget, and wasting the proceeds of sizable international loans, but could not accomplish their constitutional mission of defending the nation.

A caretaker military government realized it could no longer govern. The middle-class parties finally developed enough backbone to follow up the earlier protests of the Mothers of the Plaza de Mayo and of the

# THE POLITICAL PHILOSOPHY OF JORGE LUIS BORGES

The military debacle in the Islas Malvinas so shocked the nation that even Argentina's most renowned literary figure, Jorge Luis Borges, welcomed the fall of the military government. He had always been known for his anti-Peronist views. The famed novelist and poet counted himself among those members of the Argentine intelligentsia who, like Victoria Ocampo of the literary journal *Sur,* equated Perón with Hitler and Mussolini. He had dismissed Perón's support among the working class as a product of demagoguery and labeled Perón a dictator and tyrant despite the fact that he had won three of the most transparent elections of the 20th century. Borges even resorted to borrowing the classic dichotomy from the time of his illustrious grandfather, who had fought against Rosas: *Peronismo* represented the triumph of barbarism over civilization. Borges's views cost him a small government sinecure in 1946 when the Peronist administration "promoted" him from library clerk to chicken and rabbit inspector in the public markets.

Borges subsequently sided with numerous military men in power, praising leaders such as Francisco Franco in Spain and Augusto Pinochet in Chile. In Argentina, he observed, the generals were the "only gentlemen capable of serving the country." He was also quoted as saying, "I know I am not qualified to talk about politics, but perhaps you will allow me to say that I do not believe in democracy, that strange abuse of statistics" (González 1998, 196). Nonetheless, the Malvinas debacle had sobered him so much that in one of the last interviews of his life, he mentioned that Raúl Alfonsín's election had restored his faith in democracy—perhaps also because this had been the first free election in half a century that the Peronists did not win.

workers. The military attempted to exonerate itself with a last-minute amnesty for crimes committed by officers of the Process for National Reorganization. In December 1982, Nobel laureate Adolfo Pérez Esquivel led a huge demonstration of 100,000 people condemning the military for the "Dirty War." The generals then announced presidential elections for October 1983, fully expecting a Peronist victory. Instead, presidential candidate Raúl Alfonsín rallied the many factions of the Radical Party, refused to forgive the military of its crimes, accused the Peronists of making amnesty deals with the generals, and swept to victory with 52 percent of the vote. Even the notorious doubter of democracy, Argentina's greatest living literary figure, Jorge Luis Borges, had to concede that Alfonsín's election represented the best hope for a beleaguered and defeated nation.

# 10

# THE NEOLIBERAL AGE BEGINS

The elections of 1983 marked many transitions for Argentina: The military returned to the barracks, the first freely elected Radical president since Yrigoyen took office, and the Peronists lost their first presidential election. More important, President Raúl Alfonsín and his advisers had to confront the problems the military had bequeathed them. They now had to count the dead and missing victims of the Dirty War and prosecute those military personnel who had tortured and killed Argentine citizens and mismanaged the war in the Malvinas. The other challenge facing the new civilian administration in 1983 concerned the economy. Burdened by inflation running at more than 300 percent and by an international debt that had risen fivefold under the military government, the Alfonsín government had to get the economy to grow.

Few in Argentina could be faulted for not recognizing at the time that another, far more fundamental shift was taking shape as well. Populism had ended in bankruptcy. No longer would deficit spending stimulate domestic demand and industrial growth. No longer could the nation afford to protect inefficient industries behind high tariff walls that injured traditional agricultural exports. Sooner or later, the state would have to confront its own failure at running the core industries efficiently and begin selling them off to private investors. The economy was not going to grow without infusions of foreign capital and technology. Finally, the government had to bring down inflation and reduce the debt; indeed, the International Monetary Fund (IMF) demanded fiscal responsibility as a condition to advancing new loans to Argentina. Sharing in common high levels of debt and inflation, all other Latin American nations, except Cuba, also participated in this trend away from populist economics.

Thus was born the age of neoliberalism, so-named because its economic principles paralleled those that had held sway a century before during the liberal age. The hallmarks of neoliberalism were open markets, foreign investment, sales of state industries, lowering of trade barriers, labor flexibility, emphasis on exports, reduction of bureaucracy, relaxation of government regulation, and absorption of new technologies. Politicians swore allegiance to these principles, as the IMF looked on approvingly. But neoliberalism had its enemies in a society as fractured and discriminatory as Argentina's, and the civilian politicians would prove themselves just as inept at pursuing the neoliberal agenda as they had been at the populist one.

## The Attack on Impunity

Argentines of all classes viewed the immunity of the military as the number one national problem in 1983. The weekly march of the Mothers of the Plaza de Mayo continued into the period of electoral governments, and the public demanded accountability for the victims and perpetrators of the Dirty War. President Alfonsín, therefore, created the National Commission on Disappeared Persons. The novelist Ernesto Sábato (*On Heroes and Tombs*) presided over the commission, whose 120 employees traveled the country collecting documents and taking depositions from victims of torture and from the families of *desaparecidos*. Exiled former prisoners of the military government returned to give testimony.

Alfonsín had envisioned that the National Commission on Disappeared Persons would conclude its investigation within six months and turn over its findings to the civilian courts for the quick prosecution of the top officers in the Dirty War. If he wished to deal with the problem of the disappeared expeditiously without provoking an armed response from the military, the president had miscalculated.

From the beginning, Alfonsín's policy met resistance on all sides. Right-wing critics suggested that the process discounted the grave danger that the armed guerrillas had posed to the nation. Military officers now viewed the Radical Party as a group of communists, notwithstanding prior Radical support for the military's de-Peronization. On the left stood the Mothers of the Plaza de Mayo and Nobel laureate Adolfo Pérez Esquivel. They refused to endorse the commission because they suspected that the president really intended to limit the search for the missing and restrict the prosecution to those officers who gave the orders and not the thousands more who carried out the torturing and

251

# A VICTIM OF TORTURE
# RETURNS TO ARGENTINA, 1984

In April 1977, 20 armed men arrested journalist Jacobo Timerman in his apartment. Timerman had reported tentatively about disappearances and about guerrilla activities, two subjects the military regime had banned from publicity Timerman was also Jewish, and extremists among the ruling officers were notoriously anti-Semitic. The armed men placed a hood over his head and bundled him into the back of a sedan. One of his kidnappers placed a gun to his head and threatened, "Say goodbye, Jacobo dear. It's all up with you" (Timerman 1981, 10). Someone counted slowly to 10, then his captors broke into loud laughter.

For the next three years, Timerman was imprisoned and tortured by members of the security forces. He finally gained release through the protests of international human rights groups and left Argentina to write a celebrated chronicle of his incarceration, *Prisoner Without a Name, Cell Without a Number*. Timerman returned to Argentina following the restoration of democracy in 1984. It was a wrenching, bittersweet experience for the former prisoner of the military government.

Back in Argentina, Timerman pressed charges against two general officers and set out to find the clandestine prisons in which he had been confined for much of his time in captivity. He posed for a photo in one small cell in which he had been held incommunicado, tortured with electric currents, and poorly fed. He reflected on the renewal of democracy in the country, as well as on the search for the truth about the human rights abuses of the previous regime. Timerman expressed hope for the pursuit of justice against the military officers who had conducted the Dirty War, but he also recognized that not everyone condemned the past abuses.

Even before Timerman's return visit in 1984, apologists for the military began filling the newspapers with stories about the internationally famous Argentine journalist's former connections with suspected bankers for the Montoneros. His torturer, General Ramón Camps, even published a book linking Timerman to "communist terrorists." The publicity impugning Timerman's reputation had the impact in Argentina of justifying his kidnapping and torture.

killing. In addition, the Mothers resisted even the half-hearted attempts by the president to blame the guerrillas. He had said that their leaders, too, would be prosecuted. But the families of missing Montoneros wanted to cast their loved ones as national heroes, not as the criminal equivalent to the military officers. "[T]he future will retrieve ... the heroes and martyrs of the people, as we retrieve them," one publication of the Mothers stated, "because they were right" (Norden 1996, 89).

This whole effort was further complicated by Argentina's inadequate judicial system. The Constitution of 1853 had retained certain judicial principles dating from colonial times, when the military enjoyed its own legal jurisdiction. Officers of the armed forces for centuries had answered to crimes and civil suits only in military courts, which were notorious for hostility toward civilians, and the first military tribunals hearing the human rights allegations tended to exonerate the officers. The new government attempted to solve this age-old dilemma. Alfonsín and Congress passed a law allowing the civilian courts to review decisions of the military courts in matters relating to "the repression of terrorism."

The military could do little to deflect these encroachments on its long-cherished prerogatives. After the Malvinas debacle, the officer corps was badly divided. The military government in its last days in power had given itself amnesty for all crimes committed by its officers in fighting the guerrilla insurgency, but the outgoing regime was so discredited by its failure in the Malvinas war that the incoming Alfonsín administration quickly and easily overturned the amnesty, making Argentina's the only military dictatorship in South America to give up power without such immunity. (In the 1980s, their Brazilian, Peruvian, and Chilean brothers-in-arms had succeeded in imposing such amnesties before agreeing to elections.) Moreover, the government's economic measures slashed the military budget, and the armed forces could not replace retiring personnel. Military wages lagged so much that many officers and noncommissioned officers abandoned their posts every afternoon in order to take on second jobs.

Publication in 1984 of the report of the National Commission on Disappeared Persons set the stage for court proceedings against the military officers that went beyond measures proposed by the Alfonsín government. Its report, entitled *Never Again (Nunca Más)*, filled 50,000 pages. *Never Again* provided original documentation and gave details about specific victims of torture and murder. It chronicled the methods of torture and disappearances and identified the places where they had occurred. *Never Again* placed the number of "known" people who disappeared at 8,961. Based on this voluminous evidence, the Ministry of Justice identified 670 members of the former military government for prosecution. The human rights organizations, however, rebelled at the notion of such limited liability. They alleged that the true number of disappeared amounted to 19,000, more than twice the official government figure. By 1986, moreover, surviving victims and relatives of the disappeared had brought independent actions against approximately 1,700 officers in the civil courts. The accusations now reached deeply into the ranks of the junior officers and noncommissioned officers who had carried out the orders.

The first civilian trial of the nine generals who had served in the three military juntas from 1976 to 1983 indicated that the process would be long and divisive. Only five of the nine were convicted in an eight-month-long trial. Two former military presidents, Generals Jorge Videla and Roberto Viola, and three others received jail sentences. The Malvinas leader, General Galtieri, and three others were absolved. The human rights activists decried the "leniency" of the court decisions.

Alfonsín's advisers worried that the judicial process was taking too long and going too deeply into the lower ranks of the officer corps, so they passed two laws restricting prosecutions. One law stipulated that all new charges had to be filed within 60 days to be valid. The second piece of legislation, the Due Obedience Law, stipulated that no personnel below the rank of colonel could be prosecuted since they had just been following orders. With these laws two branches of government, the powerful executive and the subservient Congress, had in effect conspired to further limit the autonomy of the third and weakest, the judiciary.

Despite government actions favorable to their interests, the officer corps remained unrepentant. "I didn't come here to defend myself," said Admiral Emilio Massera. "No one has to defend himself for having won a just war, and the war against terrorism *was* a just war" (Lewis 2002, 219). Junior officers such as Massera's subordinate at the Navy Mechanics School, Captain Alfredo Astiz, resented having to present themselves in civilian courts even though Alfonsín's Due Obedience Law would eventually absolve them from further prosecution. Moreover, the military recoiled at the lenient treatment given to terrorists. Montonero leader Mario Firmenich received a long jail sentence, but other guerrillas convicted of killing police and military officers, and sometimes their family members, escaped punishment altogether. Some former members of the Revolutionary Army of the People even joined the Alfonsín administration as political appointees; others returned to their posts in the universities. All the while, soldiers' pay was declining.

## The Painted Faces

During Easter week of 1987, the junior officers reacted, as much against the weakness of their own general officers as against President Alfonsín. An elite group of commandos known as the Carapintada (those who painted their faces for camouflage) took over the Campo de Mayo infantry school on the outskirts of Buenos Aires. They were led by junior officers who had refused to show up for their court appearances. Military units loyal to the government refused to confront their rebel brothers-in-arms. A counterdemonstration of 300,000 human rights supporters in the Plaza de Mayo exacerbated the situation. President Alfonsín went to Campo de Mayo to confer with the rebel leader, Lieutenant Colonel Aldo Rico, who demanded an end to the "campaign of disparagement against the Armed Forces" (Norden 1996, 129).

The president later announced that the Carapintada had given up peacefully without conditions, yet the government undertook several prorebel actions soon thereafter. The defense minister and several general

*Members of the Carapintada commando unit, who seized the Infantry School on the outskirts of Buenos Aires during Easter week of 1987* (Archivo Página 12)

255

officers resigned and were replaced by nominees more to the liking of the "painted faces." The Due Obedience Law followed, exonerating all members of the armed force below the rank of colonel for their crimes against humanity. By the end of 1988, there remained a mere 20 officers being prosecuted for human rights violations.

Still, the Carapintada were not satisfied. In January 1988, Lieutenant Colonel Rico led an infantry regiment in a second rebellion in the province of Corrientes, but he and his associates were soon arrested. Finally, in December 1988, another Carapintada commander led a third rebellion. Colonel Mohammed Alí Seineldín had been an adviser to the Panamanian national guard during Rico's uprisings. When Colonel Seineldín returned to the commandos, he gained a reputation for his pro-Peronist, anti-Radical views. He was also a devout Catholic who would lead his troops in reciting the rosary at the end of each training day. Colonel Seineldín's rebellion involved more than 1,000 troops and ended in a peaceful settlement forcing another general officer into retirement and raising the pay of all soldiers. Then, the Carapintada movement gained additional support from an unexpected quarter.

Within a month of Seineldín's military rebellion, in January 1989, a group of 60 well-armed left-wing guerrillas attacked the army base of La Tablada, just outside Buenos Aires. They easily seized control of La Tablada but soon found themselves trapped inside by police and army troops. After the day-long firefight, 28 guerrillas and 11 military personnel lay dead. Fourteen terrorists were captured, and the others managed to escape. Public opinion rapidly turned against human rights activists, and the Mothers of the Plaza de Mayo hurt their own cause when they refused to condemn the attack. President Alfonsín was now nearing the end of his term without having given his nation the justice and national conciliation he had sought. He left these tasks to his successor.

The new Peronist president, Carlos Saúl Menem, did indeed provide resolution of the military and human rights problem, though he failed to satisfy everyone. After first courting the Carapintada in his successful campaign for the presidency, Menem decided that this political alliance would be too risky. He did not promote the Carapintada officers, nor did he appoint their nominees for the defense ministry and other military commands. Finally, Menem disappointed the Carapintada with his internationalist foreign policy. He especially drew close to the United States, for which Colonel Seineldín had a visceral dislike, and U.S. president George H. W. Bush soon after made a state visit to Argentina. Menem also proposed to renew diplomatic relations with Great Britain.

The frustrations of the Carapintada boiled over into another military rebellion, this one, unlike the others, ending in military casualties. In December 1990, the Carapintada seized the army headquarters building near the Casa Rosada and demanded a thorough purge of the generals as well as the promotion of Seineldín to army commander. The ensuing firefight between the Carapintada and loyal army units resulted in 14 dead and 55 injured. Subsequently, Seineldín received a life sentence for his part in the bloody rebellion, and 13 others were sentenced to prison terms of two to 20 years.

President Menem attempted to put an end to the issue of human rights and military culpability. Although 14 Carapintada and 11 attackers of La Tablada languished in jail, Menem pardoned all the junta members and other general officers who had received jail terms for crimes against humanity. President Menem also released Montonero Mario Firmenich, in an attempt to heal old animosities. Not a single guerrilla or military officer now remained in prison for their roles in the Dirty War. To this date, the military remains unrepentant, and the Mothers of the Plaza de Mayo still mount protest marches each Thursday in Buenos Aires's main square.

## The Fitful Start of Economic Reform

Perhaps the struggle to establish justice through accountability for human rights crimes would have been more successful if economic problems had not undermined the Alfonsín government and diverted attention. Inflation proved unmanageable, and the foreign debt was impossible to pay down. President Alfonsín did try the orthodox, IMF-approved fiscal remedies, but politically he could not afford to take bolder measures such as reduction of the bureaucracy and privatization of state industries. Budget deficits still equaled 15 percent of the gross domestic product. The government owed $3.2 million in back payments to foreign creditors. Per capita GDP had fallen 15 percent in the previous 10 years. Following 19 months of unsuccessful wage and price freezes and the resignation of the first economics minister, the government launched a bold stabilization project called the Plan Austral (Southern Plan).

Alfonsín's Southern Plan of 1985 met with immediate success. The government retired the worthless old peso and created a new monetary unit called the *austral*. Simultaneously, policy makers froze wages and consumer prices with the cooperation of organized labor and business groups. To trim government expenses, President Alfonsín decreed a wage freeze for all public employees, and there was a reduction in armed forces personnel and paychecks. The Plan Austral also renewed a commitment to promote settlement in the Patagonia by proposing to move the national capital from Buenos Aires to the town of Viedma on the banks of the Río Negro. The move was intended to entice *porteños* to leave the comforts of Buenos Aires in order to develop the untapped resources of the south. In addition, the government vowed to strengthen tax collection procedures to eliminate the time-honored strategies of tax evaders. Government deficits in the short term declined, and inflation came down from 360 percent to 24 percent. In 1986, the GDP shot up by 10 percent. Then reality set in once again, and government economists could not maintain sufficient self-deception.

By 1988, Alfonsín's policy makers admitted failure. The economic (and political) situation had deteriorated to the point that bureaucratic appointments multiplied rather than declined. In the 1980s, public employment rose from 484,000 to nearly 600,000, a figure representing

# THE STRANGE POLITICAL SYMBOLISM OF THE DEAD

Controversy tends to follow powerful Argentine personalities even into death. For 112 years, political opposition had prevented the return to Argentina of the remains of Juan Manuel de Rosas, the governor of Buenos Aires province from 1829 to 1852, who had fled to England when ousted from power. While campaigning for the presidency, Carlos Saúl Menem had promised to bring back Rosas. True to his word, under Menem Rosas's remains received a presidential funeral, complete with a mounted procession of gauchos in traditional garb and cavalry troops in uniforms dating from the War of Independence. President Menem had engineered the return of the notorious 19th-century caudillo to help the country "leave resentment behind." He was preparing public opinion for his forthcoming pardons of generals and guerrillas convicted for their activities during the Dirty War. It was not the first time—nor the last—that the living struggled over the bodies of famous Argentines.

Just two years before, as President Alfonsín's administration suffered its first reversals, unknown persons had plundered the tomb of Juan Domingo Perón. They stole the general's saber and cut off both his hands. They left a ransom demanding $8 million for their return. It took five hours for judicial and police authorities to reopen the coffin, for a

one in every five employees in the country. The state companies continued to lose millions of dollars each day, and private industry declined as well. Government deficits grew, and the politicians lacked the will to rigorously apply the nation's tax laws for fear of a political backlash. In 1989, only 30,000 of 30 million Argentines paid any income taxes at all. Workers' wages suffered from the resurgence of inflation (see table on page 263), which they did not accept passively. Angry workers reacted by launching 13 general strikes during Alfonsin's administration. In addition, the Peronists won the congressional elections and a majority of the governorships and thereafter obstructed many reforms of the Radical Party. With the resurgence of inflation, rebellion on the part of the Carapintada, and the recovery of the Peronist Party, President Alfonsín's administration appeared headed for failure.

The Peronists ran an adroit campaign in 1989. Their presidential candidate, Menem, had been governor of his home province of La

heavy glass cover, bolted down by 12 triple-combination locks, still protected Perón's handless corpse.

The saga of Evita Perón is the most famous case of the country's politicization of the deceased. After her death in 1952, President Perón hired a Spanish forensic doctor to prepare her body for immortality in a year-long process of embalming. Thereafter, the body came to rest in an open-casket at the headquarters of the General Labor Confederation (CGT). After ousting Perón from power, the military removed Evita's body in 1955 for a secret burial in Italy. Her remains did not return to Argentina until the Montoneros first killed the man responsible for her body's disappearance, General Aramburu, and later stole his corpse, too. Evita and Aramburu both reached their final resting places in 1974.

Ernesto "Che" Guevara shared similar controversy and tribulation after his death in 1967. Bolivian military officers snapped a famous photograph of the corpse shortly after they executed the man who had attempted to start a revolution in their country. They later removed his hands in order to provide fingerprints that would confirm Che's identity. The body then disappeared. Finally, in 1998, Fidel Castro obtained the Bolivian government's cooperation in locating Guevara's body, buried beneath the tarmac of a military airfield. Guevara's corpse returned to Cuba for a hero's funeral. He lies at rest in a magnificent tomb located at the base of the mountain out of which Che had led a victorious column of revolutionary guerrillas.

Rioja. Despite flirting with the "painted faces" during the campaign, Menem had human rights credentials: He had been imprisoned during the Dirty War. Menem ran a campaign that hewed closely to classic Peronist populism. Though the son of Syrian immigrants, he adopted the Creole persona of the interior provinces and equaled Perón himself in manipulating political symbolism. He drank *mate,* wore long side-burns in the caudillo style of Juan Manuel de Rosas, and vowed to bring back Rosas's remains from England for reburial. As governor, he had enlarged the state bureaucracy of La Rioja and undertaken many public programs with deficit spending. His lead in the polls cooled the ardor of many private investors, who expected Menem the Peronist to raise wages, spend lavishly, and retain state control of the economy.

The 1989 presidential elections gave Menem a plurality with 47 percent of the votes. The Constitution of 1853 stipulated that the president-elect wait eight months between the May elections and his December inauguration, but the quickening economic crisis rendered the outgoing president powerless. In July 1989, inflation was running at more than 1,000 percent. In the parlance of economists, Argentina had achieved "hyperinflation." Workers called for general strikes, and mobs ransacked grocery stores throughout the country in what came to be known as the IMF riots. Menem forced Alfonsin to vacate the presidency five months early.

*A looted supermarket in Rosario during the IMF riots in 1989* (Archivo Página 12)

Immediately, the inauguration of Menem calmed the nation. The new president himself assuaged his opponents with his remarkable gift for symbolism. Astor Piazzolla, for example, the country's greatest tango artist and composer since the death of Gardel, had been a vocal critic of the Peronists during the campaign and announced that he would leave Argentina if Menem was elected. The president-elect, therefore, came to a Piazzolla concert and publicly begged him

Raúl Alfonsín (left) hands over the presidency to Carlos Saúl Menem in July 1989. (Archivo Página 12)

not to leave. "Stay, Astor," he requested. "Stay, because we need you" (Christian 1989, 4). The gesture won over the musician, who remained in his homeland until his death three years later.

## Menem to the Rescue

No one was prepared for the direction that President Menem would take in his economic policy. This Peronist embraced neoliberalism. He appointed economists who had worked for the former military regime and who had liberal credentials. Privatization became the president's policy; for example, the new director of the national telephone company vowed to sell off the industry's assets to the private sector (in effect, putting herself out of a job). Menem also pledged to reduce the nation's burdensome international debt by privatizing other state industries such as the state oil company, YPF; the national railways; and the national airline, Aerolíneas Argentinas. The proceeds from these sales would be applied toward reducing the national debt. Moreover, Menem revealed plans to lower trade tariffs, streamline the bureaucracy, and remove obstacles to foreign investment. As momentous as these changes would be, the cure for inflation formed the centerpiece of Menem's economic reforms.

For his minister of economics, Menem chose Domingo Cavallo, a Harvard-trained economist. Cavallo followed some of the monetarist notions of the Chicago School of Economics identified with Nobel laureate Milton Friedman. In Chile, the "Chicago Boys" had gained recognition for helping military dictator Augusto Pinochet combat inflation

# AN INTERVIEW WITH PRESIDENT CARLOS SAÚL MENEM, OCTOBER 1989

Q. *Why are you encouraging market forces?*

Menem's Answer. Economic stagnation! In the country of cows, wheat, milk, and abundance, how can we have 9 million people out of 30 million living in poverty? It is a product of a policy that evidently has been inadequate.

Q. *What are your aims?*

A. Argentina is powerful in raw materials, food, energy, and human resources. We must liberate these resources and open our doors so foreign capital can help us grow.

Q. *Politically, critics say, you have only a few months to get results.*

A. Some sectors, particularly workers, are facing difficult conditions. But they are accepting it, except for certain groups that have not comprehended that Argentina has changed.

Q. *Your policies are likely to provoke strikes. How will you respond?*

A. We are going to take measures to challenge the union leadership in court. Those who don't work will be replaced by those who want to work. Regrettably, we have to be tough.

Q. *How about industrialists who still demand subsidies?*

A. Subsidies no longer exist. They will be as unprotected as pensioners, who will no longer travel on subways free if their pension is over $170. The same goes for power workers who pay reduced electric rates. These subsidies have disappeared forever.

Q. *What about Peronism's negative image abroad?*

A. *(Looking annoyed)* We can't spend all day telling what Peronism really is. Peronism is what is happening now in Argentina.

Q. *Who will buy the companies being privatized?*

A. Whoever wants to. They are public tenders open to international bidders.

Q. *You plan to allow private foreign ownership of oil assets. Is this a first for Latin America?*

A. I believe we are the first in Latin America to carry out something as revolutionary as what we are doing with the Argentine state oil company.

■

*("A Talk with Carlos Menem" 1989, 46)*

| Price Inflation in Argentina, 1980–2001 | | | |
|---|---|---|---|
| Year | Percent | Year | Percent |
| 1980 | 101 | 1991 | 172 |
| 1981 | 105 | 1992 | 25 |
| 1982 | 165 | 1993 | 7 |
| 1983 | 343 | 1994 | 4 |
| 1984 | 627 | 1995 | 3 |
| 1985 | 672 | 1996 | 0 |
| 1986 | 90 | 1997 | 1 |
| 1987 | 132 | 1998 | 1 |
| 1988 | 343 | 1999 | −1 |
| 1989 | 3,079 | 2000 | −1 |
| 1990 | 2,314 | 2001 | −1 |

Source: *Economist* Intelligence Unit (1980–2002)

and return the economy to growth. Cavallo adopted the strategies of the Chicago School to manage Argentina's peso. His "convertibility plan" retired the worthless austral created under Alfonsín and issued a new peso note fixed on par to the U.S. dollar. Moreover, Cavallo removed monetary control from the government (always inclined to print its way to temporary popularity). The Central Bank could not issue new paper money without having its equivalent in dollar deposits. The monetary reform provided an immediate antidote to inflation, which declined from more than 3,000 percent to less than 20 percent within three years.

In addition, the new economic team sought closer trade relations with the international community, particularly its neighbors. In 1991, Menem met with the presidents of Brazil, Paraguay, and Uruguay to form the Mercado Común del Sur (Common Market of the South), better known as Mercosur. Chile and Bolivia later joined Mercosur as associate members. This regional common market lowered or eliminated tariffs on trade between member states and established common standards for trade with other countries. Immediately, the grain and beef producers of Argentina gained access to a market of more than 215 million consumers, although manufacturers now had to compete with the

Brazilian industrial powerhouse. Trade between Mercosur countries rose fivefold in the 1990s.

This was not the economic program that Argentina had expected from the populist campaigner. Pundits began to joke that the Menem had accomplished more de-Peronization in two years than the military had in 20 years of rule. Labor bosses were split over *menemismo*. Those critical of the neoliberal policies predicted that workers once again would suffer for the economic foibles of the politicians. Their pessimism was justified, as the newly privatized industries shed redundant workers and employers no longer worried about government favoring labor. Official unemployment rose close to 20 percent; poverty rates also remained perilously high at 40 percent. Never before had the Argentine economy sustained such high rates of unemployment. At least inflation no longer threatened the real wages of those who still had jobs.

Menem's neoliberal reforms appealed to many constituencies, too. "Governments are simply not good businessmen," noted one IMF official quoted in a *New York Times* article. "Argentina was losing $5 million a day just on its railroad system, and by selling [state companies] the Government was able to get rid of thousands of unproductive workers" (Nash 1993, 6). The middle class, the elite, and the foreign bankers also approved, as did the U.S. government. For the first time in history, an Argentine president went out of his way to support U.S. policies in Latin America and the world. Menem joined the United States in its denunciations of the human rights' record of Cuban leader Fidel Castro and voiced support for the 1989 U.S. invasion of General Manuel Noriega's Panama, while his Latin American neighbors demurred. Menem also committed Argentine military assistance to Desert Storm, the U.S. military campaign against Iraq in 1991. In return, U.S. diplomats throughout Latin America spoke highly of the Argentine model of economic reforms. President Bill Clinton arrived in 1997 to pay homage to Menem's reforms.

President Menem parlayed his economic successes into a campaign for a second term. Congress cooperated in amending the Constitution of 1853 to permit his possible reelection (as Perón had done for the 1952 election). The economy cooperated. The 1990s witnessed the strongest and most consistent growth rates the nation had enjoyed since the 1940s. In the 1995 elections, therefore, the electorate returned Menem to the Casa Rosada with a majority of 55 percent of the votes. In doing so, voters overlooked some troubling signals that they soon would have to confront.

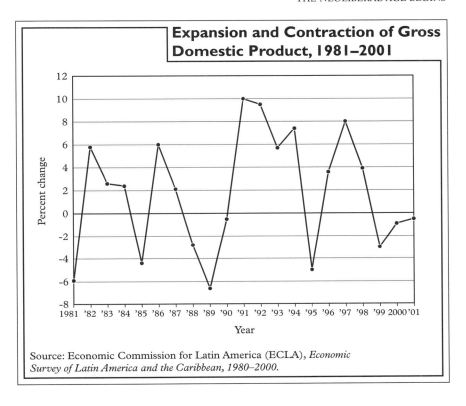

**Expansion and Contraction of Gross Domestic Product, 1981–2001**

Source: Economic Commission for Latin America (ECLA), *Economic Survey of Latin America and the Caribbean, 1980–2000.*

## The Underside of Neoliberalism

Every administration—whether military or civilian, Conservative, Radical, or Peronist—had exhibited symptoms of political corruption. Impunity had always been the handmaiden of corruption, as the judiciary historically lacked the institutional power and independence to bring corrupt ministers and legislators to justice. Argentina did however have one mechanism to expose corruption in high places. The print media (as opposed to the more regulated television media) acted as stewards of public oversight, and one could always find a full range of political discussion and analysis in the news kiosks throughout the cities. Powerful governments such as those of Perón in the early 1950s and of the military in the late 1970s effectively muzzled and intimidated the press, but few other administrations were so successful. Certainly, Menem wanted a more pliant press, but he did not get it.

Questions about corruption among the highest officials plagued Menem's administration from the beginning. The president had appointed his relatives to high government positions, which they used,

265

reporters alleged, to launder drug money. Questions also arose about the duty-free import of foreign luxury cars. A group of Italian businessmen gave President Menem, who loved fast cars, a new Ferrari. Despite the relations between Menem and the United States (which one official jestingly called "carnal" rather than "cordial"), the U.S. ambassador felt the need to go public about the amount of graft foreign businessmen had to pay. He charged that government officials held up the import of meat-processing equipment, demanding that the Swift-Armour Company first give them "substantial payments." Similarly, an accounting report on the sale of Aerolíneas Argentinas revealed charges of $80 million in "costs associated with the sale" (Christian 1991, 10; Verbitsky 1992, 21) as chronicled in a series of *New York Times* articles. Many people began to suspect that privatization merely enlarged opportunities for corruption, if graft was not, indeed its very purpose. Reporters also discovered that economics minister Cavallo received a monthly salary four times larger than his government paycheck. The difference was coming from a "think tank" supported by 400 companies doing business in Argentina.

Once again, the judiciary proved too weak to overcome the impunity enjoyed by members of the executive and legislative branches. Some of the cases came before judges appointed by Menem himself. The president had also expanded the Supreme Court and appointed a majority of the justices. Some functionaries accused of corruption brought libel suits against the newspapers and reporters who had exposed them. Government television announcers routinely attacked print reporters who wrote stories about bribery and corruption. At one moment during Menem's first term, nearly a dozen cabinet-level and senior officials had been tainted by charges of corruption. "Menem has so centralized power in the judiciary that I am very worried," said one prominent attorney quoted in yet another *New York Times* article. "But what makes me most afraid is that people don't seem to care. All they seem to be worrying about is whether there is low inflation" (Nash 1991, 15). Indeed, prosecutors eventually dropped all charges against government officials.

The president himself had escaped most of these accusations—that is, until he left office. Then, news articles began appearing that linked Menem to illegal foreign sales of Argentine-made weapons. His name also came up in connection with hush money he allegedly received from foreign terrorists to cover up a bombing in downtown Buenos Aires. In 1994, a car bomb exploded outside the city's Jewish community center, killing 86 people. Afterward, Menem reputedly filled a Swiss bank account with $10 million in bribes. For a while in 2002, the

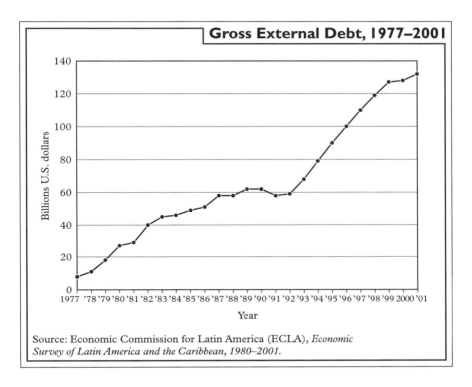

**Gross External Debt, 1977–2001**

Source: Economic Commission for Latin America (ECLA), *Economic Survey of Latin America and the Caribbean, 1980–2001.*

ex-president was under house arrest for the illegal arms sales, but charges were dropped.

As it turned out, President Menem was building economic prosperity based on borrowing from abroad, following the example of the military regime. Under Menem, the neoliberal reformer, the country's international debt obligations jumped from $62 billion to $127 billion (see figure). Ironically, the government had undertaken privatization to retire the international debt burden; however, President Menem could no more reduce government expenditures than he could cajole the well-off to pay their taxes. International borrowing made up the gap between public spending and the shortfall of tax revenues. Menem and Cavallo's neoliberal talk apparently had bamboozled the IMF and international bankers alike. Every year, they offered fresh loans.

The neoliberal reforms caused two of every five citizens to suffer. In the rush to privatize state industries in the early 1990s, thousands of employees lost their jobs in the oil, railway, and telephone industries. Between 1990 and 1998, Argentina sold 55 state companies for a total of more than $23 billion. More than 4,000 oil workers in Patagonia lost their jobs when investors purchased YPF's assets. Foreigners also bought up grazing and forest lands in Patagonia. "I used to go and camp or fish," remarked a former oil worker, "but now I hear that Ted Turner is here, Rambo there, the Terminator somewhere else. And I say, no, this is not my Argentina" (Cohen 1998, A7).

Unemployment rose steadily to become the most serious social problem faced by the country. In 1997, 17 percent of the working population had no employment. Even having a job did not ensure that members of the working class could escape impoverishment, as official poverty levels rose to 50 percent of the population. The middle class also suffered. College graduates left the country or took jobs driving taxis. Some critics spoke of the "disappearing" middle class. The largest public demonstration during Menem's two terms in office came in 1997. A reported 40,000 unemployed workers from all over the country marched on the Plaza de Mayo. In the meantime, wealthy Argentines were buying up real estate in the beach resort of Punta del Este, Uruguay. "Up to now, we haven't seen that the privatizations have brought anything good to the country," said one labor leader in Córdoba. "We only see unemployment, poverty, and that the country is left without any recourse while the external debt grows and grows" (Brown 1997, 382).

*Unemployed demonstrators block a road in Salta in 1997 as the national police prepare to clear them out.* (Archivo Página 12)

The public grew tired of Menem's ostentation and flamboyance (he also had a reputation as a womanizer, though it did not always hurt his popularity). Following his reelection, Menem had increased public expenditures, government employment, and deficit spending, and Argentina's international debt had precipitously risen as a result. So, in the 1998 elections, the electorate ignored the Peronist candidate, who did not enjoy Menem's enthusiastic support, and elected the dour and serious Radical candidate, Fernando de la Rúa. This marked only the second time the Peronists had lost a presidential election. It was clear, however, that the Radical president intended to carry on with the neoliberal economic agenda. De la Rúa appointed Domingo Cavallo once again as minister of the economy.

This time, Cavallo had to deal with the deteriorating economic situation caused in part by his own "convertibility plan" of the previous decade. The rigid linkage between the peso and the dollar had already made Argentine prices high for the rest of the world. As the dollar gained value worldwide against other national currencies, the peso also strengthened and began to deflate. Tourists to Argentina discovered that hotels and meals were expensive. Argentine agricultural exports became very costly on international markets, but imports of foreign goods became more affordable. As a result, exports declined as imports grew, to the detriment of local industries. Trade deficits mounted. Trade with its Mercosur partners developed in such a way that Brazilian industrial exports benefited while Argentine industry lost ground. The economy began to contract beginning in 1999.

President de la Rúa and Minister Cavallo also confronted an international debt that reached between $132 billion and $141 billion in 2001. They had to dedicate more and more government revenues to pay the interest on foreign loans, while failing to issue paychecks to government employees. No one wished to float the overvalued currency because devaluation would reduce the real incomes of those who still had jobs. Public protests, nonetheless, increased pressure on de la Rúa to do something. Workers launched more than eight general strikes in his first two years in office, and the unemployed marched through the streets, bearing pictures of Evita Perón. Middle-class housewives banged on empty pots and pans in their protests. In the meantime, a rash of business bankruptcies threw more and more people out of work. Cavallo resigned as economics minister.

The protests finally achieved critical mass in December 2001, as rioters again sacked supermarkets throughout the nation. These actions replicated the IMF riots of the previous decade. A massive protest

*"The Night of the Saucepans," an anti–de la Rúa demonstration by the middle class in December 2001* (Axel Laveglia)

march on the Casa Rosada led to violent clashes with police. Thirty-five people died, and thousands were arrested. President de la Rúa tendered his resignation and escaped the surrounding rioting by departing the Casa Rosada aboard a helicopter.

There followed a two-week period of constitutional uncertainty, marked by the congressional selection of three interim presidents in rapid succession. The fourth and final one, Eduardo Duhalde, had been the Peronist candidate during the presidential election of 1999. In January 2002, he had little choice but to maintain an unpopular freeze on the bank accounts of millions of citizens so that capital flight would not further sink the already weakened peso. Depositors then lost up to 40 percent of their frozen assets, as the link between the peso and the dollar was finally severed. In the meantime, the indifference of the IMF and the United States stung many Argentines. While the United States had bailed out Mexico in its 1995 monetary crisis, the U.S. secretary of the treasury, Paul O'Neill, refused to help Argentina, saying that the Argentines themselves had to solve the problems they had created. Furthermore, O'Neill claimed that Argentina had little in the way of an export industry and preferred to stay that way. Crime increased and uncertainty followed. The grandchildren

# AN ANONYMOUS VIEW FROM CYBERSPACE OF THE FALL OF PRESIDENT DE LA RÚA, 2001

Have you ever thought about the recipe for a bomb? . . . Take note:

First: Four years of recession.

Second: 40 percent of the people without possibilities of work.

Third: 14.5 million out of 37 million citizens living below the poverty line.

Slowly add a puny little fellow of small value as president who decrees unpopular laws.

Finally, rigorously mix with one sinister, lying, callous, paranoid, and "superpowerful" economics minister who devours a complicit parliament and squanders the reserve funds under the shadow of the International Monetary Fund.

You will have an unstable, hungry people and a highly explosive country.

December 19 and 20, 2001. Argentina experienced two of its darkest days. Thousands of the hungry people sacked supermarkets in order to obtain something to eat. The president decreed a state of siege.

Spontaneously and calmly, the middle class took to the streets of Buenos Aires against the state of siege decreed by an autistic government. They converged on the Plaza de Mayo and on Congress only with saucepans in their hands as weapons and the noise from the same as protest.

It was "the Night of the Saucepans" and the beginning of the fall of a system. . . .

What is the problem? Who created the bomb?

Incompetent politicians,

Bad administrators,

Corrupt deputies and senators,

Traitorous union bosses,

Avaricious entrepreneurs,

And you [for tolerating those above].

But since December 20, nothing will be the same. . . . It depends on you.

Take your saucepan in hand. And when you again see incompetent politicians, bad administrators, corrupt deputies and senators, traitorous union bosses, and avaricious entrepreneurs, do not allow them to activate a new bomb.

May God illuminate the road for the Argentine people.

*¡Viva la Argentina!*

■

*("Argentina—Diciembre 2001" e-mail)*

and great-grandchildren of Italians, Jews, and Spaniards lined up at the embassies to return to the lands of their ancestors. Yet the economy began to stabilize in mid-2002, and despite its weakened state, demand for the peso grew until in 2003 the Central Bank had to take precautionary measures in foreign-exchange markets to slow its rapid appreciation. Record exports soon proved foolish those who had proclaimed the export economy weak. The economy began to improve as output rose to 5.5 percent in 2003, inflation dropped to 4.2 percent, and employment rates flourished.

The 2003 default election of Nestor Kirchner, a Peronist, in a runoff against Carlos Menem, who dropped out, has enabled Argentina to regain the trust of the IMF and international leaders and push for a remarkable economic upturn, a pressing task for a president who entered office at a time when half of his nation's people were living at the poverty level. With the successful renegotiation of an agreement to repay the previously defaulted World Bank loan, Argentinians may look to the future with some hope as they begin to build up a nation that had teetered on the brink of financial collapse.

# 11

# CONCLUSION: HISTORY AS PREDATOR

An old joke goes something like this: After God created Earth, He discovered that the Southern Cone had received all the riches—fertile prairies, oil deposits, majestic mountains, attractive hills and lakes, rich river basins, and varied climates. Then, for the sake of balance, He populated the region with Argentines.

What is wrong with Argentina?

To answer the perennial Argentine Riddle, the historian might refer to an old adage in the Southern Cone: "The past is predator" (Feitlowitz 1998, xi). Juan Bautista Alberdi suggested that many of his countrymen of the 19th century seemed burdened by their historical legacy, defeated by "old habits." *A Brief History of Argentina* presents ample evidence to support this view. The predatory past stalks the inhabitants of Argentina in the form of two enduring behaviors. Social discrimination has become so ingrained in day-to-day relationships that Argentines easily overlook—even deny—its consequences. Meanwhile, the impunity enjoyed by those in a position of power, particularly political power, has permitted violence and corruption to become entrenched behavior. These problems did not originate in the last quarter of the 20th century; they began with the European settlement of the Río de la Plata more than 450 years ago. And the two behaviors have been mutually reinforcing.

## Social Discrimination

Argentine society has been deeply divided and conflicted since the first Spanish explorer sailed along the Paraná River, there to be riddled with the arrows of the native Charrúa. Thus began the centuries-long clash between two competing cultures, the indigenous and the European.

The civilizations developed autonomously and side-by-side across the frontier lines, interspersed with moments of mutually beneficial trade and moments of brutal savagery. The indigenous wars ended in 1879 only after General Julio A. Roca, representing "modern civilization," destroyed once and for all the indigenous civilization through force of arms. The prolonged conflict reinforced the use of violence in resolving disputes between two intractable parties.

Meanwhile, European civilization in the Río de la Plata was establishing a social order based initially on a hierarchy of race and power. Spanish-born whites monopolized the leading positions as merchants and public officials. To reinforce their status, they often used their authority to enrich themselves through fraud and corruption. A rapidly expanding stratum of native-born colonists filled out the lesser ranks of the white elites, but the Creoles, lacking the connections of their Iberian kinfolk, seethed as they observed Europeans enjoying greater access to wealth. The Creoles got their revenge during the War of Independence, when they replaced the Spaniards through force of arms.

As within the elite, the colonial working class also developed from unequal parts. European artisans tended to capture the higher-paying jobs, relegating the native peoples and mestizos to the menial tasks. Still, the colonial economy expanded with such vigor that it created a labor shortage. In the 17th century, merchants began to import African slaves, whose presence increased in the last century of the colonial period. Slaves worked in all sectors of the economy. They toiled on the farms of Tucumán and Mendoza, in the households of Spaniards and Creoles in Córdoba and Santa Fe, in the artisan shops of Buenos Aires and Salta, and on the farms and ranches of the Pampas. The system of slavery too depended on force and violence, the threat of which owners substituted for wages in order to force Africans to work.

The colonial social structure confused race with work to such an extent that hard labor became identified with dark skin, and vice versa. Poverty too became synonymous with skin color. Whites lost status in society if they had to work with their hands. Those with dark skin could rise only so far up the social hierarchy because their color marked them as peons and *obreros* (laborers). The reverse also was true: One's occupation as a menial worker marked light-skinned persons as if they were colored. Honorable white women of good family became accustomed to extracting long hours of work from house girls of color. After a while, it mattered little if the house girl actually was light skinned; the *patrona* still extracted long hours of service from her.

These are the reasons why massive European immigration beginning in the late 19th century changed social relationships and entrenched behaviors so little. Argentine landowners and businessmen favored gringos, or foreigners, over the criollo workers, although they tended to exploit the immigrant house girl and day worker as if they were mestizo or black. As soon as the upwardly mobile newcomers gained modest wealth, education, and family respectability, they adopted these same existing attitudes toward labor and color. Thus, the old animosities and resentments between unequal layers of the social hierarchy survived into the 20th century. One need only cite the working class's allure for union militancy and the pro-*descamisado* rhetoric of Juan Domingo Perón to understand how desperately those who worked with their hands, whether criollo or gringo, desired respect and dignity.

Argentine society of late has gained even greater heterogeneity and diversity. The present economic troubles have impelled the best and brightest of the middle class to emigrate, while mestizo laborers from Bolivia, Paraguay, Uruguay, and Chile have formed the new wave of immigration. The diversity and divisiveness of the social order, aided and abetted by continuing discrimination, reinforce the other historical predator stalking the nation—the authoritarian impulse.

## Impunity

Violence and corruption have a long history in Argentina because those who use force and graft in public life are not punished. They are rewarded! These conditions originated, once again, with European settlement. The evolution of the multiracial social order demanded stringent social controls. Those early settlers obtaining grants of Indian labor had to discipline their minions and show them new systems of work. In time, those born into the language and culture learned how to avoid work, except for the wandering gauchos who wanted to earn a few pesos. Slavery added new requirements to the agenda of social control. Every landowner, every employer, every shopkeeper, and every respectable *patrona* had to monitor the behavior of their employees. Everyone of substance feared a breach of discipline by the popular classes, because the latter greatly outnumbered the former. To recognize the disruptive potential of the disgruntled working classes, the elites had only to survey the pillage wrought by the popular rebellion of José Gervasio Artigas during the struggle for independence.

Authoritarianism began with the elites of the colonial period and the 19th century, but in the 20th century, the middle class has also embraced such tendencies. Middle-class youth have responded to national crises by sacking Jewish neighborhoods of Buenos Aires in 1919 and joining right-wing groups such as the Argentina Patriotic League and later the Catholic Action. Even Mario Firmenich, the accomplished and educated leader of the Montoneros, displayed little commitment to democratic principles in his leadership of guerrilla terrorists. Undoubtedly, the military serves as the greatest middle-class repository of authoritarian values. Time and again, army officers appointed themselves as "guarantors" of the constitution and "saviors" of the nation. Whenever workers promoted "chaos," military units sprang into action. Not all labor bosses consistently demonstrated support for democracy, either. Many ran their unions with iron fists and appeared willing to work with the most reactionary regimes.

As for violence, the lengthy warfare between the colonists and the native peoples justified its use. The ever-present danger to the colonists encouraged authoritarian leadership demanding total allegiance to the chieftain. Later, when the Creole caudillos of the post-independence period disputed control of resources among themselves, they resorted to violence to settle issues. Power flowed to he who successfully devoured the competitors, such as caudillo Juan Manuel de Rosas, who was not above summary execution and using thugs to intimidate opponents. The use of state terror by Rosas unfortunately had its 20th-century corollary in the Dirty War. *Patotas* acted as the modern-day *Mazorca,* disappearing those who threatened the "unity" of the nation. In the final analysis, political violence has survived into the 21st century.

The reader may have discerned in these pages the linkage between colonial and postcolonial corruption in politics. From the 17th-century governor who colluded with ship captains to import illegal cargoes to the modern-day entrepreneur who conspires with public officials to import luxury automobiles duty-free, from the 19th-century politician who used his rank to claim huge tracts of frontier land to modern-day politicos who bill foreign buyers millions of dollars for their services in privatization, the country's leaders have enriched themselves in public service. One element has changed over time, however: The modern opportunities for graft would make the colonial administrator envious. As the state grew more powerful and the foreign lenders more willing, the payoff increased faster than the international debt, yet as in the past, few corrupt functionaries or purveyors of violence have had to answer for their crimes.

The authoritarian impulse historically has emasculated the nation's judiciary. Argentina does not lack for lawyers, to be sure, but justice and rule of law are other matters. President Raúl Alfonsín intervened so successfully in the court proceedings for the crimes of the Dirty War, for example, that the trials resulted in the convictions of only a handful of generals and guerrilla leaders, and even they later received pardons. In essence, the murderers of thousands of citizens and the torturers of thousands more went free. This kind of impunity extends to corrupt politicians as well.

Competing politicians may wish to expose each other's graft in order to gain political leverage, but they do not prosecute the bribe takers, lest they too may one day end up in court. Carlos Saúl Menem further weakened the judicial system during his terms in office to such a degree that Argentines had to laugh at the irony implicit in one joke circulating in the 1990s. Menem was on a state visit to Bolivia, so the apocryphal story goes, and his counterpart was introducing the Argentine head of state to the Bolivian cabinet ministers. "And this is our minister of the navy." "Minister of the navy!" Menem exclaimed. "Bolivia is a landlocked country and has no navy. Why do you have a minister of the navy?" "Well," replied the Bolivian president, "you have a minister of justice."

## A Positive Trend

Perhaps the foregoing analysis will leave readers, particularly those who love Argentina and have good friends there, all too depressed. Some rays of light have shone through these pages, specifically the tremendous achievements of individual Argentines in the world of letters, music, sports, and international affairs. The nation has produced five Nobel laureates, after all. In politics, the electoral process has produced encouraging results. The parties have successfully and peacefully transferred power between them on numerous occasions, including during economic crises (which, admittedly, are far from over). There remains one major triumph, however, that deserves mention.

The residents of the Southern Cone have created a nongovernmental environment that encourages businesspeople and workers to produce tremendous economic growth; in fact, the economic record is the more remarkable for all the corruption, violence, civil warfare, and government regulation that have throttled innovation down through the ages. For most of the colonial period, the Spanish monarchs issued decree upon decree intending to restrict trade in the Río de la Plata. Despite this, commerce and production became so prominent that Crown officials eventually anointed them with a new political regime, the viceroyalty, which attempted both to stimulate and tax that growth. The colonials responded with frontier settlement and additional development of internal communications in order to push that growth to new heights.

The revolution and civil wars certainly disrupted economic exchanges throughout the former viceroyalty. Nonetheless, landowners, merchants, and peons exploited the new markets in northern Europe in a common effort to spread the cattle industry across the Pampean hunting grounds of the native peoples. Eventually, the secondary stimulus of Atlantic trade reached Santa Fe, Córdoba, and Mendoza, if not into the old colonial northwest. Toward the end of the 19th century, when European technology and capital became available, Argentine laborers and landowners responded yet again to market opportunities. They imported the necessary gringo ingenuity and enticed foreigners to build modern railways, port works, and urban infrastructures. Prosperity soared to new levels.

No matter what their views on populism, few people can ignore the remarkable success that Argentines garnered in the period of industrialization. The development of manufacturing preceded government assistance. Then in the 1930s through the 1950s, industrial production consistently outstripped all other sectors in its growing contributions to GDP. It is true that the turmoil of de-Peronization and the Dirty War inhibited even greater achievements, but politicians and the military share the blame for these failures, for they have consistently shown themselves incapable of efficiently carrying out either populist policies or neoliberal ones. Industrialists and workers together (though in uneasy alliance) built the infrastructure of a modern consumer society in defiance of politically inspired debts and inflation.

Time and again in the past, ordinary Argentine citizens have worked their way through national crises brought on by others. They have responded to every obstacle with humor and renewed energies in order to take the material welfare of the nation to unexpected levels—all the while burdened by the social discrimination and political impunity of a predatory past. How do they do it? Perhaps this is the real Argentine Riddle.

# APPENDIX 1

## BASIC FACTS ABOUT ARGENTINA

### Official Name
La República Argentina

### Government
Under the Constitution of 1853, Argentina is a federal republic with three branches of government, of which the presidency (executive) predominates. The president serves a four-year term and may be reelected for a consecutive term. The legislature is made up of the 257-member Chamber of Deputies and the 72-member Senate. Deputies serve four-year terms on a staggered basis so that half the chamber is elected every two years. Each state has three senators, who serve six-year terms. One-third of the Senate is elected every two years. The judiciary traditionally is the weakest branch of government. Federal judges are appointed by a Council of Magistrates, and the Senate approves all appointees to the Supreme Court by a two-thirds vote.

The two main parties are the Justicialista Party (the Peronists), the principal vote-getter for the last 60 years. The old Radical Party (officially known as the Unión Cívica Radical) has been prone to factional infighting since the 1920s. President Fernando de la Rúa, a Radical, won the last presidential election, held in 1999, with the support of a political coalition known as the Alianza por el Trabajo, la Justicia y la Educación (Alliance for Work, Justice, and Education).

### Political Divisions
Subdivisions    The republic consists of 23 provinces and one autonomous federal district.

279

Capital          Buenos Aires, a federal district since 1880, has served as the capital of Argentina since the colonial viceroyalty was established in 1776.

## Geography

Area          Covering a land area of 1.7 million square miles (2. 737 million square kilometers), Argentina encompasses subtropical and temperate forests, high deserts, snow-capped Andean mountain ranges, fertile prairies, and Antarctic wastes. It is about one-third the size of the continental United States. If this southern hemisphere country were superimposed on the northern hemisphere, its Antarctic tip would lie within the Hudson Bay of Canada, its semiarid Chaco region would rest in northern Mexico, and the capital of Buenos Aires would be located at the same latitude as Memphis, Tennessee.

Boundaries     Argentina is bounded on the east by the Atlantic Ocean, on the south by Antarctica, on the west by Chile, on the northwest by Bolivia, the north by Paraguay, and the northeast by Brazil and Uruguay.

Topography     The Andean cordillera forms a high mountain spine along Argentina's entire 3,195-mile, (5,150-kilometer) boundary with Chile. A series of foothills run through the westernmost states culminating in the province of Córdoba. The southern provinces, together forming a region known as Patagonia, are interspersed with river valleys draining eastward from the Andes directly into the South Atlantic.

The broad Pampas region, made up mainly of relatively flat plains, dominates the landscape between Córdoba, Santa Fe, Buenos Aires, and northern Patagonia. The eastern Pampas receives plentiful rainfall, while its western reaches tend to be drier. The Pampas serves as the breadbasket of southern South America. The area known as the Gran Chaco, which borders Bolivia and Paraguay, is semiarid and sparsely populated.

The great river basin made up of the Paraná, Paraguay, Bermejo, and Uruguay Rivers sustains navigation throughout the northeastern provinces of

Argentina. For centuries, these rivers have served as the principal Atlantic trade routes, through the estuary of the Río de la Plata to Paraguay and southwestern Brazil.

## Land Use

| | |
|---|---|
| Arable land | 6 percent |
| Permanent crops | 1 percent |
| Permanent pastures | 52 percent |
| Forest and woodlands | 19 percent |
| Other | 19 percent |
| Highest elevation | Cerro Aconcagua reaches 22,835 feet (6,960 meters) above sea level. |

## Demographics

| | |
|---|---|
| Population | The official 2000 figure, based on the census of 1991, estimates 37 million people, ranking Argentina as the sixth most populous country in the Western Hemisphere. Only the United States, Brazil, Canada, Mexico, and Colombia have larger populations. |
| Largest City | Gran Buenos Aires, made up of the federal capital and surrounding suburbs, has a population of 17.3 million persons. More than 46 percent of all Argentines live in this metropolitan area. |
| Language | Nearly all Argentines speak Spanish. Of the indigenous languages, only Guarani survives along the border with Paraguay, Aymara near the Bolivian border, and Mapuche among the remaining native groups in Patagonia. Some immigrant communities in the country still educate their youth in German, English, Italian, or French. |

## Religion

| | |
|---|---|
| Roman Catholic | 92 percent |
| Jewish | 2 percent |
| Protestant | 2 percent |
| Other | 4 percent |

## Economy

| | |
|---|---|
| Gross Domestic Product | The GDP of Argentina was estimated at $285 million in the year 2000. The size of its economy ranks third in Latin America, following Brazil and Mexico. |
| Economic Sectors | Finance, insurance, and property   21.2 percent<br>Commerce   15.8 percent<br>Manufacturing   16 percent<br>Agriculture, forestry, and fishing   5.3 percent<br>Mining   1.8 percent<br>Construction   5 percent<br>Electricity and water   2.6 percent<br>Other   32.3 percent |

## Most Important Sources of Foreign Revenues

Cereals, vegetable fats, and animal feeds
Petroleum exports
Machinery and transport equipment
Animal fats and meats
Chemicals

# APPENDIX 2
## CHRONOLOGY

### Pre-Columbian and Early Colonial Argentina

| | |
|---|---|
| 50,000 B.C. | Asian hunters cross Bering Straits |
| 12,000 | Migrating hunting bands arrive in Argentina |
| 200 B.C. | Guaraní begin migration from Brazil to Paraguay |
| A.D. 1492 | Christopher Columbus arrives in Caribbean Islands; approximately 900,000 native Americans inhabit Argentina |
| 1493 | Topa Inca integrates Diaguita of northwest Argentina into Inca Empire; native groups of the plains remain independent |
| 1516 | Juan Díaz de Solís explores the Río de la Plata estuary |
| 1520 | Ferdinand Magellan sails through straits now bearing his name, on first circumnavigation of the Earth |
| 1528 | Sebastian Cabot explores the Paraná River and is killed by Charrúa warriors |
| 1532 | Francisco Pizarro conquers Peru |
| 1535 | Pedro de Mendoza founds Buenos Aires |
| 1537 | Members of Mendoza expedition establish settlement at Asunción in present-day Paraguay |
| 1541 | Buenos Aires is abandoned due to indigenous hostilities |
| 1545 | Guaraní rebellion against Spaniards is repressed |
| 1553 | Santiago del Estero is founded |
| 1560 | Extensive silver production begins at Potosí (present-day Bolivia); illegal silver trade commences in Argentina |
| 1562 | Spanish settlements at Mendoza and San Juan are founded |
| 1565 | Tucumán is founded |

| | |
|---|---|
| 1573 | Spaniards drive out Comechingón people and found Córdoba; Santa Fe is founded by Spaniards from Paraguay |
| 1580 | Second founding of Buenos Aires is carried out by Spanish-speaking mestizos from Paraguay |
| 1583 | Salta and Jujuy are founded |
| 1588 | City of Corrientes is founded; first slaves are imported to Buenos Aires |
| 1591 | La Rioja is founded |
| 1596 | City of San Luis is founded |
| 1599 | Uprising of Araucanos (Mapuche) in Chile takes place |
| 1604 | Jesuits arrive in Paraguay |
| 1609 | Jesuits establish a college and *estancias* in Córdoba |
| 1620 | Export of *yerba mate* from Paraguay begins |
| 1622 | Customs are set up in Córdoba to discourage contraband |
| 1624 | The Hapsburg king denounces corruption and contraband in the Río de la Plata |
| 1626 | Jesuits found missions along the Uruguay River |
| 1629 | Brazilian slave hunters attack Jesuit missions |
| 1641 | Armed Guaraní from Jesuit missions defeat Brazilian slaving expedition |
| 1657 | Calchaquí rebellion is led by Pedro Bohórquez in Tucumán |
| 1674 | Paulista slaving expedition destroys Villa Rica in Paraguay; 4,607 persons live in Buenos Aires |
| 1680 | Portuguese found port of Colonia do Sacramento in Uruguay |
| 1681 | City of Catamarca is founded |
| 1702 | French company obtains monopoly to import slaves |
| 1704 | Spanish-Guaraní forces from Paraguay seize Colonia from the Portuguese |
| 1713 | First Bourbon monarch ascends throne of Spain; British company obtains monopoly to import slaves to Spanish America |
| 1714 | Colonia reverts to Portuguese; 30 Jesuits missions have 120,000 inhabitants |
| 1721 | Rebellion of Comuneros in Paraguay takes place and governor of Asunción is executed; Montevideo (modern-day Uruguay) is founded |
| 1735 | *Comunero* rebellion in Paraguay is suppressed |

| 1740 | Araucano (Mapuche) chieftains lead indigenous rebellion on the Pampas |
| 1750 | Treaty of Madrid is signed; Colonia reverts to Spain; Spanish Jesuits move seven missions out of Brazil; approximately 130,000 persons inhabit Jesuit missions |
| 1751 | Abipón warriors loot Santa Fe; Portuguese refuse to leave Colonia |
| 1753 | Indigenous rebellion breaks out in missions on the Pampas |
| 1754 | Three-year rebellion of the Guaraní mission begins |
| 1762 | Spanish forces retake Colonia |
| 1764 | Spain returns Colonia to Portugal under the Peace of Paris |
| 1767 | Jesuits are expelled from colonial Spanish America |

## The Viceroyalty and Independence

| 1776 | Viceroyalty of the Río de la Plata is established; Córdoba is the region's most populous city at 40,000 residents |
| 1777 | Spain legally reoccupies Colonia |
| 1778 | "Free trade" is permitted between the colonies and 13 Spanish ports |
| 1780–83 | Tupac Amaru rebellion rages in Andean highlands |
| 1786 | Intendancies are instituted in the viceroyalty to collect taxes |
| 1787 | The Filipinas Company gains monopoly to import slaves to Buenos Aires; large slave market is constructed |
| 1791 | Free trade is established on the import of slaves |
| 1797 | Blandengues rural police force is established in the Banda Oriental; Spanish tax agents collect 5.8 million pesos throughout the viceroyalty; British blockade Spanish trade |
| 1806 | 2,733 slaves are imported legally; first British invasion of Montevideo and Buenos Aires takes place |
| 1807 | Second British invasion occurs; Santiago Liniers is named viceroy; Creole militias expel British troops while Spanish merchants trade with the enemy; Napoléon invades the Iberian Peninsula |
| 1809 | Liniers is replaced as viceroy by Spanish authorities |
| 1810 | *Cabildo abierto* establishes Creole government at Buenos Aires; slave trade is outlawed |

| 1811 | Paraguayans repel invasion from Buenos Aires, overthrow Spanish governor, and declare independence; first invasion of Bolivia takes place |
|------|------|
| 1813 | Law of the Free Womb is passed to phase out slavery; second invasion of Bolivia is undertaken |
| 1815 | José Gervasio Artigas becomes "protector" of the interior provinces; *porteño* troops invade Bolivia for third time |
| 1816 | Representatives in Tucumán declare independence and establish the United Provinces of the River Plate; José de San Martín defeats royalist invasion from Peru |
| 1817 | San Martín liberates Chile |

## Age of *Caudillos*

| 1820 | Buenos Aires government is overthrown; *caudillos* rule provinces |
|------|------|
| 1821 | University of Buenos Aires is founded |
| 1822 | San Martín gives up command of Peruvian campaign to Simón Bolívar |
| 1824 | San Martín departs from Buenos Aires for exile in Paris; Baring loan of 1 million pounds sterling is acquired in England |
| 1825 | War with the empire of Brazil breaks out |
| 1826 | United Provinces defaults on Baring loan |
| 1828 | War with Brazil ends; Uruguay becomes independent; *porteño* troops rebel and Buenos Aires governor Manuel Dorrego is assassinated |
| 1829 | Juan Manuel de Rosas becomes governor of Buenos Aires province |
| 1832 | English writer Charles Darwin tours the Pampas |
| 1835 | Rosas appointed governor of Buenos Aires for second time, with dictatorial powers |
| 1838 | France blockades port of Buenos Aires |
| 1845 | Great Britain begins three-year blockade of Buenos Aires |
| 1852 | Rosas is deposed by Justo José de Urquiza |
| 1853 | Constitution establishes the Republic of Argentina; slaves are emancipated; national army is formed |
| 1859 | Urquiza resigns after losing the battle of Pavón |
| 1862 | President Bartolomé Mitre encourages railway building |

| | |
|---|---|
| 1865 | Five-year war begins against Paraguay |
| 1872 | *Martín Fierro,* written by José Hernández, is published |
| 1876 | Last great raid by indigenous war parties occurs |
| 1879 | Conquest of Desert under General Julio A. Roca marks the end of indigenous resistance; southern Pampas and Patagonia become open for settlement |

## Age of Liberalism

| | |
|---|---|
| 1880 | Roca becomes president; City of Buenos Aires is federalized |
| 1890 | Opponents of the Generation of Eighty Revolt; University of La Plata is founded |
| 1891 | Banco de la Nación Argentina is established |
| 1893 | Financial crisis occurs; farmers revolt; President Miguel Juárez Celman resigns |
| 1895 | Monument is built to La Difunta Correa |
| 1902 | Workers launch first general strike in Buenos Aires; law is passed to expel foreign-born "troublemakers" |
| 1905 | Radicals revolt |
| 1909 | Porteño police chief is assassinated by anarchist |
| 1910 | More than 15.5 million acres (6.3 million hectares) of wheat are cultivated |
| 1912 | Farm tenants strike in Entre Ríos; electoral laws are reformed |
| 1914 | Railways consist of 21,400 miles (34,500 kilometers) of track; 30 percent of country's inhabitants are immigrants; Buenos Aires has 1.5 million residents |
| 1916 | Hipólito Yrigoyen is elected president; Conservative Party peacefully transfers power to Radical Party |
| 1917 | Labor strikes reach crescendo; singers Carlos Gardel and José Razzano revive "criollo" music; Bernardo Hussay wins Nobel Prize in medicine |
| 1918 | University strikes erupt; student admissions are expanded; universities are founded in Santa Fe and Tucumán |
| 1919 | Right-wing vigilantes kill hundreds in Jewish neighborhoods of Buenos Aires during the Semana Trágica |
| 1922 | Army suppresses workers' strikes in Patagonia; YPF is founded as the state oil company; Unión Ferroviaria is founded to represent railway workers; Marcelo T. de Alvear becomes president |

| 1928 | Yrigoyen is elected president for second time |
|------|-----------------------------------------------|
| 1929 | YPF establishes uniform price system for oil products |

## Age of Populism

| 1930 | Export prices plummet; General José F. Uriburu ousts Yrigoyen in first military coup of 20th century |
|------|------|
| 1932 | General Augustín Justo is elected president after some voting irregularities; Radicals prevented from participating in election |
| 1934 | Roca-Runciman Treaty preserves British markets for Argentine exports |
| 1936 | Buenos Aires grows to 2.4 million residents; tango great Gardel dies; Carlos Saavadra Lamas wins Nobel Peace Prize |
| 1938 | Electoral fraud is widespread in presidential election of Conservative Roberto M. Ortiz |
| 1941 | Fabricaciones Militares is established under military control to manufacture war supplies |
| 1943 | Nationalist army officers lead coup d'etat; Juan Domingo Perón takes over Labor Department |
| 1945 | Massive demonstration denounces Perón's prolabor policies; workers demonstrate on October 17 to free Perón from arrest |
| 1946 | Perón is elected president |
| 1947 | Women gain voting rights; 4.7 million out of 16 million Argentines live in Buenos Aires |
| 1948 | Perón nationalizes railway industry by buying out British companies |
| 1950 | Union membership reaches 2 million; blue-collar workers receive 50 percent of national income |
| 1952 | Perón is reelected; Evita Perón dies; drought and recession produce 80 percent inflation; workers protest austerity plans |
| 1953 | Victoria Ocampo is arrested and jailed for 26 days |
| 1954 | Catholic Action leads opposition to Perón; church-state relations deteriorate |
| 1955 | Military takes power in the Revolución Libertadora; Perón lives in exile the next 18 years |

| | |
|---|---|
| 1956 | General Pedro E. Aramburu and military junta begin de-Peronization; Evita's body disappears for next 17 years; workers resist; Ernesto "Che" Guevara meets Fidel Castro in Mexico |
| 1958 | Peronists are prevented from participating in elections; Arturo Frondizi is elected president |
| 1960 | S.I.A.M. produces first and only Argentine-engineered automobile |
| 1961 | Guevara makes secret visit to Buenos Aires |
| 1962 | Military removes Frondizi from the presidency |
| 1963 | *Peronistas* are again excluded from elections as Arturo Illia wins as president |
| 1966 | Military coup replaces Illia as president with General Juan Carlos Onganía; Police invade university campuses during the Night of the Long Pencils |
| 1967 | Guevara is captured and executed in Bolivia |
| 1969 | Cordobazo strike is held by workers and students; Montonero guerrillas kidnap and execute Aramburu |
| 1970 | Luis Federico Leloir wins Nobel Prize in chemistry |
| 1972 | U.S. investments reach $1.8 billion; 23 foreign car companies manufacture in Argentina |
| 1973 | Peronists win presidential elections; guerrillas are released from jail; Perón returns to the presidency despite violence between factions of his supporters |
| 1974 | Perón dies and his wife, Isabel, succeeds as president; Montoneros declare war against government; Argentine Anticommunist Alliance (Triple A) begins counterterrorist activities; Evita's body is returned |
| 1976 | Inflation reaches 600 percent; military coup deposes Isabel Perón as president; *patota* squads begin to eliminate leftist "suspects" |
| 1977 | Mothers of the Plaza de Mayo begin first protests against military terror |
| 1978 | Argentina hosts World Cup; home team wins |
| 1979 | Workers organize general strike to protest military government |
| 1982 | Military government invades Falkland Islands; British expeditionary force defeats Argentina; Nobel laureate Adolfo Pérez Esquivel leads huge antimilitary demonstration |

## The Age of Neoliberalism

| | |
|---|---|
| 1983 | Inflation rises to 343 percent; international debt reaches $45 billion; Paúl Alfonsín of the Radical Party wins presidential election |
| 1984 | *Nunca Más* is published; prosecution of military officers for human rights abuses begins; César Milstein wins Nobel Prize in medicine |
| 1886 | Plan Austral reduces inflation to 80 percent |
| 1887 | Carapintada commando troops rebel for first time |
| 1989 | Left-wing guerrillas attack an army base; inflation rises to 3,000 percent; IMF riots break out; Carlos Saúl Menem of the Peronist Party wins election; body of Rosas is repatriated; privatization begins |
| 1990 | Final Carapintada rebellion precedes visit of President George H. W. Bush; Convertibility Plan pegs the peso to the dollar |
| 1991 | Mercosur is formed by Argentina and three neighbors; news stories appear concerning high-level corruption |
| 1994 | Car bomb destroys Jewish community center in Buenos Aires and kills 86 people |
| 1995 | Inflation declines to 3 percent; Menem is reelected for second presidential term |
| 1997 | Official unemployment rate reaches 17 percent; 40,000 unemployed workers join protest march |
| 1999 | Economic recession commences; Radical election victory puts Fernando de la Rúa in the presidency |
| 2001 | Recession completes third year; international debt reaches $132 billion; second IMF riots occur; de la Rúa resigns; after three other interim presidents come and go during a two-week period, Eduardo Duhalde, a Peronist, becomes interim president |
| 2002 | Peso is severed from dollar and falls in value by 40 percent |
| 2003 | Nestor Kirchner assumes the presidency after winning a runoff election from which Carlos Menem dropped out; 40 former military officers are held for alleged crimes against humanity during the military years of 1976–83; laws allowing former military officers immunity from prosecution overturned in Congress; World Bank repayment negotiated, ameliorating relations with the IMF |

# Appendix 3

## Bibliography

Alberdi, Juan Bautista. *The Life and Industrial Labors of William Wheelwright in South America. Translated from the Spanish.* Boston: A. Williams, 1877.

Anderson, Jon Lee. *Che Guevara: A Revolutionary Life.* New York: Grove Press, 1997.

Anderson, Martin. *Dossier Secreto: Argentina's Desaparecidos and the Myth of the "Dirty War."* Boulder, Colo.: Westview Press, 1993.

Andrien, Kenneth J., and Lyman L. Johnson. *The Political Economy of Spanish America in the Age of Revolution, 1750–1850.* Albuquerque: University of New Mexico Press, 1994.

Angelis, Pedro de, ed. *Colección de obras y documentos relativos a la historia antigua y moderna de las provincias del Río de la Plata.* 3 vols. 1835. Reprint, Buenos Aires: Editorial Plus Ultra, 1969.

Anna, Timothy E. *The Fall of the Royal Government in Peru.* Lincoln: University of Nebraska Press, 1979.

Baily, Samuel L., and Franco Ramella, eds. *One Family, Two Worlds: An Italian Family's Correspondence across the Atlantic, 1901–1922.* Trans. John Lenaghan. New Brunswick, N.J.: Rutgers University Press, 1988.

Beaumont, J. A. B. *Travels in Buenos Ayres, and the Adjacent Provinces of the Río de la Plata.* London: J. Ridgeway, 1828.

Bethell, Leslie, ed. *The Cambridge History of Latin America.* Vol. 1, *Colonial Latin America.* Cambridge, England: Cambridge University Press, 1984.

———. *The Independence of Latin America.* Cambridge, England: Cambridge University Press, 1987.

Boczek, Barbara Aniela. "Early, Self-Proclaimed Nationalists in Argentina, 1928–1932: Historical Ties and Contemporary Nemeses." M. A. report, University of Texas at Austin, 1991.

Bourvard, Marguerite Guzmán. *Revolutionizing Motherhood: The Mothers of the Plaza de Mayo.* Wilmington, Del.: Scholarly Resources, 1994.

Brand, Charles. *Journal of a Voyage to Peru.* London: H. Colburn, 1828.

Brennan, James P. *The Labor Wars in Córdoba, 1955–76: Ideology, Work, and Labor Politics in an Argentine Industrial City.* Cambridge, Mass.: Harvard University Press, 1994.

Brown, Jonathan C. "British Petroleum Pioneers in Mexico and South America." No. 89–17, Texas Papers on Latin America. Institute of Latin American Studies, University of Texas at Austin.

———. "What Historians Reveal About Labor and Free Trade in Latin America." *Work and Occupations* 24, no. 3 (August 1997): 381–98.

———. "Juan Bautista Alberdi y la doctrina del capitalismo liberal en Argentina, *Revista Ciclos* 3, no. 4 (1993): 69–74.

———. *A Socioeconomic History of Argentina, 1776–1860.* Cambridge, England: Cambridge University Press, 1979.

———, ed. *Workers' Control in Latin America, 1930–1979.* Chapel Hill: University of North Carolina Press, 1997.

Campbell, J. *An Account of the Spanish Settlements in America.* Edinburgh, Scotland: A. Donaldson & J. Reid, 1762.

Canabrava, Alice Piffer. *O comércio portugues no Rio da Prata, 1580–1640.* São Paulo: Universidad de São Paulo, 1944.

Carbonell de Masy, Rafael. *Estrategias de desarrollo rural en los pueblos guaraníes (1609–1767).* Barcelona: Antoni Bosch, 1992.

Carlos II. "Resumen de las consultas en que su majestad resolvió fundar y extinguir la Audiencia de Buenos Aires … [c. 1672]". Document number 318, Manuel E. Gondra Manuscript Collection. University of Texas Library, Austin.

*Censo industrial y comercio.* Boletín no. 17. Buenos Aires: Oficina Meterológica Argentina, 1913.

Chiaramonte, José Carlos. *Nacionalismo y liberalismo económico en Argentina, 1860–1880.* Buenos Aires: Solar/Hachette, 1971.

Christian, Shirley. "Bluntly Put, It's Graft: U.S. Envoy Speaks Out." *New York Times,* January 16, 1991, 10.

———. "Tango with Peronist? Who's Afraid?" *New York Times,* July 4, 1989, 4.

Cochran, Thomas C., and Ruben E. Reina. *Capitalism in Argentine Culture: A Study of Torcuato Di Tella and S.I.A.M.* Philadelphia: University of Pennsylvania Press, 1962.

Cohen, Roger. "Argentina Sees Other Face of Globalization." *New York Times,* February 6, 1998, A1, A7.

Collier, Simon. *Ideas and Politics of Chilean Independence, 1808–1833.* Cambridge, England: Cambridge University Press, 1969.

————. *The Life and Times of Carlos Gardel.* Pittsburgh, Pa.: University of Pittsburgh Press, 1986.

Comandrán Ruiz, Jorge. *Evolución demográfica argentina durante el período hispánico (1535–1810).* Buenos Aires: Editorial Universitaria de Buenos Aires, 1969.

Comisión Directiva del Censo. *Segundo censo de la República Argentina, 1895.* 3 vols. Buenos Aires: Taller de la Penitenciaría Nacional, 1898.

Comisión Nacional de Censos. *Tercer censo nacional, 1914.* 10 vols. Buenos Aires: L. J. Rossi, 1916–1919.

Concolorcorvo (Alonso Carrió de la Bandera). *El Lazarillo: A Guide for Inexperienced Travelers Between Buenos Aires and Lima, 1773.* Trans. Walter D. Kline. Bloomington: Indiana University Press, 1965.

Coni, Emilio. *Historia de las vaquerías del Río de la Plata (1555–1750).* Madrid: Tipografía de Archivos, 1930.

Cook, Noble David. *Born to Die: Disease and New World Conquest (1492–1650).* Cambridge, England: Cambridge University Press, 1998.

Cook, Noble David, and W. George Lovell, eds. *"Secret Judgments of God": Old World Disease in Colonial Spanish America.* Norman: University of Oklahoma Press, 1992.

Cooney, Jerry W. *Economía y sociedad en la intendencia del Paraguay.* Asunción: Centro Paraguayo de Estudios Sociológicos, 1990.

Cox, Lisa Diane. "Repression and Rank-and-File Pressure during the Argentine Process of National Reorganization, 1976–1983." M.A. thesis, University of Texas at Austin, 1995.

Crites, Byron. "Native Railroad Workers and Foreign Businesses in Argentina: 1916–1930." M.A. report, University of Texas at Austin, 2001.

Crump, W. B. *The Leeds Woollen Industry, 1720–1820.* Leeds, England: The Thoresby Society, 1931.

Cushner, Nicholas P. *Jesuit Ranches and the Agrarian Development of Colonial Argentina, 1650–1767.* Albany: State University of New York Press, 1983.

Darwin, Charles. *The Voyage of the* Beagle. New York: Bantam, 1858.

Denevan, William D., ed. *The Native Population of the Americas in 1492,* 2d ed. Madison: University of Wisconsin Press, 1992.

Díaz Alejandro, Carlos F. *Essays on the Economic History of the Argentine Republic.* New Haven, Conn.: Yale University Press, 1970.

Di Tella, Guido, and Carlos Rodríguez Braun. *Argentina, 1946–1983: The Economic Ministers Speak.* New York: St. Martin's Press, 1990.

———. *Argentina under Perón, 1973–1976.* London: Macmillan, 1981.

Di Tella, Guido, and Rudiger Dornbusch, eds. *The Political Economy of Argentina, 1946–83.* Basingstoke, England: Macmillan, 1989.

Di Tella, Guido, and D. C. M. Platt, eds. *The Political Economy of Argentina, 1880–1946.* Basingstoke, England: Macmillan, 1986.

Di Tella, Torcuato S. *Historia argentina desde los orígenes hasta nuestros días.* 2 vols. Buenos Aires: Editorial Troquel, 1995.

———. *Historia social de la Argentina contemporánea.* Buenos Aires: Troquel, 1998.

Di Tella, Torcuato S., Gino Germani, and Jorge Graciarena, eds. *Argentina: Sociedad de masas.* 3d ed. Buenos Aires: Editorial Universitaria de Buenos Aires, 1966.

Dobritzhoffer, Martin. *An Account of the Abipones, an Equestrial People of Paraguay.* 3 vols. London: J. Murray, 1822.

du Biscay, Acarete. *Account of a Voyage up the River de la Plata and Thence Overland to Peru.* 1698. Reprint, North Haven, Conn.: Institute Publishing, 1968.

*Economist* Intelligence Unit. *Country Report: Argentina.*

Faddis, Matthew James. "Getting Away with Murder: Actions by the Argentine Military to Escape Culpability for Crimes Committed During the Process of National Reorganization." M.A. report, University of Texas at Austin, 1997.

Falkner, Thomas. *A Description of Patagonia, and the Adjoining Parts of South America.* 1774. Reprint, Chicago: Armann & Armann, 1935.

Feitlowitz, Marguerite. *A Lexicon of Terror: Argentina and the Legacies of Torture.* New York: Oxford University Press, 1998.

Fisher, Jo. *Mothers of the Disappeared.* Boston: South End Press, 1989.

Florescano, Enrique, ed. *Haciendas, latifundios y plantaciones en América Latina.* Mexico City: Siglo Ventiuno, 1975.

Fradkin, Raúl O., ed. *La historia agraria del Río de la Plata colonial: Los establecimientos productivos.* Buenos Aires: Centro Editor de América Latina, 1993.

Furlong, Guillermo. *Entre los pampas de Buenos Aires.* Buenos Aires: Talleres Gráficos "San Pablo," 1938.

———. *Misiones y sus pueblos de guaraníes.* Buenos Aires: Imprenta Balmes, 1962.

Gandía, Enrique de. *Francisco de Alfaro y la condición social de los indios: Río de la Plata, Paraguay, Tucumán y Perú, siglos XVI y XVII.* Buenos Aires: Librería y Editorial "El Ateneo," 1939.

Ganson, Barbara A. "Better Not Take My Manioc: Guaraní Religion, Society, and Politics in the Jesuit Missions of Paraguay, 1500–1800." Ph.D. diss., University of Texas at Austin, 1994.

Garaveglia, Juan Carlos. *Economía, sociedad y regiones.* Buenos Aires: Ediciones de la Flor, 1987.

Garaveglia, Juan Carlos, and Jorge Gelman, eds. *El mundo rural rioplatense a fines de la época colonial.* Buenos Aires: Biblos/Fundación Simón Rodríguez, 1989.

García, Juan Agustín. *La ciudad indiana: Buenos Aires desde 1600 hasta mediados del siglo XVIII.* 1955. Reprint, Buenos Aires: Editorial Universitaria, 1966.

Gelman, Jorge. *Campesinos y estancieros.* Buenos Aires: Editorial Los Libros Riel, 1998.

Goldman, Noemi, and Ricardo D. Salvatore. *Caudillismos rioplatenses: Nuevas miradas a un viejo problema.* Buenos Aires: Eudeba, 1998.

Gómez, Jesús Fernando. "Military Rule in Argentina, 1976–1983: Suppressing the Peronists." M.A. thesis, University of Texas at Austin, 2001.

Góngora, Mario. *Los grupos de conquistadores en Tierra Firme (1509–1530).* Santiago: Universidad de Chile, 1962.

González, José Eduardo. *Borges and the Politics of Form.* New York: Garland, 1998.

Graham-Yooll, Andrew. *A State of Fear: Memories of Argentina's Nightmare.* London: Eland Books, 1986.

Groot, José Manuel. *Historia eclesiástica y civil de Nueva Granada.* 5 vols. Bogotá: Casa Editorial de M. Rivas, 1889–93.

Guy, Donna J. *Sex and Danger in Buenos Aires: Prostitution, Family, and Nation in Argentina.* Lincoln: University of Nebraska Press, 1991.

Halperín Donghi, Tulio. *Reforma y disolución de los imperios ibéricos, 1750–1850.* Madrid: Alianza Editorial, 1985.

———. *Revolución y guerra: Formación de una élite dirigente en la Argentina criolla.* Buenos Aires: Siglo Vientiuno, 1972.

Hammond, Gregory Sowles. "The Institution of Eva Perón: Extensions of the State in Argentina." M.A. thesis, University of Texas at Austin, 2000.

Harrison, Margaret H. *Captain of the Andes: The Life of Don Jose de San Martin, Liberator of Argentina, Chile and Peru.* New York: Richard R. Smith, 1943.

Hernández, Isabel. *Los indios de Argentina.* Madrid: Editorial Mapfre, 1992.

Hernández, José. *The Gaucho Martín Fierro.* Trans. C. E. Ward. Albany: State University of New York Press, 1967.

Hibbert, Edward. *Narrative of a Journey from Santiago de Chile to Buenos Ayres.* London: J. Murray, 1824.

Hsiao, Yao-sung Thomas. "Perón, Leaders and Centralization of Labor Unions." M.A. report, University of Texas at Austin, 1992.

James, Daniel. *Resistance and Integration: Peronism and the Argentine Working Class, 1946–1976.* Cambridge, England: Cambridge University Press, 1994.

Jara, Alvaro. *Guerra y sociedad en Chile: La transformación de la guerra de Arauco y la esclavitud de los indios.* Santiago, Chile: Editorial Universitaria, 1971.

Johnson, Lyman L., and Enrique Tandeter. *Essays on the Price History of Eighteenth Century Latin America.* Albuquerque: University of New Mexico Press, 1990.

Josephy, Alvin M., Jr. *America in 1492: The World of the Indian Peoples Before the Arrival of Columbus.* New York: Vintage Books, 1993.

Kelly, Kevin James. "Juan Manuel de Rosas: Nineteenth Century Argentine Populist." Ph.D. diss., University of Texas at Austin, 1988.

Kinsbruner, Jay. *Independence in Spanish America: Civil Wars, Revolutions, and Underdevelopment.* Albuquerque: University of New Mexico Press, 1994.

Kon, Daniel. *Los Chicos de la Guerra: The Boys of War.* London: New English Library, 1983.

Larden, Walter. *Estancia Life: Agricultural, Economic, and Cultural Aspects of Argentine Farming.* London: T. Fisher Unwin, 1911.

Levene, Ricardo. *El genio político de San Martín.* Buenos Aires: Editorial Guillermo Kraft, 1950.

Levillier, Roberto, ed. *Gobernación del Tucumán: Probanzas de méritos y servicios de los conquistadores.* 3 vols. Madrid: Sucesores de Rivadeneyra, 1919.

Lewis, Colin M., and Nissa Torrents, eds. *Argentina in the Crises Years (1983–1990): From Alfonsín to Menem.* London: Institute of Latin American Studies, 1993.

Lewis, Paul. *The Crisis of Argentine Capitalism.* Chapel Hill: University of North Carolina Press, 1990.

———. *Guerrillas and Generals: The "Dirty War" in Argentina.* Westport, Conn.: Praeger Publishers, 2002.

Liss, Peggy K. *Atlantic Empires: The Network of Trade and Revolution, 1713–1826.* Baltimore: Johns Hopkins University Press, 1982.

Luna, Félix *Historia integral de la Argentina.* 10 vols. Buenos Aires: Planeta, 1995.

Lynch, John. *Argentine Dictator: Juan Manuel de Rosas, 1829–1852.* Oxford, England: Oxford University Press, 1981.

———. *The Spanish American Revolutions, 1808–1826.* 2d ed. New York: W. W. Norton, 1987.

MacCann, William. *Two Thousand Miles' Ride Through the Argentine Provinces.* 2 vols. London: Smith, Elder, 1853.

McGann, Thomas F. *Argentina, the United States, and the Inter-American System.* Cambridge, Mass.: Harvard University Press, 1957.

Magnusson, Wayne Peter. "Institutionalizing State-Sponsored Terrorism: A Decade of Violence in Argentine Terrorism, 1970–1979." M.A. thesis, University of Texas at Austin, 1998.

Mansilla, Lucío V. *An Expedition to the Ranquel Indians.* Trans. Mark McCaffrey. Austin: University of Texas Press, 1997.

Martínez Savasola, Carlos. *Los hijos de la tierra: Historia de los indígenas argentinos.* Buenos Aires: Emecé Editores, 1998.

Masini, José Luis. *La esclavitud negra en Mendoza, época independiente.* Mendoza, Argentina: D'Accurzio, 1965.

Maura, Juan Francisco. *Women in the Conquest of the Americas.* Trans. John F. Deredita. New York: P. Lang, 1997.

Mayo, Carlos A. *Estancia y sociedad en la pampa, 1740–1820.* Buenos Aires: Editorial Biblos, 1995.

Mayo, Carlos A., and Amalia Latrubesse. *Terratenientes, soldados y cautivos: La frontera (1736–1815).* Mar del Plata, Argentina: Universidad Nacional de Mar del Plata, 1993.

Méndez, Jesús. "Argentine Intellectuals in the Twentieth Century." Ph.D. diss., University of Texas at Austin, 1980.

Meyer, Doris. *Victoria Ocampo: Against the Wind and the Tide.* Austin: University of Texas Press, 1990.

Mirelman, Victor A. *Jewish Buenos Aires, 1890–1930: In Search of an Identity.* Detroit: Wayne State University Press, 1990.

Moreno, Mariano. *Representación que el apoderado de los hacendados de las campañas del Río de la Plata dirigió al Exmo. Sr. Virey D. Baltasar Hidalgo de Cisneros.* Bueno Aires: Imprenta Especial, 1874.

Morison, Samuel Eliot. *The European Discovery of America: The Southern Voyages, 1492–1619.* New York: Oxford University Press, 1974.

Mosconi, Enrique. *La batalla del petróleo: YPF y las empresas extranjeras.* Buenos Aires: Ediciones Problemas Nacionales, 1957.

Moutoukias, Zacarías. *Contrabando y control colonial en el siglo XVII: Buenos Aires, el Atlántico y el espacio peruano.* Buenos Aires: Centro Editor de América Latina, 1988.

Moya, Jose C. *Cousins and Strangers: Spanish Immigrants in Buenos Aires, 1850–1930.* Berkeley: University of California Press, 1998.

Moyano, María José. *Argentina's Lost Patrol: Armed Struggle, 1969–1979.* New Haven, Conn.: Yale University Press, 1995.

Nash, Nathaniel C. "Argentines Escape an Economic Mire: A Success Story, Yes, but No Miracle." *New York Times,* July 25, 1993, 6.

———. "Justice Proves to Be Sluggish in Argentina's Corruption Cases." *New York Times,* December 15, 1991, 15.

Nicolau, Juan Carlos. "Comercio exterior por el puerto de Buenos Aires: Movimiento marítimo (1810–1855)." MS.

Norden, Deborah L. *Military Rebellion in Argentina: Between Coups and Consolidation.* Lincoln: University of Nebraska Press, 1996.

*Papeles Ventura Miguel Marcó del Pont.* Benson Latin American Collection. University of Texas Library, Austin.

Parish, Woodbine. *Buenos Ayres and Provinces of the Rio de la Plata: Their Present State, Trade, and Debt.* London: J. Murray, 1852.

Parry, John H. *The Age of Reconnaissance.* New York: Mentor Books, 1974.

Parry, John H., and Robert G. Keith. *New Iberian World: A Documentary History of the Discovery and Settlement of Latin America to the Early 17th Century.* 5 vols. New York: Times Books, 1984.

Perón, Juan Domingo. *Peron Expounds His Doctrine.* Trans. Argentine Association of English Culture. Buenos Aires: n.p., 1948.

Pierce, Barbara Eleanor. "The Argentine Military Junta's Ideology in the Dirty War: The Ongoing Battle to Conquer Barbarism." M.A. thesis, University of Texas at Austin, 1993.

Poenitz, Alfredo Juan Erich. "Conflict for Labor Leadership in Latin America, 1918–1955." M.A. thesis, University of Texas at Austin, 1990.

Potash, Robert A. *The Army and Politics in Argentina.* 3 vols. Stanford, Calif.: Stanford University Press, 1969–1996.

Qamber, Rukhsana. "Government Policy towards Public Land: Mexico and Argentina, 1880–1910." Ph.D. diss., University of Texas at Austin, 1992.

Ramírez, Gilberto, Jr. "The Reform of the Argentine Army, 1890–1904." Ph.D. diss., University of Texas at Austin, 1987.

Randall, Laura. *A Comparative Economic History of Latin America.* Vol. 1, *Argentina.* Ann Arbor, Mich.: University Microfilms, 1977.

———. *An Economic History of Argentina in the Twentieth Century.* New York: Columbia University Press, 1978.

*Registro estadístico de Buenos Aires, 1854.* Buenos Aires, 1855.

Rochford, David John. "In Search of a Popular Mission: The Argentine Catholic Church under Juan Perón, 1946–1955." M.A. report, University of Texas at Austin, 1992.

Rock, David. *Argentina, 1516–1987: From Spanish Colonization to Alfonsín.* Berkeley: University of California Press, 1987.

Ross, Stanley R., and Thomas F. McGann, eds. *Buenos Aires: 400 Years.* Austin: University of Texas Press, 1982.

Roulet, Florencia. *La resistencia de los Guaraní del Paraguay a la Conquista Española [1537–1556].* Posadas, Argentina: Editorial Universitaria Universidad Nacional de Misiones, 1993.

Saguier, Eduardo R. *Mercado inmobiliario y estructura social: El Río de la Plata en el siglo XVIII.* Buenos Aires: Centro Editor de América Latina, 1993.

Sala de Tourón, Lucía, Nelson de la Torre, and Julio C. Rodríguez. *Artigas y su revolución agraria, 1811–1820.* Mexico City: Siglo Vientiuno, 1978.

Salvatore, Ricardo D., and Carlos Aguirre, eds. *The Birth of the Penitentiary in Latin America: Essays on Criminology, Prison Reform, and Social Control, 1830–1940.* Austin: University of Texas Press, 1996.

Salvatore, Ricardo D., and Jonathan C. Brown. "The Old Problem of Gauchos and Rural Society." *Hispanic American Historical Review* 69, no. 4 (1989): 733–45.

Salvatore, Ricardo Donato. "Class Struggle and International Trade: Río de la Plata's Commerce and the Atlantic Proletariat, 1790–1850." Ph.D. Diss., University of Texas at Austin, 1987.

Sarmiento, Domingo F. *Life in the Argentine Republic in the Days of the Tyrants, or Civilization and Barbarism.* New York: Hafner Press, 1974.

Sarobe, José M. *Memorias sobre la revolución del 6 de septiembre de 1930.* Buenos Aires: Ediciones Gure, 1957.

Schmidl, Ulrich. *The Conquest of the River Plate (1535–1555).* London: Hakluyt Society, 1891.

Scobie, James R. *Argentina: A City and a Nation.* 2d ed. New York: Oxford University Press, 1971.

———. *Revolution on the Pampas: A Social History of Argentine Wheat, 1860–1910.* Austin: University of Texas Press, 1964.

Sempat Assadourian, Carlos. *El sistema de la economía colonial: El mercado interior. Regiones y espacio económico.* Mexico City: Editorial Nueva Imagen, 1983.

———. *El tráfico de esclavos en Córdoba, 1588–1610.* Córdoba, Argentina: Universidad Nacional de Córdoba, 1965.

Sempat Assadourian, Carlos, Guillermo Beato, and José Carlos Chiaramonte. *Argentina: De la conquista a la independencia.* Buenos Aires: Paidós, 1972.

Service, Elman R. *Spanish-Guaraní Relations in Early Colonial Paraguay.* Ann Arbor: University of Michigan Press, 1954.

Simpson, John, and Jana Bennett. *The Disappeared and the Mothers of the Plaza: The Story of the 11,000 Argentinians Who Vanished.* New York: St. Martin's Press, 1985.

Smith, Peter H. *Politics and Beef in Argentina: Patterns of Conflict and Change.* New York: Columbia University Press, 1969.

Socolow, Susan Migden. *The Merchants of Buenos Aires, 1778–1810: Family and Commerce.* Cambridge, England: Cambridge University Press, 1978.

Solberg, Carl. "Entrepreneurship in Public Enterprise: General Enrique Mosconi and the Argentine Petroleum Industry," *Business History Review* 56, no. 3 (1982): 389.

———. *Immigration and Nationalism: Argentina and Chile, 1890–1914.* Austin: University of Texas Press, 1970.

———. *Oil and Nationalism in Argentina.* Stanford, Calif.: Stanford University Press, 1979.

Spears, Andrea Lynn. "Labor's Response to Centralization and Rationalization: The Argentine Railway Strikes, 1950–1951." M. A. thesis, University of Texas at Austin, 1990.

Steward, Julian H., ed. *Handbook of South American Indians.* 7 vols. 1946. Reprint, 8 vols. New York: Cooper Square Publishers, 1963.

Street, John. *Artigas and the Emancipation of Uruguay.* Cambridge, England: Cambridge University Press, 1959.

Studer, Elena F. S. de. *La trata de negros en el Río de la Plata durante el siglo XVIII.* Buenos Aires: Universidad de Buenos Aires, 1958.

Supplee, Joan Ellen. "Provincial Elites and the Economic Transformation of Mendoza, Argentina, 1880–1914." Ph.D. diss., University of Texas at Austin, 1988.

Szuchman, Mark D., and Jonathan C. Brown, eds. *Revolution and Restoration: The Rearrangement of Power in Argentina, 1776–1860.* Lincoln: University of Nebraska Press, 1994.

"A Talk with Carlos Menem: 'Subsidies No Longer Exist.'" *Business Week* (October 2, 1989): 46.

TePaske, John Jay, and Herbert S. Klein. *The Royal Treasuries of the Spanish Empire in America.* Vol. 3, *Chile and the Río de la Plata.* Durham, N.C.: Duke University Press, 1982.

Timerman, Jacobo. *Prisoner Without a Name, Cell Without a Number.* New York: Alfred A. Knopf, 1981.

Tjarks, Germán O. E., and Alicia Vidaurreta. *El comercio inglés y el contrabando: Nuevos aspectos en el estudio de la política económica en el Río de la Plata, 1807–1810.* Buenos Aires: Self-published, 1962.

Tornquist, Ernesto. *The Economic Development of the Argentine Republic in the Last Fifty Years.* Buenos Aires: Tornquist y Cía, 1919.

Verbitsky, Horacio. "Argentina Retreats from Democracy." *New York Times,* October 3, 1992, 21.

———. *Medio siglo de proclamas militares.* Buenos Aires: Editora 12, 1987.

Videl, E. E. *Picturesque Illustrations of Buenos Aires and Montevideo.* London: R. Ackerman, 1820.

Villalobos R., Sergio. *Comercio y contrabando en el Río de la Plata y Chile, 1700–1811.* Buenos Aires: Editorial Universitaria de Buenos Aires, 1965.

———, ed. *El comercio y la crisis colonial: Un mito de la independencia.* Santiago: Universidad de Chile, 1968.

Walker, John, ed. *The South American Sketches of R. B. Cunningham.* Norman: University of Oklahoma Press, 1978.

Walter, Richard J. *Politics and Urban Growth in Buenos Aires, 1910–1942.* Cambridge, England: Cambridge University Press, 1993.

Wirth, John D., ed. *Latin American Oil Companies and the Politics of Energy.* Lincoln: University of Nebraska Press, 1985.

Wright, Winthrop R. *British-Owned Railways in Argentina: Their Effect on Economic Nationalism, 1854–1948.* Austin: University of Texas Press, 1974.

# APPENDIX 4

## SUGGESTED READING

The following lists the best up-to-date books and sources in English on Argentine history and contemporary affairs. It is neither exhaustive nor definitive, yet these books will assist specialists and nonspecialists alike in learning more about this fascinating country.

### For Contemporary Issues

*Buenos Aires Herald* (newspaper). Available online: http://www.buenosairesherald.com

*Current History* (journal). Philadelphia: Current History, Inc. Available in libraries

*Country Report: Argentina.* London: The *Economist* Intelligence Unit. (journal). Available in libraries

### General Overview

Ferns, H. S. *Argentina.* New York: Praeger Publishers, 1969.

Lewis, Daniel K. *The History of Argentina.* Westport, Conn.: Greenwood Press, 2001.

McGann, Thomas F. *Argentina: The Divided Land.* Princeton, N.J.: Van Nostrand, 1966.

Randall, Laura. *A Comparative Economic History of Latin America.* Vol. 1, *Argentina.* Ann Arbor, Mich.: University Microfilms, 1977.

Rock, David. *Argentina, 1516–1987: From Spanish Colonization to Alfonsín.* Berkeley: University of California Press, 1987.

Romero, José Luis. *A History of Argentine Political Thought.* Trans. Thomas F. McGann. Stanford, Calif.: Stanford University Press, 1963.

Ross, Stanley R., and Thomas F. McGann, eds. *Buenos Aires: 400 Years.* Austin: University of Texas Press, 1982.

Scobie, James R. *Argentina: A City and a Nation.* 2d ed. New York: Oxford University Press, 1971.

## The Colonial Period and Wars of Revolution, 1776–1830

Concolocorvo. *El Lazarillo: A Guide for Inexperienced Travelers between Buenos Aires and Lima, 1773.* Trans. Walter D. Kline. Bloomington: Indiana University Press, 1965.

Cushner, Nicholas P. *Jesuit Ranches and the Agrarian Development of Colonial Argentina, 1650–1767.* Albany: State University of New York Press, 1983.

Ganson, Barbara. *The Guaraní under Spanish Rule in the Río de la Plata.* Stanford, Calif.: Stanford University Press, 2002.

Halperín Donghi, Tulio. *Politics, Economics, and Society in Argentina in the Revolutionary Period.* Trans. Richard Southern. Cambridge, England: Cambridge University Press, 1975.

Lynch, John. *Spanish Colonial Administration, 1782–1810: The Intendant System in the Viceroyalty of the Río de la Plata.* 2d ed. Westport, Conn.: Greenwood Press, 1969.

Morner, Magnus. *The Political and Economic Activities of the Jesuits in the La Plata Region, Hapsburg Era.* Trans. Albert Read. Stockholm: Institute of Ibero-American Studies, 1953.

Palmer, Colin. *Human Cargoes: The British Slave Trade to Spanish America, 1700–1739.* Campaign-Urbana: University of Illinois Press, 1981.

Service, Elman R. *Spanish-Guaraní Relations in Early Colonial Paraguay.* Ann Arbor: University of Michigan Press, 1954.

Socolow, Susan Migden. *The Bureaucrats of Buenos Aires, 1790–1810: Amor al real servicio.* Durham, N.C.: Duke University Press, 1987.

———. *The Merchants of Buenos Aires, 1778–1810: Family and Commerce.* Cambridge, England: Cambridge University Press, 1978.

Steward, Julian H., ed. *Handbook of South American Indians.* 8 Vols. New York: Cooper Square Publishers, 1963.

White, Richard Alan. *Paraguay's Autonomous Revolution, 1810–1840.* Albuquerque: University of New Mexico Press, 1978.

## Age of Caudillos, 1820–1880

Adelman, Jeremy. *Republic of Capital: Buenos Aires and the Legal Transformation of the Atlantic World.* Stanford, Calif.: Stanford University Press, 1999.

Amaral, Samuel. *The Rise of Capitalism on the Pampas.* Cambridge, England: Cambridge University Press, 1999.

Andrews, George Reid. *The Afro-Argentines of Buenos Aires, 1800–1900.* Madison: University of Wisconsin Press, 1980.

Brown, Jonathan C. *A Socioeconomic History of Argentina, 1776–1860*. Cambridge, England: Cambridge University Press, 1979.

Burgin, Miron P. *The Economic Aspects of Argentine Federalism, 1820–1852*. Cambridge, Mass.: Harvard University Press, 1946.

Bushnell, David. *Reform and Reaction in the Platine Provinces, 1810–1852*. Gainesville: University of Florida Press, 1983.

De la Fuente, Ariel. *Children of Facundo: Caudillo and Gaucho Insurgency During the Argentine State-Formation Process (La Rioja, 1853–1870)*. Durham, N.C.: Duke University Press, 2000.

Ferns, H. S. *Britain and Argentina in the Nineteenth Century*. Oxford, England: Clarendon Press, 1960.

Kroeber, Clifton B. *Growth of the Shipping Industry in the Río de la Plata Region, 1794–1860*. Madison: University of Wisconsin Press, 1957.

Lynch, John. *Argentine Dictator: Juan Manuel de Rosas, 1829–1852*. Oxford, England: Oxford University Press, 1981.

Martínez Estrada, Ezequiel. *X-Ray of the Pampa*. Trans. Alain Swietlicki. Austin: University of Texas Press, 1971.

Reber, Vera Blinn. *British Mercantile Houses in Buenos Aires, 1810–1880*. Cambridge, Mass.: Harvard University Press, 1979.

Sabato, Hilda. *Agrarian Capitalism and the World Market: Buenos Aires in the Pastoral Age, 1840–1890*. Albuquerque: University of New Mexico Press, 1992.

———. *The Many and the Few: Political Participation in Republican Buenos Aires*. Stanford, Calif.: Stanford University Press, 2001.

Sarmiento, Domingo F. *Life in the Argentine Republic in the Days of Tyrants, or Civilization and Barbarism*. New York: Hafner Press, 1974.

Shumway, Nicolas. *The Invention of Argentina*. Berkeley: University of California Press, 1991.

Slatta, Richard W. *Gauchos and the Vanishing Frontier*. Lincoln: University of Nebraska Press, 1982.

Szuchman, Mark D. *Order, Family, and Community in Buenos Aires, 1810–1860*. Stanford, Calif.: Stanford University Press, 1988.

Szuchman, Mark D., and Jonathan C. Brown, eds. *Revolution and Restoration: The Rearrangement of Power in Argentina, 1776–1860*. Lincoln: University of Nebraska Press, 1994.

Whigham, Thomas. *The Politics of River Trade: Tradition and Development in the Upper Plata, 1780–1870*. Albuquerque: University of New Mexico Press, 1991.

Williams, John Hoyt. *The Rise and Fall of the Paraguayan Republic, 1800–1870*. Austin: University of Texas Press, 1979.

## Age of Liberalism, 1880–1930

Adelman, Jeremy, ed. *Essays in Argentine Labour History, 1870–1930.* Houndsmills, England: Macmillan, 1992.

Agullo, Juan Carlos. *Eclipse of an Aristocracy: An Investigation of the Ruling Elites of Córdoba.* Trans. Betty Crouse. Tuscaloosa: University of Alabama Press, 1976.

Alonso, Paula. *Between Revolution and the Ballot Box: The Origins of the Argentine Radical Party.* Cambridge, England: Cambridge University Press, 2000.

Baily, Samuel L. *Immigrants in the Lands of Promise: Italians in Buenos Aires and New York City, 1870–1914.* Ithaca, N.Y.: Cornell University Press, 1999.

Brennan, James P., and Ofelia Pianetto, eds. *Region and Nation: Politics, Economics, and Society in Twentieth Century Argentina.* New York: St. Martin's Press, 2000.

Cochran, Thomas C., and Ruben E. Reina. *Capitalism in Argentine Culture: A Study of Torcuato Di Tella and S.I.A.M.* Philadelphia: University of Pennsylvania Press, 1962.

Collier, Simon. *The Life and Times of Carlos Gardel.* Pittsburgh, Pa.: University of Pittsburgh Press, 1986.

Crawley, Eduardo. *A House Divided: Argentina, 1880–1980.* London: C. Hurst, 1984.

Díaz Alejandro, Carlos F. *Essays on the Economic History of the Argentine Republic.* New Haven, Conn.: Yale University Press, 1970.

Di Tella, Guido, and D. C. M. Platt, eds. *The Political Economy of Argentina, 1880–1946.* Basingstoke, England: Macmillan, 1986.

Gallo, Ezequiel. *Farmers in Revolt: The Revolutions of 1893 in the Province of Santa Fe, Argentina.* London: Athlone Press, 1976.

Guy, Donna J. *Sex and Danger in Buenos Aires: Prostitution, Family, and Nation in Argentina.* Lincoln: University of Nebraska Press, 1991.

Hora, Roy. *The Landowners of the Argentine Pampas: A Social and Political History, 1860–1945.* Oxford, England: Clarendon Press, 2001.

Lewis, Colin M. *British Railways in Argentina, 1857–1914: A Case Study of Foreign Investment.* London: Athlone Press, 1983.

McGann, Thomas F. *Argentina, the United States, and the Inter-American System.* Cambridge, Mass.: Harvard University Press, 1957.

McGee Deutsch, Sandra. *Counterrevolution in Argentina: The Argentine Patriotic League.* Lincoln: University of Nebraska Press, 1986.

Moya, Jose C. *Cousins and Strangers: Spanish Immigrants in Buenos Aires, 1850–1930.* Berkeley: University of California Press, 1998.

Munck, Ronaldo, Ricardo Falcón, and Bernardo Galitelli. *Argentina from Anarchism to Peronismo: Workers, Unions, and Politics, 1855–1985*. London: Zed, 1987.

Plotkin, Mariano Ben. *Freud on the Pampas: The Emergence and Development of a Psychoanalytic Culture in Argentina*. Stanford, Calif.: Stanford University Press, 2001.

Randall, Laura. *An Economic History of Argentina in the Twentieth Century*. New York: Columbia University Press, 1978.

Richmond, Douglas. *Carlos Pelligrini and the Crisis of the Argentine Elites, 1880–1916*. Westport, Conn.: Greenwood, 1989.

Rock, David. *Politics in Argentina, 1890–1930: The Rise and Fall of Radicalism*. Cambridge, England: Cambridge University Press, 1974.

Scobie, James R. *Buenos Aires: Plaza to Suburb, 1870–1910*. London: Oxford University Press, 1974.

———. *Revolution on the Pampas: A Social History of Argentine Wheat, 1860–1910*. Austin: University of Texas Press, 1964.

———. *Secondary Cities of Argentina: The Social History of Corrientes, Salta, and Mendoza*. Stanford, Calif.: Stanford University Press, 1993.

Smith, Peter H. *Argentina and the Failure of Democracy: Conflict among Political Elites*. Madison: University of Wisconsin Press, 1974.

———. *Politics and Beef in Argentina: Patterns of Conflict and Change*. New York: Columbia University Press, 1969.

Solberg, Carl. *Immigration and Nationalism in Argentina and Chile, 1890–1914*. Austin: University of Texas Press, 1970.

———. *Oil and Nationalism in Argentina*. Stanford, Calif.: Stanford University Press, 1979.

Szuchman, Mark D. *Mobility and Integration in Urban Argentina: Córdoba in the Liberal Era*. Austin: University of Texas Press, 1980.

Walter, Richard J. *Politics and Urban Growth in Buenos Aires, 1910–1942*. Cambridge, England: Cambridge University Press, 1993.

———. *The Province of Buenos Aires and Argentine Politics, 1912–1943*. Cambridge, England: Cambridge University Press, 1985.

———. *The Socialist Party of Argentina, 1890–1930*. Austin: University of Texas Press, 1977.

———. *Student Politics in Argentina: The University Reform and Its Effects, 1918–1964*. New York: Basic Books, 1968.

Wright, Winthrop. *British-Owned Railways in Argentina*. Austin: University of Texas Press, 1974.

## Age of Populism, 1930–1983

Aizcorbe, Roberto. *Argentina, the Peronist Myth: An Essay on the Cultural Decay of Argentina after the Second World War.* Hicksville, N.Y.: Exposition Press, 1975.

Alexander, Robert J. *Juan Domingo Perón: A History.* Boulder, Colo.: Westview Press, 1979.

———. *The Perón Era.* New York: Columbia University Press, 1965.

Anderson, Jon Lee. *Che Guevara: A Revolutionary Life.* New York: Grove Press, 1997.

Baily, Samuel L. *Labor, Nationalism and Politics in Argentina.* New Brunswick, N.J.: Rutgers University Press, 1967.

Barnes, John. *Evita, First Lady: A Biography of Eva Perón.* New York: Grove Press, 1978.

Brennan, James P., ed. *Peronism and Argentina.* Wilmington, Del.: Scholarly Resources, 1998.

Brown, Jonathan C., ed. *Workers' Control in Latin America, 1930–1979.* Chapel Hill: University of North Carolina Press, 1995.

Crassweller, Robert D. *Perón and the Enigmas of Argentina.* New York: W. W. Norton, 1987.

Di Tella, Guido, and Rudiger Dornbusch, eds. *The Political Economy of Argentina, 1946–83.* Oxford, England: Macmillan, 1989.

Dujovne Ortiz, Alicia. *Eva Perón: A Biography.* Trans. Shawn Fields. New York: St. Martin's Press, 1996.

Falcoff, Mark, and Ronald H. Dolkart. *Prologue to Perón: Argentina in Depression and War.* Berkeley: University of California Press, 1975.

Francis, Michael J. *The Limits of Hegemony: U.S. Relations with Argentina and Chile During World War II.* Notre Dame, Ind.: University of Notre Dame Press, 1977.

Fraser, Nicholas, and Marysa Navarro. *Evita: The Real Life of Eva Perón.* New York: W. W. Norton, 1996.

Germani, Gino. *Authoritarianism, Fascism, and National Populism.* New Brunswick, N.J.: Transaction Books, 1978.

Hodges, Donald C. *Argentina, 1943–1976: The National Revolution and Resistance.* Albuquerque: University of New Mexico Press, 1976.

Horowitz, Joel. *Argentine Unions, the State and the Rise of Peronism, 1930–1945.* Berkeley, Calif.: Institute of International Studies, 1990.

Kirkpatrick, Jeane J. *Leader and Vanguard in Mass Society: A Study of Peronist Argentina.* Cambridge, Mass.: M.I.T. Press, 1971.

Lewis, Paul. *The Crisis of Argentine Capitalism.* Chapel Hill: University of North Carolina Press, 1990.

Meyer, Doris. *Victoria Ocampo: Against the Wind and the Tide.* Austin: University of Texas Press, 1990.

Navarro, Marysa. *Evita.* Buenos Aires: Ediciones Corregidor, 1981.

Page, Joseph A. *Perón: A Biography.* New York: Random House, 1983.

Paz, Alberto Conil, and Gustavo Ferrari. *Argentina's Foreign Policy, 1930–1962.* Notre Dame, Ind.: University of Notre Dame Press, 1960.

Peralta-Ramos, Mónica. *Political Economy of Argentina: Power and Class since 1930.* Boulder, Colo.: Westview Press, 1992.

Perón, Eva Duarte de. *Evita: Eva Duarte Peron Tells Her Own Story.* London: Proteus, 1978.

Perón, Juan Domingo. *Peron Expounds His Doctrine.* Trans. Argentine Association of English Culture. Buenos Aires: n.p., 1948.

Rock, David. *Authoritarian Argentina: The Nationalist Movement, Its History and Its Impact.* Berkeley: University of California Press, 1993.

Rock, David, ed. *Argentina in the Twentieth Century.* Pittsburgh, Pa.: Pittsburgh University Press, 1975.

Tamarin, David. *The Argentine Labor Movement, 1930–45: A Study in the Origins of Peronism.* Albuquerque: University of New Mexico Press, 1987.

Taylor, Carl C. *Rural Life in Argentina.* Baton Rouge: State University of Louisiana Press, 1948.

Taylor, J. M. *Eva Perón: The Myths of a Woman.* Chicago: University of Chicago Press, 1979.

Wynia, Gary W. *Argentina in the Post-War Era: Politics and Economic Policymaking in a Divided Society.* Albuquerque: University of New Mexico Press, 1978.

## Military Governments, 1955–1983

Anderson, Martin E. *Dossier Secreto: Argentina's Desaparecidos and the Myth of the "Dirty War."* Boulder, Colo.: Westview Press, 1993.

Bourvard, Marguerite Guzmán. *Revolutionizing Motherhood: The Mothers of the Plaza de Mayo.* Wilmington, Del.: Scholarly Resources, 1994.

Brennan, James P. *The Labor Wars in Córdoba, 1955–76: Ideology, Work, and Labor Politics in an Argentine Industrial City.* Cambridge, Mass.: Harvard University Press, 1994.

Brysk, Alison. *The Politics of Human Rights in Argentina: Protest, Change, and Democratization.* Stanford, Calif.: Stanford University Press, 1994.

Burdick, Michael A. *For God and Fatherland: Religion and Politics in Argentina.* Albany: State University of New York Press, 1995.

Ciria, Alberto. *Parties and Power in Modern Argentina.* Trans. Carlos A. Astiz and Mary F. McCarthy. Albany: State University of New York Press, 1974.

Dabat, Alejandro, and Luis Lorezano. *Argentina: The Malvinas and the End of Military Rule.* Trans. Ralph Johnstone. London: Verso Editions, 1984.

Di Tella, Guido. *Argentina under Perón, 1973–1976.* London: Macmillan, 1981.

Di Tella, Torcuato. *Latin American Politics: A Theoretical Approach.* Rev. ed. Austin: University of Texas Press, 2001.

Feitlowitz, Marguerite. *A Lexicon of Terror: Argentina and the Legacies of Torture.* New York: Oxford University Press, 1998.

Fillol, Tomás Roberto. *Social Factors in Economic Development: The Argentine Case.* Cambridge, Mass.: MIT Press, 1961.

Fisher, Jo. *Mothers of the Disappeared.* Boston: South End Press, 1989.

Freedman, Lawrence, and Virginia Gamboa-Stonehouse. *Signals of War: The Falklands Conflict of 1982.* Princeton, N.J.: Princeton University Press, 1991.

Gillespie, Richard. *Soldiers of Perón: Argentina's Montoneros.* New York: Oxford University Press, 1982.

Goldwert, Marvin. *Democracy, Militarism, and Nationalism in Argentina, 1930–1966.* Austin: University of Texas Press, 1969.

González, José Eduardo. *Borges and the Politics of Form.* New York: Garland Publishers, 1998.

Graham-Yooll, Andrew. *A State of Fear: Memories of Argentina's Nightmare.* New York: Hippocrene, 1986.

Hodges, Donald C. *Argentina's "Dirty War."* Austin: University of Texas Press, 1991.

Imaz, José Luis de. *Los que mandan: Those Who Rule.* Albany: State University of New York Press, 1970.

James, Daniel. *Resistance and Integration: Peronism and the Argentine Working Class, 1946–1976.* Cambridge, England: Cambridge University Press, 1994.

Kennedy, John J. *Catholicism, Nationalism and Democracy in Argentina.* Notre Dame, Ind.: University of Notre Dame Press, 1958.

Kon, Daniel. *Los chicos de la guerra: The Boys of War.* London: New English Library, 1983.

Lewis, Paul. *Guerrillas and Generals: The "Dirty War" in Argentina.* Westport, Conn.: Praeger Publishers, 2002.

O'Donnell, Guillermo. *Bureaucratic Authoritarianism: Argentina, 1966–1973, in Comparative Perspective.* Berkeley: University of California Press, 1988.

Mallon, Richard D., and Juan Sourrouille. *Economic Policy Making in a Conflict Society, the Argentine Case.* Cambridge, Mass.: Harvard University Press, 1975.

Mendez, Juan E. *Truth and Partial Justice in Argentina: An Americas Watch Report.* New York: Americas Watch Committee, 1987.

Moyano, María José. *Argentina's Lost Patrol: Armed Struggle, 1969–1979.* New Haven, Conn.: Yale University Press, 1995.

Naipaul, V. S. *The Return of Eva Perón.* London: André Deutsch, 1980.

Pion-Berlin, David. *The Ideology of State Terror: Economic Doctrine and Political Repression in Argentina and Peru.* Boulder, Colo.: Lynne Rienner Publishers, 1989.

Potash, Robert A. *The Army and Politics in Argentina.* 3 vols. Stanford, Calif.: Stanford University Press, 1969–96.

Reina, Rubén E. *Paraná; Social Boundaries in an Argentine City.* Austin: University of Texas Press, 1973.

Simpson, John, and Jana Bennett. *The Disappeared and the Mothers of the Plaza: The Story of the 11,000 Argentinians Who Vanished.* New York: St. Martin's Press, 1985.

Smith, William. *Authoritarianism and the Crisis of the Argentine Political Economy.* Stanford, Calif.: Stanford University Press, 1991.

Sobel, Lester A., ed. *Argentina and Peron, 1970–75.* New York: Facts On File, 1975.

Snow, Peter. *Political Forces in Argentina.* Boston: Allyn & Bacon, 1971.

Timerman, Jacobo. *Prisoner Without a Name, Cell Without a Number.* New York: Alfred A. Knopf, 1981.

Tulchin, Joseph S. *Argentina and the United States: A Conflicted Relationship.* Boston: Twayne, 1990.

Verbitsky, Horacio. *The Flight: Confessions of an Argentine Dirty Warrior.* Trans. Esther Allen. New York: New Press, 1996.

Whiteford, Scott. *Workers from the North: Plantations, Bolivian Labor, and the City in Northwest Argentina.* Austin: University of Texas Press, 1981.

## Age of Neoliberalism, 1983 –

Collier, Simon. *Le Grand Tango: The Life and Music of Astor Piazzolla.* Oxford, England: Oxford University Press, 2000.

Corradi, Juan. *The Fitful Republic: Economy, Society, and Politics in Argentina.* Boulder, Colo.: Westview Press, 1985.

Lewis, Colin M., and Nissa Torrents, eds. *Argentina in the Crises Years (1983–1990): From Alfonsín to Menem.* London: Institute of Latin American Studies, 1993.

McGuire, James. *Peronism without Perón: Unions, Parties, and Democracy in Argentina* (Stanford, Calif.: Stanford University Press, 1997.

Norden, Deborah L. *Military Rebellion in Argentina: Between Coups and Consolidation*. Lincoln: University of Nebraska Press, 1996.

*Nunca Más: A Report by Argentina's National Commission on Disappeared People*. Boston: Faber & Faber, 1986.

Peralta-Ramos, Mónica, and Carlos H. Waisman, eds. *From Military Rule to Liberal Democracy in Argentina*. Boulder, Colo.: Westview Press, 1987.

Ruggiero, Kristin Hoffman. *And Here the World Ends: The Life of an Argentine Village*. Stanford, Calif.: Stanford University Press, 1988.

Tulchin, Joseph S., and Allison M. Garland, eds. *Argentina: The Challenges of Modernization*. Wilmington, Del.: Scholarly Resources, 1998.

Turner, Frederick J., and Enrique Miguens, eds. *Juan Perón and the Reshaping of Argentina*. Pittsburgh, Pa.: University of Pittsburgh Press, 1983.

Waisman, Carlos. *Reversal of Development in Argentina: Postwar Counterrevolutionary Policies and Their Structural Consequences*. Princeton, N.J.: Princeton University Press, 1987.

Wynia, Gary W. *Argentina: Illusions and Realities*. New York: Holmes & Meier, 1986.

# INDEX

Page numbers followed by the letter *f* refer to illustrations; the letter *m* indicates a map; the letter *t* denotes a table.